Social Suffering

Essex Studies in Contemporary Critical Theory

Series Editors: Peter Dews, Professor of Philosophy at the University of Essex; Lorna Finlayson, Lecturer in Philosophy at the University of Essex; Fabian Freyenhagen, Professor of Philosophy at the University of Essex; Steven Gormley, Lecturer in Philosophy at the University of Essex; Timo Jütten, Senior Lecturer in Philosophy at the University of Essex; and Jörg Schaub, Lecturer in Philosophy at the University of Essex.

Essex Studies in Contemporary Critical Theory: This series aims to develop the critical analysis of contemporary societies. The series publishes both substantive critical analyses of recent and current developments in society and culture and studies dealing with methodological/conceptual problems in the Critical Theory tradition, intended to further enhance its ability to address the problems of contemporary society

Titles in the Series

Social Suffering

Sociology, Psychology, Politics

Emmanuel Renault
Translated by Maude Dews

R O W M A N *&*
L I T T L E F I E L D
——————————— INTERNATIONAL

London • New York

Published by Rowman & Littlefield International, Ltd.
Unit A, Whitacre Mews, 26-34 Stannary Street, London SE11 4AB
www.rowmaninternational.com

Rowman & Littlefield International, Ltd. is an affiliate of Rowman & Littlefield
4501 Forbes Boulevard, Suite 200, Lanham, Maryland 20706, USA
With additional offices in Boulder, New York, Toronto (Canada), and London (UK)
www.rowman.com

British Library Cataloguing in Publication Information Available
A catalogue record for this book is available from the British Library

ISBN: HB 978-1-78660-072-1
ISBN: PB 978-1-78660-073-8

Library of Congress Cataloging-in-Publication Data

Names: Renault, Emmanuel, 1967 - author.
Title: Social suffering : sociology, psychology, politics / Emmanuel Renault ; translated by Maude
    Dews.
Description: Lanham : Rowman & Littlefield International, 2017. | Series: Essex studies in contem-
    porary critical theory
Identifiers: LCCN 2017018513 (print) | LCCN 2017028203 (ebook) | ISBN 9781786600745 (Elec-
    tronic) | ISBN 9781786600721 (cloth : alk. paper) | ISBN 9781786600738 (pbk : alk. paper) |
    ISBN 9781786600745 (electronic : alk. paper)
Subjects: LCSH: Suffering—Social aspects. | Suffering—Political aspects.
Classification: LCC HM1131 (ebook) | LCC HM1131 .R4713 2017 (print) | DDC 301—dc23
LC record available at http://lccn.loc.gov/2017018513

Printed in the United States of America

Contents

Introduction

The question of suffering has a paradoxical political topicality. For at least the past few years, we have been accustomed in France to hearing our politicians speak of the 'people's suffering' and sometimes, in self-criticism, condemn the lack of attention governments and major parties pay to the 'France that is suffering'. And in Spain, 'Podemos' has made the politicization of social suffering one of its aims. In the social sciences too, whether in the work of Pierre Bourdieu and Christophe Dejours in the French-speaking world, for example, or in that of Veena Das, Nancy Scheper-Hughes and Arthur Kleinman in the English-speaking world, describing the lived reality of suffering has been proposed as a fundamental political task. However, in parallel, there has been an increasing reluctance to admit that the term 'suffering' can designate real social problems and that it can be employed in a politically useful way.

At the very moment when it was introduced into everyday political and social discourse, the term 'suffering' became the common target of theoretical criticism running across almost the entire spectrum of political views. Some supporters of neoliberalism condemn the framing of issues in terms of suffering as based on a vision of individuals reduced to the status of powerless victims, a view that supposedly keeps the excluded trapped in the role of those who need help instead of encouraging their efforts at integration. As for the supporters of political liberalism, they condemn the paternalism of a state that under the guise of fighting against suffering claims to take responsibility for individual happiness—a confusion of morality and law that supposedly replaces a politics of social justice with a mixture of paternalism and utilitarianism.

Among opponents of mainstream political thought as well, rejection of the theme of social suffering is widespread. The followers of Arendtian republicanism see in references to suffering a straightforward version of a politics of pity against which they put forward a definition of politics as an active joy in being together. Foucault's heirs, for their part, see in the emergence of the discourse of suffering a new face of biopower in which dominance, control and monitoring are attained by defining the norms of a good life and of health, through psychologization and the medicalization of the social domain. Finally, among critical thinkers who still make reference to Marx, there are many for whom the issue of suffering blocks an accurate perception of the structural weight of domination and exploitation.

Hence while the political uses of suffering seem ever more numerous, a paradoxical consensus has been established between political enemies. The objective of this book is to disentangle this paradox and demonstrate that a political reference to suffering can contribute to a revival of social criticism. To be sure, not all references to suffering have the same political interest, but description of the lived reality of the suffering linked to domination, violence and injustice is nevertheless a significant issue. Reporting on experienced suffering, making it an object of narration and knowledge, allows us in particular to oppose the reduction of political confrontations to the narrow circle of issues relating to economic efficiency or equal respect for universal rights and aids in bringing whole sections of society out of invisibility. It helps to give back to the individuals concerned the capacity to make demands and act collectively to transform the conditions of their existence.

Contrary to widely held assumptions, the discourse of suffering does not lock individuals into the position of victims; rather, silence and the inability to express suffering are what condemn people to powerlessness. The discourse of suffering does not simply buttress a biopower that binds individuals by making their bodies and minds the application point for a technology of health; it is also a means of contesting technocratic definitions of health and the narrow politics that draws inspiration from them. If we want to change the world, we must, as Marx himself remarked, analyse not only its structures, but also the way people live in them.

It is only as social suffering that suffering can play a role in social criticism. But what exactly should we understand by 'social suffering'? To answer this question, this book embarks upon a critical analysis of theoretical models with which not only sociology and psychology, but also political economy, social medicine and medical anthropology have attempted to describe the conditions, effects and social dimension of suffering. When sociology rejects the study of 'social suffering' because the scope of this subject is too psychological or too cultural, it indirectly participates in the technocratic discourse that leaves aside the question of experienced injustice and domination because these cannot be made the object of scientific scrutiny. When psychology or psychoanalysis refuses to analyse the social factors at work in suffering, they contribute indirectly to confirming the idea that suffering is of purely individual significance and that any criticism of social suffering can consist only, and inevitably, in psychologization or an illegitimate moralization.

However, the concept of social suffering must not be understood only in a critical sense: it does not have the sole function of criticizing all attempts, ordinary or expert, to exonerate society from the suffering it produces. If the task of speaking about the world as it is experienced, including those of its aspects passed over in silence by society, is a clear political requirement, it also defines a question that is fundamental to clarifying the relationship of disciplines such as sociology and psychology to their objects, and the status of their theories. Social suffering is a subject which can be defined and analysed rigorously, whose theorization poses the general problem of the relationship that disciplines such as sociology and psychology maintain with society as it is experienced. In this sense, the question of social suffering brings to light the limitations, both political and epistemological, of certain research programmes which dominate psychology and sociology.

This book has two main objectives: first, to determine how a consideration of social suffering can contribute to a revival of criticism suited to the current form of the social question, and second to establish that social suffering is far from being a false problem, while identifying the theoretical terms on which it can be recognized.

By way of a general introduction, the first chapter describes the theoretico-political context of the problem. It raises the question of the obstacles encountered by any study of social suffering, which have to do with the different possible meanings of the term 'social suffering' and how the theme of social suffering can be addressed by a critical theory of society.

Chapter 2 focuses on the political aspect of the problem. It shows that, contrary to common prejudice, the term 'suffering' does in fact belong to the lexicon of modern social criticism. More specifically, the emergence of the social question in the nineteenth century was accompanied by descriptions and denunciations of suffering. It would have been possible to give other illustrations, focusing for example on how Mao developed political procedures for investigating the suffering of the peasantry and for the 'expression of grievances'.[1] If this book had been written more recently it could also have referred to how the movement 'Podemos' in Spain has pursued the goal of contributing to the politicization of social suffering.

The following chapter deals with the strictly theoretical aspect of the problem. It begins by examining how the early social sciences encountered the question of the social dimension of suffering by focusing on classical political economy and social economy, then on the beginnings of social medicine. It concludes by offering a synthesis of different forms of sociological and psychological theorization within a general conception of suffering which sheds light on the current debates in the field of the psychopathology of work and of exclusion.

The final chapter seeks to determine what kind of social criticism the theme of suffering leads us toward, and how this theme can be useful to us in the era of neoliberal capitalism.

These different chapters each adopt a specific point of view on a particular aspect of the social problem of suffering. Chapter 1 takes the perspective of the epistemology of human sciences. Chapter 2 discusses some uses of the term 'suffering' from the perspective of the history of political ideas. Chapter 3 explores the theme of social suffering from the point of view of the history of the humanities, before proposing a conceptualization that combines the approaches of psychoanalysis, social psychology, sociology and clinical psychology. Finally, chapter 4 reviews the discussion from the standpoint of social and political philosophy. Although integrated into an overall argument, these chapters have an internal consistency that allows each of them to be read independently.

This book is the result of work begun in the 2004–2005 academic year at the Institut für Sozialforschung in Frankfurt, supported by a grant from the Humboldt Foundation, and also benefitted from the institutional support of UMR 5206 of the CNRS (*Triangle*). It was published in French in 2008. The English reader will encounter a shortened version: the last section of chapter 2 has been greatly reduced, and almost all of chapter 3, which focused on the emergence of the problematic of social suffering in France in the years from 1980 to 1990, and the last two sections of chapter 4, which focused on Durkheim and Freud, have been removed, the rest being merged with what was chapter 5. Initially composed of six chapters, the book now only has four. The rest remains unchanged.

At the end of this introduction, it only remains to me to thank F. Freyenhagen, who took the initiative for the English edition of *Social Suffering*, and M. Dews, who kindly undertook the work of translation. Finally, I repeat my thanks to all those who kindly read and discussed initial versions or parts of this book, and who gave me the opportunity to present the project in the context of symposia or seminars: V. Houillon, C. Gautier, Ch. Dejours, S. Haber, J. Guilhaumou, C. Laval, A. Honneth, L. Frobert, C. Hanna, H. Bentouhami, B. Cenatus, J.-P. Deranty, D. Zeneidi, Ch. Zurn, B. Ravon, J. Furtos, P. Molinier, F. Neyrat, S. Laugier, O. Voirol, B. Ogilvie, E. Dorlin, Ch. Lazzeri, B. Binoche, L. Vincenti, J.-C. Bourdin, T. Périlleux, M. Otero, S. Henry and H. Jallon.

NOTE

1. On these points, see E. Renault, 'Dewey, Hook, and Mao: On Some Affinities between Marxism and Pragmatism', http://www.cairn-int.info/article.php?ID_ARTICLE=E_AMX_054_0137.

Chapter One

Obstacles and Problems

I feel it imperative from a personal and ethical perspective, as well as from an analytic and theoretical one, to expose the horrors I witnessed among the people I befriended, without censuring even the goriest details. The depth and overwhelming pain and terror of the experience of poverty and racism . . . needs to be talked about openly and confronted squarely, even if that makes us uncomfortable.
—Ph. Bourgois, *In Search of Respect: Selling Crack in El Barrio*, 46

If the study of a society requires a study of its pain, then so far as there is an absence of languages of pain in the social sciences—which is, after Veena Das's text, to say, languages in which pain is acknowledged, in which its existence is known ('witnessed' is the term she offers us, correctly and frighteningly)—social science participates in the silence, and so extends the violence it studies. . . . So, I understand Veena Das's more or less implicit claim to be a double one, namely that the study of social suffering must contain a study of a society's silence towards it (or, say, the degree of its incapacity to acknowledge it) and that the study of that suffering and that silence must contain an awareness of its own dangers in mimicking the social silence that perpetuates the suffering.
—S. Cavell, 'Comments on Veena Das's Essay "Language and Body: Transactions in the Construction of Pain"', in *Social Suffering*, ed. A. Kleinman, V. Das, and M. Lock, 94–95

During the last fifteen years, at least in France, the topic of social suffering has gradually become more widespread, both in the public arena and in the social sciences. At the same time, questions have been posed concerning the issues raised by this topic, issues which are at once sociological (What is the meaning of the current 'sensitivity' to suffering, of the mode of expression of affects in terms of suffering, of the characterization of inequalities in terms of suffering?), psychological (Is the problem of suffering related to a change in the aetiology or even the nosology of subjective harm?) and political (Is concern for social suffering a sign of new forms of domination and social control or the opportunity for a revival of social criticism?).[1]

The contemporary debate concerns the political, but also epistemological, value of the issue of social suffering: Can it be used positively in the framework of an analysis of social processes and subjective harm or should it simply be analysed and demystified? The complexity of the debate—its sometimes confused nature—is due on the one hand to the intertwining of political and theoretical issues, and on the other to the intersection of psychological, sociological and epistemological lines of argument. Some authors are led to reject the sociological, political and epistemological relevance of the theme of social suffering. They claim that the paradigm of suffering corresponds to a social construction that hides the reality to which it refers, that it is merely a new mode of social control by medicalization and that it is not based on any rigorous conception of suffering in general, and of suffering of social origin in particular.[2] Others try instead to produce explanatory models that allow this topic a certain degree of relevance from a psychological and sociological point of view (they claim it describes certain kinds of subjective harm[3] as well as transformations affecting social intersubjectivity and public action[4]) as well as from a political point of view (they claim it allows us to take a critical view of some aspects of a new social question[5]).

The analyses developed in this book belong to this second perspective. They aim, in fact, to defend the principle of a reference to social suffering from a point of view both theoretical (specifically epistemological, inasmuch as the theoretical argument takes the form of a reflection on the theoretical models proposed by the human sciences) and political. They also start from the assumption that the critical analysis of the theoretical aspects of the problem should not be isolated from the critical analysis of its political aspects: first, because it is the task of theory to establish that the term 'social suffering' denotes an object which is a valid target of social criticism, and not a false problem; second, because theoretical debates about social suffering are freighted with political conflicts that must be considered as such; and finally, because theory here has a political objective not only to defend the legitimacy of a *study* of social suffering in itself, as a subject insufficiently taken into account by the human sciences and calling for the development of new knowledge, but also to defend the principle of a *critique* of social suffering.

Does the concept of social suffering really merit an entire book? The question is bound to arise, as social suffering appears to be a vague and confusing object, a topic often seen as being as elusive as it is politically dangerous. This chapter begins by showing that all the ways of rejecting the issue of social suffering or giving it ready-made answers simply circumvent or deny a problem (1). It then proceeds to work through the various possible meanings of the term 'social suffering' (2). Lastly, moving from the analytical to the political field, it specifies in what sense critiques of suffering fit into a model of social pathology (3) and attempts in conclusion to explain why and how an investigation of social suffering can form part of the intellectual tradition critical theory and renew its aims (4).

OBSTACLES TO THE ANALYSIS OF SOCIAL SUFFERING

It is striking that 'suffering' appears at first glance too indeterminate as a subject to be considered in a serious theoretical work and too elusive to be entitled to feature in a model of social criticism. This spontaneous reaction is made up of disciplinary, political, psychological and social prejudices: so many reasons to raise suspicion.

If social suffering seems inconsistent with serious theory, this is mainly because it does not fit well into the deep disciplinary divide that reserves the study of individual representations and affects for psychology and the study of individuals' interaction with other people and with institutions for sociology. In speaking about social suffering, we are indeed discussing a psychological reality with a social dimension and therefore designating a subject that cannot easily be classified under the alternative either of the individual mind or of collective phenomena.

There would certainly be little justification for subjecting the distinction between psychology and sociology to a general criticism. Indeed, the hypotheses of the social world as a reality *sui generis* or of social action as a specific object or a method of analysis have enabled the development of many sociological theories with strong explanatory and descriptive power, while different branches of psychology have at the same time developed fruitful theories by designing concepts and methods irreducible to those of sociology. However, although the methodological separation of sociology and psychology has proven fruitful, it does not follow that psychological and social phenomena must necessarily fit into this separation. As noted in G. Devereux, 'the isolation of phenomena is a fundamental strategy in science, but the amputation of core characteristics of reality only enables us to fit it into the procrustean bed of scholastic sterility'.[6] In saying this he was deploring the fact that human science researchers too often tend to recognize as worthy of interest only those phenomena that immediately raise the questions recognized as legitimate within their disciplines, instead of taking up the challenge thrown down by phenomena that fit them only imperfectly. These remarks apply very directly to the study of social suffering.

The term 'social suffering' in fact refers to a set of phenomena which psychology perceives only with difficulty because psychology as such cannot have a complete theory of the social conditions and social effects of the problems it studies.[7] Similarly, this set of phenomena is not easily handled by a sociology which, as such, cannot have a conception of suffering as such, that is to say, of suffering as affect. Assuming, as a first approximation, that the term 'social suffering' refers to some type of negative social experience in which the subjective dimension of experiences (subjective harm) is inseparable from the social context of which these experiences form an integral part, we can say that this term denotes the challenge posed to sociology and psychology by their common borders.

Certainly, the challenge has been met in different ways, in particular via the channels of social psychiatry, ethnopsychiatry, medical anthropology, social psychology or clinical sociology and sociology of morality. However, none of the doctrines developed within these theoretical frameworks has provided any satisfactory model for the study of social suffering. Moreover, they remain exceptions that should not hide the strength of the prejudice that maintains that social suffering is unworthy of theoretical attention. This prejudice is expressed in different ways which do not necessarily lead to wholesale rejection of the problem of social suffering, but still lead to forms of discreditation.

Sociology offers many illustrations of this. The most classic involves emphasizing that because the objective study of phenomena must assume the burden of proof, subjective elements that are not amenable to quantification must be set aside. It is striking that a classic book like *Marienthal: The Sociology of an Unemployed Community*, which is largely devoted to the subjective collapse resulting from the negative social experience of unemployment and partly based on participant observation, nonetheless opens with the following statement: 'We tried to reduce the subjective element that is inherent in any description of social phenomena to a minimum by discarding all impressions for which we had no objective support'.[8]

A symmetrical form of discreditation is to reduce social suffering to a collective representation awaiting explanation by the cultural or institutional context, which involves transcribing its emotional reality into the well-established framework of the sociology of knowledge (or the emerging framework of medical anthropology).[9] A third form of the scholarly discreditation involves arguing explicitly that if sociology should turn its focus to suffering, this must be suffering not as disorders of individual subjectivity, but as social dysfunction; it must focus on the mismatch between aspirations and opportunities (the functionalist explanation) or the distortion of the normal 'role distance' of individuals in relation to their social roles (the interactionist explanation).[10]

More generally, it is noticeable that the social sciences tend to favour the study of order and patterns, while at the same time interpreting violence and suffering as the irruption of disorder—the pure form of this bias is perhaps the Weberian argument that the explanation of social action in terms of psychological reasons should be considered only when the logics of rational action in terms of value rationality and tradition are prove ineffectual.[11] Even when it is taken into account, suffering tends to be confined to the margins by the social sciences, which are thus pushed in spite of themselves into an irenic vision of the social context.[12] But examples of scholarly disqualification are not restricted to these disciplines, as evidenced by the strong resistance in psychiatry and psychoanalysis to dealing with the specific problems of exclusion or work, for example on the ground that these problems are not amenable to the conventional technique of psychoanalytic treatment.[13]

While most theories that have dealt with the issue of social suffering may appear epistemologically problematic or theoretically questionable, perhaps this is—as it is convenient to believe—because suffering is nothing more than a way like any other to represent our social difficulties, or even a mere social construction. But perhaps it is rather because of the difficulty of positions on the borders of disciplines, positions which are uncomfortable both from a theoretical viewpoint (since conceptual foundations and established principles are lacking) and from a social viewpoint (since they complicate interaction in the order of legitimate discourse).

The epistemological obstacles that the study of social suffering must face do not simply have to do with a questioning of the disciplinary divide between psychology and sociology (and with the invitation to place these disciplines in relation to medicine and anthropology[14]). They also refer to the fact that it is generally difficult, in scholarly discourse as in ordinary speech, to express, to describe and to understand suffering, be it our suffering or that of others. This difficulty is doubtless due to psychological constraints, which will be discussed shortly, but also to constraints specific to the process of social interaction.

As emphasized by E. C. Hughes, 'concealment and ego-protection are of the essence of social intercourse'.[15] As social roles are at the same time modes of social regulation and of protection, it seems that institutionalized language is modelled on the normal functioning of interaction and that it is poorly suited to the expression of private experiences of violence and deprivation which result from malfunctions of socialization and interaction or which are in danger of making them worse.[16] The term 'suffering' clearly refers to one of the elements of our experience which is partially inexpressible by means of ordinary language and to an aspect of the experience of others that we know is always partially inaccessible to us and that we continually subject to routines of euphemization.[17] These can be explained in part by psychological processes and social logics, and they doubtless also reflect the limits of the expressive capacity of ordinary language. Perhaps the logic of the psyche and the modes in which linguistic interactions are recorded conspire to limit the capacity to represent suffering in general. From these limits to expression, representation and even symbolization, it is possible to elaborate a new argument not only to explain, but also to legitimize the silence of the human sciences as regards social suffering. In the last analysis, it would be futile to try to develop sociological or psychosocial theories of suffering. Rather, we should recognize that it structurally evades rationality and simply make do with ethnographic descriptions of the different forms of its social expression.[18]

Suffering at least partially defeats the expressive capacity of ordinary language and of culture but, insofar as the theoretical study of suffering is among the most traditional objects of psychology, it is difficult to agree that by nature it evades any theoretical approach. Just as the groups affected by suffering work to invent new forms to express it, so it should probably be admitted that suffering in general, and social suffering in particular, are among the subjects for the sake of which theoretical discourse can and must break with common conceptions, developing concepts that are not reducible to socially available notions, in order to provide the means not only of expression, but also of understanding (is this not precisely the approach used by psychoanalysis?).

The link between suffering and interaction can lead to another way of rejecting the study of social suffering on the ground that the concept of social suffering supposedly misses its purpose. Instead of simply analysing how failures of interaction produce a set of psychological and social problems for individuals, we may, so the argument runs, be led by the theme of social suffering to reduce the variety of failed interpersonal relationships and subsequent difficulties to a simple psychological essence: suffering. As an illustration of this alleged substantialist simplification, an illustration sometimes mentioned by critics of the topic of 'social suffering', it could be mentioned that it is social workers who work with the socially excluded who say that these people are suffering and sometimes even ask them to express their social difficulties in terms of suffering. Thus it is their own social difficulties that they are psychologizing and substantializing, attributing them to their interaction partners. The socially excluded, however, would in reality have no use for a description of their situation in terms of suffering.[19]

To this type of objection we could reply that, far from illustrating an improper psychologization of a certain type of interaction, this example rather brings to light the relational dimension of the concept of social suffering. In the human sciences more so than in the natural sciences, it is a crucial fact that the object observed by a subject is also observing the observing subject. As pointed out by Devereux, that which is observed is never merely an object but always also a subject observing the observer and producing in him or her emotional effects that can be counted among the components of the observation. Devereux concluded that instead of pursuing the vain hope of defensively developing an objective conceptuality following the model of the natural sciences (before the quantum revolution), the behavioural sciences should consider all of the emotions projected onto their objects of study (countertransference) as a means of accessing them and as material to be analysed.[20] More generally, they should doubtless consider that the specific nature of the human sciences may not be due to the existence of any object or method that is common to them, but to the need they all share to deal with problems arising from the solidarity of the subject and object of knowledge or, in Adornian terms, from the mediation of the subject of knowledge by its objects.[21]

These brief methodological remarks suffice to emphasize that the concepts of the human sciences always have a relational dimension, a characteristic that is particularly evident for psychological concepts. Indeed, the psychological point of view on social relations is usually triggered by a malfunction of our interactions with others.[22] It is when the behaviour of others no longer fits into our social models of interpretation (the interpretive frameworks based on tacit knowledge of general social rules of engagement and specific social roles) that others cease to appear to us only as interaction partners, becoming individuals made distinctive by their character traits (themselves identified with abnormal action profiles).

The description of others in psychological terms is part of a type of interaction crisis and it is no wonder, then, that the term 'suffering' has been used by social workers to refer to failures in their interaction with people in difficulty. Moreover, the fact that these failures are related not only to social maladjustments (a mismatch between what is being offered by institutions and the expectations and behaviour of the people involved) but also to the specific psychological difficulties of persons benefiting from social assistance is enough to give a first degree of legitimacy to the use of the psychological concept of suffering (it would furthermore be wrong to argue that these people never spontaneously take up the discourse of suffering in describing themselves[23]). Nor is the fact that individuals facing these people in difficulty are in turn contaminated by these difficulties surprising. As for the idea that scientific knowledge of situations should disregard this kind of cognitive and affective solidarity, it is, as we have said, more than dubious.

To the strictly epistemological obstacles can be added the political obstacles that lead to an almost spontaneous reluctance to criticize societies in psychological terms. There is a widespread feeling that the issue of social suffering could lead to a transformation of social problems into psychological problems and an appeal to medical expertise at the expense of collective deliberation. At first glance, these fears seem misplaced because, on the one hand, the suffering in question is precisely called *social* and because in this sense it does not lead to a depoliticization of the social so much as to a politicization of the psychological and because, on the other hand, as social suffering is not included in any psychiatric nosology, it is unclear what medical specialism could take on responsibility for it.

But from behind the critique of medicalization and psychologization there emerges a critique of the notion of victimhood. Opponents of the concept of social suffering consider that an approach in terms of social suffering is intrinsically dangerous because it pushes those who suffer injustice to conceive of themselves as victims to be rescued rather than participants in the process of transformation or reparation of injustice.[24] Certainly the language of suffering can lead to individualized social representations that rob individuals of their capacity for political action, but it can also promote a sharing of experiences through which to build solidarity and collective action. Finally, critiques of victimization, psychologization and the medicalization of the social seem to function rather like 'smokescreen arguments'.[25]

In their attempts to reduce the psychologization of social factors to the effect of an inadequate form of problematization, these critiques are silent on the social processes that psychologize the experience of domination and injustice, leading individuals to see themselves as responsible for their own difficulties and to conceive of themselves as mere victims. Similarly, by refusing to take into account the specific reality of subjective harm related to certain negative social experiences, these criticisms indirectly encourage the treatment of the experience of exclusion, poor working conditions or poverty with antidepressants and fine sentiments.[26]

The psychological effects of exclusion, violence or extreme poverty tend in particular to inhibit protest action. Now, the term 'suffering' allows us to denote this inhibiting aspect (this is the sense in which we generally grant suffering the power to isolate individuals and weaken their capacity for action). Such suffering gives rise especially to the shame and guilt that tend to be caused by long-term unemployment and repeated and often ineffective attendance at various employment centres.[27] The term 'suffering' not only describes the effects of certain social situations on individual subjectivity, it also helps to account for the impact of these psychological effects on the social group that suffers domination and poverty. Notably, the dynamics of suffering can lead to the transformation of social violence and distress undergone by individuals into violence against the group. A politically decisive question is therefore how to struggle against the psychological effects of domination and injustice and against the very real impact of suffering on social action. This question cannot be resolved by mere criticism of psychologizing views on social issues.

In addition, the social invisibilization of suffering contributes to reinforcing it, which is an additional obstacle to collective mobilization. When the social sciences reject the issue of social suffering, their discourse prolongs the silence of the public political sphere concerning the experience of the dominated and the dispossessed, while they could instead contribute to the development of a discursive framework for sharing this experience. Invisibilization, unease in articulating a claim and obstacles to mobilization together cause a spiral effect.[28] The absence of social descriptions of a social condition results both in a lack of representation and a lack of language; it hinders the narration which enables the sharing of experience and engagement, and which is the only means of forcing access to the political public sphere and thus to visibility. It is not insignificant that in *Weight of the World*, Bourdieu makes precisely the category of suffering, understood as social suffering, serve the threefold purpose of displaying hidden poverty, criticizing the inadequacy of the language of the political public sphere and clarifying the social causes of guilt complexes with a view to neutralizing their sources as well as their effects:[29] describing the social process of suffering helps us to stop assigning responsibility to ourselves as individuals and contributes to a co-construction of suffering with others.

From a similar perspective, Veena Das has for her part emphasized, first, that the individualizing and weakening effects of suffering are all the more profound when they cannot be expressed and, second, that obstacles to the expression of suffering may arise both from the absence of adequate social or cultural resources and from genuine collective denial. In her work, these themes are illustrated in particular by the mass rape linked to the partition of India (the number of cases being estimated at over 100,000), by which the colonized attained the basic status of autonomous citizens at the same time that they collectively became rapists. Faced with such a phenomenon, the ethnographer of social suffering is positioned both as a spokesperson for a suffering too crushing to be expressed and brought into the public space by the victims, as a social critic struggling against the denial of the lived reality of violence and as an actor in the co-construction of a discourse on suffering making it possible to liberate individuals from its pathogenic influence.[30] To describe social suffering is also to provide linguistic resources to aid escape from a position characteristic of 'subalternity' in which it is speech itself that suffering renders inaccessible.[31]

It is quite possible that the collective denial of suffering may be a more ordinary social experience than it seems: the 'defensive ideology' that work collectives built to withstand the arduous nature of their specific activity could provide illustrations of this.[32] And the problem of the invisibilization of suffering is doubtless just as prevalent. What are the factors that contribute to this problem? It has been observed that the public sphere has been characterized, since the advent of the bourgeoisie as the dominant social class, by an invisibilization of the experience of poverty,[33] an invisibilization whose political challenge is evident as soon as poverty ceases be regarded as a general characteristic of human nature and the social order claims to guarantee the rights of individuals against inequality and domination.[34] Like violence, suffering is among the phenomena that immediately raise the question of the legitimacy of the social order in which they develop. Because the social invisibilization of the experience of poverty and domination is required in order to justify a social order based on inequality, one might think it is one of the forms of expression of an ideological coercion in the public sphere, or, if preferred, of class structure, or of a social polarization through forms of domination at once economic, social and symbolic.

Let us note on this point that the study of social suffering allows us to question a presupposition of the usual conception of ideology. This is not solely the loquacious expression of social interests through rhetoric, but also different forms of silence and denial of all that tends to challenge the authority and position even of dominant social groups.[35] And let us note that the existence of such social processes of invisibilization is enough to show how little weight there is to the recurring argument that opposes the critique of domination and injustice to an approach in terms of social suffering: the social order distributes unequally painful negative experiences (injustice) and their invisibilization plays a role in the reproduction of these inequalities (domination).

To this general process of the invisibilization of domination and poverty, specific to modernity, are added the dynamic characteristics of neoliberalism. The end of the society of salaried labour typical of Fordist capitalism has caused the development of subjective harm related to exclusion and new forms of work. As regards the effects of exclusion, Marcel Jaeger has reported that 'the phenomena of psychological collapse amongst the long-term unemployed and those dependent upon social assistance have already been emphasised by several researchers: disproportionately high morbidity is particularly clear with regard to depressive illnesses, anxiety disorders with somatisation, the consumption of alcohol, drugs, tobacco. It is clearer still for the homelesss, in terms of the prevalence of psychiatric disorders'.[36]

Similarly, in the work domain, we have seen the development of diseases of overwork (burnout, *karoshi*, musculo-skeletal disorders) and pathologies of harassment (that is to say, situations experienced as harassment and resulting in depressive syndromes, confusional syndromes, delusions of persecution and various psychosomatic effects).[37] The transition to neoliberalism has also resulted in new forms of inequality in response to suffering in the countries on the periphery. While in the countries at the centre of the world economy suffering emerges today mostly as depression and anxiety disorders, poverty and malnutrition, violence and the struggle for survival that they cause remain the major form of suffering in the countries of the periphery. Poverty and malnutrition are increasing on every continent: almost half of the world population lives on less than $2 a day, a fifth on less than a dollar and an estimated 800 million people are suffering from malnutrition.[38]

In such a context it is not surprising that new forms of denial of suffering are developing, whether through the invisibilization of work or workers, modes of representation of unemployment and exclusion that concentrate on the economic aspects (the quantitative question of 'unemployment') or moral aspects (the 'responsibility' of the unemployed) and ignore the lived experience of individuals in the countries at the centre of the world economy, or whether through the representation of poverty in an exoticized form (it concerns 'other' societies) or a spectacularized form (its horror is so great that it can only be an exceptional phenomenon) in the countries on the periphery. The invisibilization of suffering related to insecurity, unemployment, exclusion and poverty appears as a structural feature of the contemporary world.

Negative experiences that are related to new forms of work ('suffering at work' has recently given rise to what has sometimes been seen as an 'epidemic' of workers' suicides[39]), poverty (in the shape of the working poor, precarious workers and the unemployed) and extreme social situations (homelessness, slums, the extreme poverty of peasants who sometimes experience, as in India, 'epidemics' of suicide[40]) spontaneously appear as very direct objections to the existence of the social order in which they occur; whether and how to describe them is what is at stake in a conflict over legitimation, in which the different possible strategies are invisibilization, euphemization and naturalization, while criticism is the counterstrategy.

Regarding forms of suffering characteristic of societies at the centre of the world economy, justification may there consist in producing descriptions in which the world appears as a place of enjoyment and freedom rather than suffering. Legitimation may also include stating that expressed suffering can be explained exclusively by semantic transformations (a new language) that are actually integral to objective changes which are emancipatory in themselves. Legitimation can consist, finally, in all the attempts to claim that the suffering of individuals is merely caused by timidity in the face of social changes or by a temporary failure to adapt or to set up in contrast to real suffering (for example that of the unemployed) difficulties that are only relative (for example, those of the precariously employed).

Regarding the suffering associated with forms of poverty and extreme violence restricted to certain populations on the periphery of the world economy, a similar conflict over justification can be observed. Nancy Scheper-Hughes has pointed out how much the bodies and deaths of the poor can be rendered invisible in pockets of extreme poverty in Brazil.[41] Arthur and Joan Kleinman have noted that the structural invisibilization of extreme rural poverty and the forms of indigence and routinized violence that are the hallmark of life in the slums is paradoxically accompanied by staging them as a spectacle and by a veritable professionalization of the representation of suffering (through television reports, photographs and advertisements).[42]

Similarly, Nancy Scheper-Hughes has emphasized that exhibition as a spectacle produces a kind of emotional neutralization and appearance of fatalism in response to which the social sciences cannot be content to remain in the position of neutral observers: they should rather become aware that their own descriptions of social suffering are part of a 'politics of representation'.[43] In particular, she has analysed how the violence and dehumanization that are characteristic of the favelas are not only aggravating factors of the social suffering within these socially marginalized areas, but also provide the argument justifying the armed violence inflicted on their inhabitants by the rest of society (unlimited police repression, death squads, etc.).[44] A description in terms of social suffering allows us to offer a different view of the origin of violence and counter such ideological effects and such distorting representations of socially caused suffering.[45]

But when describing social suffering challenges domination and poverty, new political objections arise. On the one hand, should social criticism not focus on the forms of resistance that domination and poverty bring about, instead of describing their ability to damage subjectivity? On the other hand, is it not a weakness of the theme of social suffering that it places on the same level the question of domination and that of poverty, whereas resistance to domination seems politically more fruitful (and frequent) than resistance to poverty? Examining these objections requires some terminological clarification.

Domination and poverty are partially independent and partially overlapping realities. They are independent to the extent that some forms of domination affect economically privileged individuals (gender domination, and more rarely the domination of 'race'), while some forms of extreme poverty are characterized by a certain kind of outsider status with regard to what constitutes the core of class domination (exploitation): some of the excluded are excluded even from the common forms of exploitation. However, poverty remains largely dependent on domination, first because the concept of poverty refers to the effect of class domination (the confinement of certain people in a subordinate economic and social position), and second because the intensification of poverty is usually accompanied by the intensification of gender and race domination, as well as exposure to various forms of violence related to social relations of class, gender and race.

In addition, the concept of poverty means some form of vulnerability to domination and violence to the extent that the capacity to resist is diminished by the weakness of collective resources, isolation or even subjective collapse that characterize poverty. It does not seem legitimate, therefore, to attempt to oppose the perspective of the critique of domination to that of the critique of poverty. Yet in various sectors of the left, criticism of poverty has a worse reputation than criticism of domination and the political disqualification of the problem of poverty has repercussions for that of social suffering.

The most obvious explanation for this bad reputation has to do with the fact that the category 'poverty' does not denote a dynamic of transformation: poverty is a social situation that does not either spontaneously or easily become political struggle against the established order. If we believe H. Arendt, struggles against poverty, unlike resistance to oppression, have only ever led to uprisings without political results.[46] Similarly, in the Marxist tradition, the passivity of a peasantry in the grip of destitution is generally opposed to the revolutionary energy of a proletariat resisting capitalist exploitation.

It seems that, in the work of some authors at least, the idea of suffering may have been discredited because it specifically referred to the passivity that kept the poor, especially poor peasant farmers, out of the movement of history.[47] But after the working proletariat failed to establish itself as the subject of history and at a time when the progress of democracy and justice on the world scale is being spurred on by movements such as the Landless Workers' Movement in Brazil or governments whose social base is the indigenous peasantry, as in Bolivia, at a time when the dead end of any hierarchy of domination and its effects cannot be ignored, the political disqualification of the peasantry cannot be treated as a matter of course. The same is true of suffering.

Even in the struggles of the proletariat against class domination, the privilege granted to activity over passivity tended to exclude the problem of suffering, according to a logic which clearly bears the mark of gender domination. If suffering has been excluded from politically decisive phenomena, this is doubtless also due to a heroic vision in which politics is played out in large group clashes in the male public sphere (strikes, demonstrations, conquests of power), themselves disconnected from the space reserved for women of daily life and daily accommodations made with the lived reality of domination and poverty. It has thus been possible to show all the differences between the official story, that is to say the male story, of the labour movement in Minneapolis between the First and Second World Wars, in which politics was a matter of battles guided by ideas and organizations, and women's account of the same events, in which demonstrations and protest culture were much more rooted in a 'community of suffering'.[48] We could add that even today, if the theme of suffering at work can enter trade union circles only with difficulty, this is particularly due to the vision of unionism as struggle and of the trade union member as someone who resists adversity and remains invulnerable to the pressures of the managerial hierarchy and the difficulties of labour.[49]

When one argues that criticism must be based on the practices of resistance to domination rather than the harm to subjectivity domination causes, ultimately one presupposes a whole set of false oppositions. From the perspective of social theory, one presupposes the opposition of domination and poverty, whereas in fact the second is hardly thinkable without the first. From the perspective of the theory of action, one sets up activity and passivity in opposition one another, whereas in fact social action always involves forms of passivity and interpassivity[50]—that social struggles can have roots in the 'suffering of communities' illustrates this principle.

Finally, from the perspective of political theory, one sets up in opposition to one another the respective value of resistance to domination and of revolts against suffering. To reveal the unconvincing nature of this opposition, we could refer to the Foucaldo-Deleuzian theme that as resistance is caused by power, it always risks speaking the language of power and being reabsorbed by it.[51] By contrast, suffering can be among the factors leading to lines of flight, to the extent that it always has to do with a failure of inclusion in social forms. But rather than reverse the opposition of resistance and suffering and overstate the value of the latter, we will limit ourselves in what follows to challenging this opposition by proceeding from the following two arguments: struggles against domination are often struggles against suffering and suffering provides a critical perspective when social struggles are lacking.

A final set of political difficulties is attributable to the problems posed by the ways in which suffering is publicly articulated. Such an articulation is already problematic in the sense that suffering always seems to be experienced on a level below public language, in affects and in individuals' bodies. This difficulty is redoubled when we try to articulate the social dimension of a suffering experienced in the singularity of a body and an individual story. The concrete forms of these challenges depend on the resources that societies offer to people to represent and express their suffering. Societies do not only render suffering invisible, they also offer modes of representation of suffering, and in this they may also sometimes hinder the expression of suffering and increase rather than heal it. Mourning rituals imposed on women provide a paradigmatic illustration of this,[52] such as in South Africa, where the many prohibitions are accompanied by the marking of women's bodies (for example, by shaving the head).[53]

An additional problem is posed by the diversity of the ways in which public recognition of suffering can be achieved. The problem for any spokesperson for suffering is to become aware of both the political and psychological effects of the public expression of suffering. It is clear that the expression of suffering and its recognition by others cannot be the main vector of a grieving process. On the contrary, they may constitute obstacles to the psychic recovery that victims are trying to obtain from silence and oblivion. But conversely, such a grieving process always risks leading to a minimization of the horror of the past situation, locking the victims in guilt fostered by collective denial by only offering them superficial and precarious resilience and leaving intact the social conditions of the past catastrophe. In a way, a spokesperson for suffering intervenes in favour of the victims and against certain psychological solutions which they adopt. This challenge takes the form of an aporia when the discourse of suffering is addressed to members of society who participated in generating this suffering, even if only indirectly, for example in the case of Indian women raped by Muslims if they were Hindus or Sikhs or by Hindus and Sikhs if they were Muslims. In this instance all men appear simultaneously as both the intended audience of the discourse of suffering and as potential rapists.[54]

Though spokespersons for social suffering expose themselves through their role to the contradiction between the logic of mourning and that of social criticism, and though they should doubtless give up the ideal of a perfectly adequate expression of suffering and take the risk of substituting for silence modes of social representation which can make things worse, they would be accomplices of invisibilization and denial if they gave up expressing suffering and proceeding with its joint construction with the people concerned.[55] It is futile to seek to circumvent the political difficulties involved in issues of social suffering; we must face them. This applies to these political obstacles as much as to the epistemological obstacles mentioned earlier. And just as much as such epistemological obstacles, the political obstacles are rooted in the very notion of social suffering.

Suffering as a simple fact challenges the social order in which it emerges. To put it in Adornian terms, the experience of suffering is that of the refusal of suffering, and although it is the experience of the singularity of this suffering, it is also the experience of the refusal of the world that caused this suffering or made it possible.[56] The question of social suffering is both descriptive and evaluative, and it is as much in its descriptive component as its normative component that the concept of social suffering has a critical dimension. This critical dimension explains why the concept of social suffering is essentially 'contested'.[57] The political conflicts concern its descriptive component insofar as both legitimation and social critique depend on establishing that there are social factors in suffering. The controversy is also normative insofar as, even though the social factors of suffering may be attested, the usefulness and legitimacy of social criticism in terms of suffering can be questioned. Because political conflicts manifest themselves within 'essentially contested' concepts in the form of aporias, it is mistaken to claim to be able to handle these concepts or do without them without directly confronting such aporias. To the extent that these aporias are inseparably epistemological and political, it is unrealistic to try to resolve them from a purely speculative point of view: it is rather a theoretical articulation of an epistemological solution and a political position that should be aimed for.[58]

At the beginning of a theoretical work on social suffering, it would be awkward to hide the fact that the use of this concept for such negative social experiences also expresses the deep malaise that must be overcome by anyone who wants to study them: here we encounter strictly psychological obstacles. Here again, Devereux is enlightening: he stressed that the study of human behaviour can produce anxiety to which the simplest response is the establishment of defences such as the omission, underestimation or overplaying of disturbing details, fetishization of 'the facts' and methodological fundamentalism. These considerations apply to the study of some of the negative experiences related to domination and poverty, not only to the study of distant cultures or that of mental illness. Because of the invisibilization to which these experiences are generally subject, because of the non-permeability of the social spaces in which they develop, because of the distance which separates them from the social standards considered normal, it is only possible to study them seriously by way of anthropological engagement and participant observation or of clinical psychology. But still, the clinician and anthropologist studying areas where social distress is prevalent, where the subproletariat are confined, spaces of structural poverty or severe precarity, face the spectacle of forms of violence and psychological degradation that make them likely to give in and give up the study. The difficulty of enduring the suffering of others is then connected with the sharing of suffering and combines with a difficulty in allowing one's own suffering access to expression.[59]

Ethnographic studies like those of Philippe Bourgois on New York crack sellers, David Lepoutre and Pascale Jamoulle on socially marginalized neighbourhoods, Emily Hermant on reintegration centres, Djemila Zeneidi on the homeless or Patrick Declerck on the tramps of Paris bear witness to these difficulties in various ways.[60] The discomfort, even suffering, of the observer is always present. These can be discussed explicitly and bring about reflection on how the investigator must accept being 'affected' by the object of the study while protecting his or her 'mental and physical health'[61] as in the study Pascale Jamoulle devoted to 'working-class families overwhelmed by the risky behavior of one of their members'. But this suffering can also be dealt with by defensive mechanisms of dramatization or denial which have the effect of distorting further the features of reality that prompted them.

WHAT DO WE MEAN BY SOCIAL SUFFERING?

The idea of social suffering assumes the connection between a psychological reality, suffering, and a social factor. In itself, it says nothing either of the nature of the suffering in question or of the nature of this social factor, nor of the nature of the link between them. In the final analysis, it only asks three questions, and there are many conceptions of social suffering that can result from the combination of their answers. We must now analyse these various conceptions of social suffering and specify those which will be retained in this book. We will not be discussing these conceptions in themselves, but only organizing the meanings they give the idea of social suffering. However, to the extent that most of the meanings have been taken up by particular types of theorization, the ordering of meanings will be accompanied by an attempt at theoretical articulation of the most relevant of them, that is, at an outline conceptualization (the actual conceptualization being postponed to chapter 3).[62] It may be useful to refer in advance to figure 1.1 to track the movement of the typology which is described below.

What kind of suffering is implied by the idea of social suffering? This question concerns both the understanding and the scope of the term 'suffering'. Because uses of this term are inflationary and a traditional objection to any theoretical and political reference to suffering is that the notion necessarily remains indeterminable, let us start with the restrictions. The most obvious is based on the classic distinction between *suffering* and *pain*.

Pain is generally understood as meaning a physiological phenomenon and a physical sensation, while the notion of suffering has a more truly psychological dimension that can either accompany the pain or come from an independent source: all pain can be experienced as suffering, but some suffering can be of strictly psychological origin.[63] Although suffering tends to be experienced physically, we must distinguish suffering where the cause is pain felt as subjective harm, and in this sense resulting from the dynamics of pain, and pain resulting from a process of somatization, and in this sense resulting from the process of psychological harm: the exacerbating subjective resonances of pain are different from an exacerbation of psychic suffering that is experienced somatically, although the two are often intertwined. Clearly, the distinction between pain and suffering cannot be understood as a real distinction, which would separate the phenomena into two watertight categories. But if it is understood as a semantic distinction, it seems quite legitimate.

A second criterion for distinguishing pain and suffering lies in the types of temporality and magnitude proper to each. We commonly distinguish between time-limited harm of very high intensity (pain) and lasting harm of high intensity (we speak of 'great suffering', we say that we have 'suffered very much', while this type of description is less common for pain). The fact that there are various types of subjective investment in pain indeed makes it possible to speak of gradations of suffering; involved here are Freudian issues of the psychic resonance of pain and defences against suffering. Let us further note that the temporality involved in suffering cannot be reduced to its permanence, but also consists in various forms of distortion in relationships to the present and the future: suffering has the ability to cut me off from my past and my future by locking me in a disturbing and demeaning present.

To define the meaning assignable to suffering, it is not necessary to engage further in the analysis of types and subtypes of suffering. But we must now state that it involves neither simply a physical feeling nor simply an emotion, but always also what we call an affect. This statement can already be rendered plausible in terms of phenomenological analysis. Saying 'I am suffering' is not at all to describe an emotion in the sense in which we normally understand this expression to mean acute and transient states such as anger, fear, etc. Saying 'I am suffering' does not amount only to expressing a feeling in the sense that this usually suggests a milder and more sustained state, such as shame, happiness, etc. To say that I 'suffer' is also to pass judgement on a reality that we are generally aware of as overflowing the boundaries of the current consciousness that we have of it, in contrast to emotions and feelings—and in this respect suffering could be compared to the passions. It is also significant that this judgement is spoken in the past tense ('I suffered a great deal') or in an objectifying manner ('there is much suffering in X') more often than in the first person present indicative.

It is however in a more precise sense that the concept of affect is called upon, in the sense in which, in Freud's work, this concept does not operate on the level of psychological analysis (to which belongs the distinction between emotions, feelings and passions) but on that of metapsychological analysis: that of the theory of psychic life, and especially of the emotions, feelings and passions. The term affect refers to the quality (the pleasure/displeasure polarity) and the quantity of energy ('quantum of affect') mobilized by the drives and their destinies: repression, qualitative change (for example, the conversion of libido into 'tender love') or transposition into another affect (for example, the transformation of repressed affect into anxiety affect).[64] If it makes sense to describe suffering in terms of affect, we must presuppose the working of affects to explain the special power of suffering, its ability to mobilize our conscious life, its ability to transform our models for interpreting ourselves, our interactions with others and our consciousness of time.

These preliminary definitions are not yet enough to understand how suffering can be an element of social criticism. For it to gain critical power, a further distinction is necessary: that between *normal* and *abnormal* suffering. Individuals are often able to integrate their own suffering into satisfactory subjectivation processes; then it becomes a normal part of their lives. But the term 'suffering' has a critical dimension when it refers to the fact that people's lives 'stop going right', when it denotes the process in which individuals 'feel badly' because their relation to themselves and to the world is undermined, as are the relationships without which life loses value and quality, or when it denotes the processes that send individuals 'overwhelmed with grief' down the slippery slope of an unbearable relationship with themselves and the world.

One can indeed wonder whether the distinction between *normal* and *abnormal* suffering is legitimate, and there is a serious temptation to reduce any and all suffering to a normal part of existence (as in Nietzsche, where it is the fact of no longer suffering or no longer being able to face suffering that is abnormal[65]) or, conversely, to a potentially pathological suffering (as in Schopenhauer, where suffering is always the sign of the fundamental irrationality of the will that we should strive to negate[66]). The strength of these two positions is entirely in their one-sidedness, which is also their weakness.

But we can also wonder about the nature of the criteria for distinguishing normal and abnormal suffering. Should what is abnormal be decided based on criteria internal to the psyche (in the sense of the creation of pathological or pathogenic structures of the psyche, loss of capacity of the self and the associated freedoms, the weakening or breaking down of identity), based on the social effects of suffering (the narrowing down of social relations, the collapse of horizons of expectation) or based on ethical or moral standards (suffering that is unacceptable, unbearable, serves no purpose, is unevenly distributed in society)? The question of the criteria is easily resolved if we rely on a medical definition of suffering (if we identify abnormal suffering with pathological suffering) or if we retain for our definition only the acute suffering caused by traumatic situations of violence or extreme poverty (as in Kleinman or Das[67]). But it will undoubtedly arise if the term 'social suffering' is applied to more common forms of suffering. It is precisely on the recognition of this suffering that the extension of the concept of social suffering depends, an extension which decides whether it is of interest to social criticism.

A fact decisive for the idea of social suffering is that, in general, the term 'suffering' can be understood either in the sense of one of the conditions constitutive of the human condition or in the sense of an abnormal phenomenon. Clearly suffering defines a normal part of life, but clearly there are also different qualities of suffering, and it seems legitimate, even necessary, to distinguish in principle normal and abnormal suffering (even though the criteria for making this distinction operative may be lacking).

Most uses of the concept of social suffering refer to abnormal suffering that is understood as a pathological disorder or as nonpathological harm severe enough to be taken into account as part of a negative definition of mental health (suffering that is extreme, incapacitating, crippling, alienating etc.[68]). When suffering is understood in the sense of abnormal suffering, the concept of social suffering, which in this case denotes the social dimension of severe subjective harm, can be used in a critical sense: critical of suffering itself as well as of its social context. This is not the case when social suffering is understood in the sense of the social dimension of normal suffering or suffering constitutive of the human condition (see 1 in figure 1.1). It is in this latter sense especially that Freud speaks of a 'suffering of social origin' in *Civilisation and Its Discontents*: society always produce suffering, and in this respect social suffering belongs to normal suffering, even if it is also the case that specific types of civilization produce types of abnormal suffering.[69]

When suffering is understood in the sense of abnormal suffering, different types of connections between 'suffering' and 'social' are possible depending on whether these terms are taken in a literal or relatively figurative sense (analogous or metaphorical or metonymic). In this regard we propose to distinguish between suffering *of* the social body, suffering *in* the social body and social suffering in the strict sense.

By *suffering of the social body*, we mean a metaphorical use of the idea of suffering to refer to disorders or dysfunctions which are located in a specifically social entity but are—by analogy only—considered suffering. This use of the concept is proper to theories that rely on an interpretation of the social context through the metaphor of the social body and that propose an analogy between social unrest on the one hand and the organic disorders and suffering it leads to on the other. We find an illustration of this in organicist social theories such as those of Lilienfeld[70] and Müller-Lyer[71] (see 2 in figure 1.1).

The notion of *collective suffering*, or suffering that is in a society rather than of that society, allows us for its part to recognize another connection between the terms 'social' and 'suffering'. When the idea of social suffering is called upon within a public health framework, for example, the term 'suffering' is used in a literal sense to denote psychological or organic disorders of individuals and the term 'social' is taken in a loose sense because it denotes the social as a collective phenomenon (we could speak here of a metonymic use to point out that though all social suffering has a collective dimension, the reverse is not true) (see 4 in figure 1.1).

In the framework of this conception, the definition of suffering is independent of that of the social. When suffering is defined in strictly medical terms, for example, it is connected to the social context only externally (in indicators of collective morbidity or mortality, for instance). But the issue of collective suffering can also be understood in reference to a nonmedical definition of suffering, as when it is placed in the category of individual feelings. We could refer in this respect to the construction of quality of life indicators, still in the context of public health. In the one case as in the other it is through aggregation procedures that suffering is raised to the status of a collective entity. What defines the idea of collective suffering in society is, first, the reference to individual suffering (whether defined in a medical way or in terms of quality of life) and second, the aggregation of individual suffering into collective suffering.

The flaws of theoretical undertakings whose topic is the 'suffering of the social body' and 'collective suffering in society' are clear. The first meaning, 'suffering of the social body', understands 'suffering' in an indeterminate, purely analogical sense, whose legitimacy is impossible to justify: if the aim is only to denote social 'disorders', then the use of psychological or medical vocabulary brings nothing decisive to the theory and can only cause confusion. The metaphor of the social body is just as detrimental. The second meaning, 'collective suffering', has, on the contrary, the advantage of rigour because it confers a medical or psychological meaning on the term 'suffering' while giving a quantitative definition of what should be meant by social. This rigour has, however, a corresponding narrowness. On the one hand, there is no reason to think that the aggregation of individual phenomena is the best way to account for the social dimension of phenomena. On the other hand, and there will be an opportunity to return to this point, there is every reason to believe that the domain of suffering is broader than that of pathological suffering and of suffering experienced as such on which public health concentrates.[72]

Let us add that the first two conceptions can be associated with each other in different ways. We can note with H. P. Dreitzel that one of the most common defects of the theoretical construct of social suffering is to associate in a purely analogous way a concept of suffering *in* society with a suffering *of* society (see 3 in figure 1.1), in other words, to juxtapose a conception of individual pathology with an organic conception of social pathology without explaining the link between them.[73]

Let us from now on reserve the term 'social suffering' to usages of 'social suffering' that take social and suffering in their proper senses, denoting the truly *social dimension* of subjective harm which can be said to belong to the category of suffering in the proper sense of the term, insofar as it belongs to the affective lives of individuals. It is immediately apparent that this social dimension can be understood in two ways: first, from a *psychological perspective*, that of an analysis of the social components of subjective disorders, and second, from a *sociological perspective* (in the broad sense of the social sciences), that of a theory of the social conditions of suffering, of how it is experienced in the social context and the feedback effect it has on interactions and institutions. Each of these perspectives leads to different elaborations of the problem of social suffering.

The properly psychological study of the social component of subjective disorders can be viewed in two different ways depending on whether this component is understood in the sense of social conditioning (or nondeterminant conditions) or in the sense of social causation (or determinant conditions). The psychological approach can aim at describing the *social conditioning* of psychological disorders in general, in which case the social dimension of suffering only denotes the social part of any abnormal suffering (see 5 in figure 1.1). This is the specific objective of the supporters of sociogenesis of mental disorders because they oppose the assumptions of physiogenesis or psychogenesis,[74] but it is also an objective that can be pursued within the framework of a psychogenic theory of disorders, following the Freudian suggestion that social psychology should be considered as the foundation of individual psychology[75] or following the hypothesis of an 'ethnic segment' of the unconscious.[76] In all of these cases, suffering is not specifically social, even if social factors have a part in its origin.

Analysis of the social component of subjective disorders can also lead us to describe forms of pathological or nonpathological suffering whose distinguishing characteristic is that they are *caused by the social context*. Some kinds of abnormal suffering may be *distinguished* from others in the sense that *specific social processes* have a decisive share in their aetiology (see 6 in figure 1.1). This is the path that L. Le Guillant has taken in his work on the issue of work-related neuroses.[77] It is, then, certain specific psychological disorders, not all psychological disorders, which are taken into consideration.

As part of the sociological approach, the problematization of social suffering differs according to whether the concept of social suffering is intended to clarify the social *experience* or the social *dynamics* of suffering. The analysis of the social experience of suffering is centred on how each society builds modes of expression for—and specific responses to—suffering. Such analysis has been especially developed in the field of medical anthropology and sociology of health. It can consist of a simple study of the social construction of suffering: each society has its own definition of what is bearable and unbearable,[78] each society gives specific forms and functions to the social representations of suffering, and offers different social responses to what is identified as suffering.[79] But it is also possible to give a more political dimension to this study on the premise that suffering is a problem that challenges societies themselves and to which they must therefore attempt to respond with different forms of social and cultural creation (the anthropological analysis of 'social suffering'[80]) (see 7 in figure 1.1).

The dynamic analysis of suffering focuses in turn on the analysis of interactions between suffering and the social context (the action of the social context on individual and collective suffering, as well as the reaction of this suffering on the social context). These two approaches are not mutually exclusive, if only because the experience of suffering is directly related to the interactions in which individuals are engaged, indeed is related also to the modifications of these interactions under the influence of this suffering.[81] In fact, the anthropological analysis of 'social suffering' concerns as much the processes that produce suffering as the interactions in which it is experienced and how these interactions can be modified by suffering. But the core of the analysis consists mainly in the meaning that cultures give to suffering, the latter being understood above all in the sense of pathological suffering and of extreme suffering produced by events such as wars and collective violence as well as severe poverty. All these are characteristics that distinguish the anthropological-ethnographic and medical study of 'social suffering' from strictly sociological approaches to suffering which, in turn, tend to focus on the interaction between suffering and sociale processes and take into account especially suffering induced by (or involved in) routinized social relations. These studies take a dynamic view of suffering that can lead us to consider it either as a structural effect or as the specific characteristic of certain social actions.

The structural approach to suffering can make suffering an effect of stabilized social forms (theories of structural anomie,[82] of symbolic violence,[83] of stigmatization[84]) (see 9 in figure 1.1). In this case, it is usually either *social norms* that shape collective representations and practices or specific *social relations* in which individuals are engaged, which play a causal role. It is clear that suffering can also be explained by a third level of social reality, that of the *symbolic structures* of social life, although a focus on this is more often the result of a social psychology inspired by psychoanalysis than of sociology.[85]

Suffering can also be explained by the destabilization of general social forms[86] due to their internal transformations (these may produce various patterns of temporary anomie) (see 10 in figure 1.1) or exogenous events that deserve to be called 'social' because of their social restructuring effects (the model of collective trauma, of which we also find a use and deconstruction in the anthropological analysis of 'social suffering'[87]) (see 11 in figure 1.1).

Moreover, it is a totally different sociological perspective which is developed within the framework of an 'interpretive sociology', which, in the context of a reformulation of the pragmatist approach of 'social careers',[88] focuses on describing 'trajectories of suffering' in which the suffering of individuals is both cause and effect of catastrophic social trajectories, involving a series of misalignments with the everyday world and with others (see 8 in figure 1.1).

These are the main mechanisms characteristic of trajectories of suffering according to Fritz Schütze: 1) 'the progressive construction of a framework of conditions favourable to the development of a trajectory (made up, on the one hand, of predispositions determined by injuries suffered during an individual's life and, on the other hand, of a constellation of severely unfavourable circumstances in the current situation)', 2) 'the sudden crossing of the activation threshold of the developmental potential of the trajectory (experience of shock and of disorientation)', 3) 'the attempt at establishing an unstable equilibrium in learning to manage a new daily reality', 4) 'the destabilisation of this unstable equilibrium (the individual becomes a stranger to himself: he no longer understands himself, because he can no longer act in the same way as before)', 5) 'the collapse of the organisation of his daily life and of his capacity to orient himself (the individual loses confidence in himself and in his significant others)'.[89] Schütze's approach comes under the more general heading of studies of life paths, which actually lie on the border between sociology and psychology. One of their specific features is the central use of the concept of 'social trajectory', which is understood in both a both sociological and a psychological sense.[90]

In order to develop a mode of problematization relevant to the negative social experiences that are the subject of this book, to which of these eleven meanings should we refer?

To the extent that these experiences blur the boundaries of sociology and psychology, it is necessary to articulate psychological and sociological points of view on social suffering. Sociology can undertake the study of the social factors of suffering, but it cannot claim to identify the aetiology of suffering

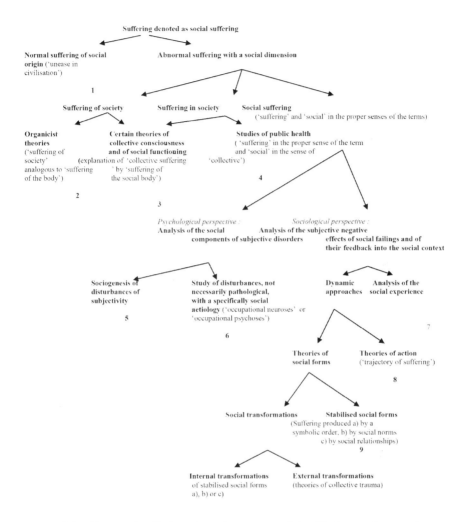

Figure 1.1. Forms of suffering given the name social suffering. Source: Author's own.

as long as it refuses to engage in the analysis of psychological processes which are superimposed on social processes. Psychology and psychoanalysis can claim to supplement it on this point, but generally they will not go so far as to develop a real sociological analysis when working to theorize the specific subjective effects of specific social processes. Just as the experience of suffering is one of the forms of interweaving of the social and psychological factors of experience,[91] so the content of the idea of social suffering calls for a shift in psychology towards sociology and a shift in sociology towards psychology. In sociology as in psychology, such shifts are sometimes considered, and it is by building on these theoretical proposals that it is possible to sketch out modes of conceptualization and general theorization of social suffering.[92]

Even though suffering is always given in and through meanings, representations and social practices, the term 'suffering' refers to a reality that always goes beyond the social techniques available for expressing and controlling it: it is a part of the reality of social experience that is irreducible to a categorization, a meaning or a mode of interaction: in short, that is irreducible to a social construction.[93] Conversely, society cannot be reduced to the social context in which suffering can occur. It is a multilayered reality that can contribute in many ways to the occurrence of suffering. Society is a set of standards recognized as legitimate by individuals who use them and a set of social relations that individuals continuously interpret, confirm and repair through interaction. It also consists of a set of social relations of domination (which cannot be reduced to the symbolic structures through which they are perpetuated or in which they have their roots), of intersubjective networks of support and of material objects (which themselves cannot be reduced to the technical objects we use as a means of action) capable of satisfying needs. Actualization of domination in the form of constraints within interactions or in that of symbolic violence, weakening of intersubjective supports (disaffiliation) and unsatisfied needs connected with the physical constraints that objects exert on our actions are three dynamic factors of social suffering that belong to the reality of social experience.

Just as social experience carries the weight of social relations, events and material objects that are always liable to undermine our representations and our aspirations by condemning us to a more or less unbearable dissatisfaction from which we seek to rescue ourselves,[94] so affects are at work within social experience that are always liable to subvert the meanings of our representations and to defeat our plans of action.[95] If the study of suffering therefore should always consider the inextricably social and political efforts by which societies strive to represent and control the suffering they produce, it will also have to keep from reducing the experience of suffering to a social construction and strive to account for the psychological and social reality of this experience.

The idea of social suffering aims in particular at characterizing some of the negative social experiences most typical of our time (such as suffering at work related to new forms of work, psychological suffering linked to exclusion at the centre of the world economy and suffering related to extreme structural poverty on the periphery) which seemingly cannot to be reduced to the transient effect of social transformations that are underway (we left behind the crisis of Fordism and entered neoliberalism three decades ago now). Although the effect of social change on life transitions undeniably plays a role, in order to identify these specific negative social experiences of our time we will focus on the *social aetiology of specifically social* and not necessarily pathological subjective harm and on the subjective harm produced by *stabilized social structures*. In other words, we will understand the concept of social suffering mainly as a way of bridging the gap between sociology and psychology that finds its centre of gravity in the combination of meanings 6 and 9 of figure 1.1. But it is clear that in order to capture these negative experiences as experiences, such a conception of social suffering must also consider the achievements of the anthropology of 'social suffering' and the analysis of trajectories of suffering. In other words, the combination of meanings 6 and 9 will be conditioned by meanings 7 and 8.

Certainly, the project of a theory whose center of gravity is fixed *both* by psychological disorders with a specific social component *and* by the subjectively negative effects of stabilized social structures is problematic. It first raises a number of methodological difficulties having to do with the terms on which sociological and psychological issues are linked together. There would be little sense in developing a 'discourse on method' concerning how sociology and psychology can complement one another by being applied to the same object, and it is better to postpone consideration of this issue until we analyse the various specific problems associated with it. However, let us mention two symmetrical pitfalls that must be avoided as far as possible.

The first is to content ourselves with combining concepts from independent theoretical frameworks, some from certain sociological theories, the others from certain psychological theories, without justifying either the choice of a particular concept in the sense used by a particular theory or the choice of this or that theory, and without justifying the legitimacy and coherence of combining them other than from an instrumentalist perspective—a pitfall that is specific to 'social philosophy' in the pejorative sense of the term.

The second pitfall would be to compete with sociology and psychology on behalf of a new science that is supposed to cover the phenomena of both the one and the other, assuming an interweaving of the psychological and the social in a homogeneous type of reality, whereas the logics of the psychic and of the social are irreducible and heterogeneous.[96]

More serious still than the methodological difficulties are the problems arising from the fact that the respective extensions of the two concepts of social suffering that we have identified as crucial (meanings 6 and 9) do not overlap: the phenomena that psychologists and psychiatrists attempt to explain when describing psychological disorders with specific social components are not the same as those to which the framework of negative subjective effects produced by stabilized social structures applies, for example those to which Bourdieu refers when integrating social suffering into a theory of 'the subjective experience of domination'.[97] While the specifically social aetiology of certain psychological disorders now applies, for example, to subjective harms related to increased precarity, negative experiences related to general forms of socialization come under the heading of more widespread subjective harm which should not necessarily be considered as psychological disorders in the strict sense. However, there is no reason to exclude the possibility that these two conceptions of social suffering could develop complementary analyses.

Freud had already noted that the neuroses, unlike infectious diseases, have no specific cause.[98] By taking up his argument, the psychopathology of work transformed itself into the psychodynamics of work. It abandoned the issue of 'occupational neuroses' to develop one of 'suffering at work'. It also emphasized that it is impossible to attribute a causal role to the social context of work without considering the conditions of life outside work and the background negative social experiences in a person's life history: the concept of suffering at work means, therefore, a transversal reality that cannot be understood only in the context of work.[99] In clinical studies of severe precarity, what is required is to take into account jointly the social and biographical contexts in question. Hence it has often been pointed out that loss of employment and the various social supports related to it is not sufficient to explain a slide into severe precarity and its associated disorders.[100]

Let us note that in clinical studies of work and of exclusion, analysis simultaneously adopts a point of view that is both biographical and contextual, but at the same time one that is both static (describing current psychological and social structures) and dynamic, describing the trajectories of individuals in social contexts: those trajectories that lead from suffering at work to decompensation and sometimes dramatic outcomes, from the suffering of ordinary socialization up to the suffering of exclusion, even that of life on the street. To think of suffering in this way, in terms of trajectories of suffering, allows us to connect social suffering in the sense of the subjective harm of ordinary socialization (meaning 9) and social suffering in the sense of psychological disorders with a specifically social aetiology (meaning 6). And we see here not only that the sociological and psychological approaches relate to epistemic objects that are complementary, but that they even adopt complementary viewpoints on their respective objects. Indeed, these complementary perspectives must be mobilized conjointly by each of these approaches when they seek to give an account of their own specific object. Just as pathological destinies of work and precarity also actually have their roots in the structures of ordinary socialization, so the way in which social trajectories are part of the social experience of individuals always assumes the interweaving of different types of social conditions and psychological dynamics.

As Howard Becker notes, because of its use of statistics with multiple variables, sociology often tends to take the view that all the social causes that influence individual behavior act simultaneously, whereas in fact they act in sequence: the social factors in their behavior depend on how individuals successively move through different social contexts and how the effects of past contexts alter the responsiveness of individuals to new social influences.[101] Social suffering is a subject which, more than any other, can only be understood properly through a sequential model or in a processual way: first because the social causes of suffering are never instantaneous and second because trajectories of suffering are social trajectories whose individual dimension is irreducible.

Studying this subject also requires that another common assumption of sociology be abandoned: the one claiming that social actors are influenced by their childhood only insofar as it constitutes the deep phase of their socialization and thus *positively* determines their social destiny. The analysis of social suffering focusing on the negative experiences of socialization highlights the fact that in childhood there are also in play the conditions determining the reactions of these individuals to potential failures of their social destiny. And what is crucial, then, is not just childhood as social destiny, but also as a structuring of the individual *psyche* that cannot be reduced to a simple principle of variation of social destiny, as Bourdieu claims.[102] Sequential analysis of suffering not only concerns an individual considered as a carrier of internalized social logics, but also considered as a personality inducing a specific kind of response to the negative social experiences in which these internalized logics are no longer able to organize the social experience.

Sociology seems less well prepared than 'clinical psychology' to undertake such an analysis of social suffering. Indeed, the purpose of clinical psychology is to study the reactions of an individual, considered as a total personality, to the social contexts of his or her existence. [103] Clinical studies of work and exclusion, analysing *in situ* the effects of specific social contexts on individuals with a specific life history and the practical responses and discourse patterns that go along with them, confirm the fruitfulness of this type of focus on social suffering. But it is doubtless possible to take the view that the clinical approach—generally defined as a study based on the analysis of specific characteristics of individuals, assuming the involvement of the subject of knowledge, combining research and intervention, and making negative experiences into a privileged mode of access to knowledge—can be adopted by social sciences other than psychology alone. [104]

The clinical approach may indeed have two opposite orientations: a hermeneutical analysis of social trajectories, where the main challenge is to capture the uniqueness of an individual life history, or, conversely, an attempt to reconstruct the weight of the social context from individuals' trajectories. In this case, the analysis seeks to move from simple understanding to comprehensive explanation both of a particular life trajectory and of the action of social forces on individual behaviour. To do this, it still relies, implicitly or explicitly, on an analysis of psychological processes (or a metapsychology) and a general theory of social processes (or general sociology). But conversely, it is likely that the clinical analysis of the effects of these processes on general negative social experiences decisively contributes to the general theory of these processes. Let us illustrate the different dimensions of a comprehensive explanation of social trajectories by turning to the clinical study of work and severe precarity.

Although catastrophic trajectories that lead to homelessness can typically be explained by a demeaning or unstable social environment and a fragile identity that can be captured hermeneutically, these contextual conditions produce different effects according to the type of psychic fragility specific to individuals. In addition, the type of effect produced by these contextual and biographical factors itself depends on a macrosocial framework that concepts such as 'domination' and 'disaffiliation' allow us to identify. It is clear in fact that vulnerabilities caused by a loss of social support will be overdetermined by the specific vulnerability of individuals to class, gender and race domination—the effects of these being reenacted specifically in a catastrophic trajectory (for example, the social and psychological problems of a woman trying to survive on the street are not the same as those of a man[105]).

Similarly, if analysis of suffering at work involves taking into account together the work situation and the subjective coping resources of individuals, contextual and life history–based analysis must also be supplemented by the factoring in of structural social constraints. The broad forms of domination (class, gender and race) are reenacted in the work context, meaning that, for example, the violence generated by degraded working conditions tends to fall first and most heavily on the least qualified immigrant women.[106] It is also evident that breakdowns in a life history that originate from the intertwining of professional activity and private life tend to have worse effects in a general context of disaffiliation.[107]

In one case as in the other, what is at stake in clinical analysis seems also to concern more general theoretical issues: those concerning metapsychological hypotheses that can account for subjective disabilities that are not taken into consideration within the framework of classical psychology and the integration of new forms of exclusion, precarity and domination into general social theory.

From the analyses of clinical sociology and the ethnography of poverty, as from those of the psychodynamics of work and psychopathology of exclusion, it is clear that the concept of social suffering must be conceived as a transversal concept, dynamic and contextual. It denotes the *social context* of subjective harm which cannot be identified by simple snapshot findings, but whose reality must instead be grasped from the *dynamic* point of view of the social trajectories that they bring about or maintain and the psychological processes they induce (defence against suffering or sublimation of suffering), processes that can cause displacement of suffering (we will see that it will sometimes be necessary to speak of unconscious suffering) or its transference (for example, the transformation of nonpathological suffering into pathological suffering in an episode of decompensation). *Transversal*: this word is apt for the concept of social suffering because it involves setting in relation with one another various different viewpoints (static and dynamic) and different areas of investigation (description of the social structures of domination and disaffiliation, of the social context and relational environments, description of metapsychological processes, clinical description of individual behaviour). In this sense, the concept of social suffering denotes a *type of investigative method* for subjective harms related to certain negative social experiences, more than a psychological category of a nosographic or aetiological kind or a sociological concept intended to explain social regularities.

Rather than as a unified concept, then, we will take the term 'social suffering' as a *means of problematization* of a number of phenomena at the intersection of life histories and the social context, of work and life outside of work, of social integration and social exclusion. On one hand, this problematization leads to a broadening of the questions of mental health by taking into account a set of subjective harms and social processes that fall outside the traditional concerns of public health. On the other hand, it leads us to question the ordinary forms of socialization from the perspective of the negative experiences associated with them.

A CRITIQUE OF SOCIAL PATHOLOGIES?

In what follows, the concept of suffering will thus be understood as a means of problematizing phenomena that fit poorly into established disciplinary divides and the forms of ordinary language and public representation, but that raise political issues which are too important to be ignored. We must now show how social suffering understood in this sense can form part of a social critique. To the extent that the idea of social suffering is reminiscent of social pathology, it seems that social criticism which takes suffering as a connecting thread is part of the model of criticism of social pathologies. But the term 'social pathology' can have varied psychological and sociological interpretations, and although it is a model of social criticism as old as the 'social question' itself, it remains a model whose legitimacy is still under suspicion. Therefore let us specify the general logic and the specific nature of this type of social criticism.

From its first explicit formulations, which appear to come from social medicine, the concept of social pathology has linked together the three ideas of a diagnosis, an aetiology and a treatment, all related to the social context.[108] When social medicine began to use this term, it used it to signify a crisis (the 'social question') that can be measured particularly by its impacts on the health and living conditions of the poor. But the conjunction of diagnosis of a crisis with aetiology and treatment is found well beyond medical references to health. Indeed, one could argue that the idea of social pathology is essential to the development of the original problem of sociology: that of a diagnostic crisis specific to postrevolutionary societies and industrialization, that of a reflection on the causes that make these social changes no longer compatible with the maintenance of satisfactory social relations, that of a reflection on how progress could nevertheless be ensured and on ways to limit the harmful effects of the disorders of modern civilization.[109]

More generally, the idea of social pathology can be understood as a general mode of social criticism, no longer as simply a theoretical tool used by a particular human or medical science. This mode of social criticism is characterized by the following properties. First, this critique relies on diagnoses of the state of societies, or 'historical diagnoses': these identify a state of crisis that they then interpret as pathological using a medical model or metaphor, while addressing a specific historical conjuncture. Second, they engage in an analysis of the causes and effects of the crisis: they are elaborating a sociological analysis of social processes, while producing an assessment based upon the effects of these processes on social and individual life. Third, the criticism has a therapeutic dimension; that is to say, it is directly focused on defining remedies which are intended to address the social causes of the crisis, to transform society.[110] A criticism attentive to specific historical processes, based on analysis of effects rather than on principles, aimed at transformation and not simply judgement: these are all characteristics that distinguish the criticism of social pathologies from more conventional forms of social criticism.

The advantage of this type of criticism is clear: it seems capable of being applied to the social and historical detail that makes up the substance of politics, but that discussions of justice and injustice, of human rights and their violation, of the effectiveness or dysfunction of institutional orders sometimes tend to lose sight of. However, the advantage conferred by the effects of such a criticism seems weakened by the apparent vagueness of the criteria and standards that could legitimize it. The concept of crisis is inherently ambiguous and the identification of crisis with pathology is not a self-evident route to take. What are the criteria for identifying a crisis? What are the standards that allow us to propose crisis as a state capable of legitimating a critique, rather than seeing in it, for example, a transitional stage in a process of useful adaptation to necessary changes?[111]

The justification for this type of social criticism has an interdisciplinary dimension: a philosophical one, if we are to establish the legitimacy of a reference to health, to clarify its status and to articulate its norms and standards; a sociological one, if we need to identify the causes of a crisis and the possible social transformations; a medical one, if we need to analyse effects on health or simply to explain which concept of health can be taken as a critical model. From this come a significant number of conceptual problems. The sociological uses of the concept of social pathology raise the problem of the legitimacy of focusing on the social context in medical terms; its medical uses raise the problem of the legitimacy of the idea of 'social causes of disease'; its philosophical uses that of the modalities of linking philosophy with the human and medical sciences. More generally, the problem will be to join a critical judgement to a social theory identifying pathogenic factors and establishing the possibility and consequences of their transformation: How to ensure that pathological phenomena have been traced back to their actual causes, how to prove that these are not elements necessary to social functioning and that their transformation would indeed constitute some kind of social therapy?

Two crucial problems seem to emerge. On the normative level, we must determine and find a basis for the criteria for identifying pathologies. On the descriptive level, we must justify the transition from diagnosis to treatment, which involves at the same time a determination of the social causes of pathology and the possibility of transforming these causes. We do not propose here to list all the culturalist, psychoanalytic and sociological models of social pathology,[112] only to categorize the possibilities using distinctions between types of criteria and types of causal attribution. By retaining these variables, it is possible to distinguish three major models, according to whether the criteria for identifying social pathologies are sought in a definition of social normality, in a definition of health or in a theory of normal human life. We will see that each of these models requires different ways of diagnosing social suffering and deciding on the remedies that may be applied (see table 1.1).

As part of a sociological model (or one proper to social theories), pathologies of the social context are identified by the criterion of social normality (first column of table 1.1). Some social theories make it possible to identify abnormal situations with 'illnesses' of the social body itself, which requires either some form of organicism or a functionalism, or a theory of normative presuppositions of social life.

Durkheim's arguments in *Professional Ethics and Civic Morals* (they could be contrasted on this point to those in *Suicide*[113]) provides an illustration of the organicist type of conception. Analysing the development of an economic activity free from any specific moral regulation, Durkheim contests in the first part of the book the economic doctrines that, considering this state of affairs as normal, merely 'raise . . . a *de facto* state of affairs which is unhealthy to the level of a *de jure* state of affairs'.[114] The different economic activities should in fact be seen as elements of a functionally articulated whole or of an 'organism'. And it is also this organic conception which gives to the solutions that are advocated the form of therapeutic remedies. As the crisis is a similar form of disruption to an organic disorder ('the forces thus released can have no guidance for their normal development, the forces that have been identified no longer know what is their normal development. . . . There is a head-on clash when the moves of rivals conflict, as they attempt to encroach on another's field or beat him down or drive him out'[115]), so the remedies consist of reestablishing the organization on the basis of the activity of the organs ('All these various interrelations cannot remain in a perpetually instable state of equilibrium. A system of ethics, however, is not to be impro-vised. It is the task of the very group to which they are to apply'[116]). Whether according to an organicist or a functionalist model,[117] the reference to medi-cal vocabulary remains purely an analogy and is based on a highly question-able social ontology: a principle of social unity, an exclusion of conflict and a substantial definition of dysfunction and deviance.

In the work of authors such as Honneth, there is another definition of social pathology which, starting from the idea that every interaction has communicative conditions that constitute its normative core, identifies a number of relationships of recognition of the normative presuppositions of social life.[118] This conception could be compared with how Goffman impli-citly identifies total institutions with pathological forms, in that they deprive individuals of the ability to express both distance from their roles and forms of resistance to the institution, possibilities found in normal conditions of interaction.[119] It is, in the one case as in the other, through the terms of the engagement of individuals in their social activities and the manner in which they experience their own forms of socialization that the normal and the pathological are distinguished from one another.

According to the sociological model, the relationship of disease with the concept of suffering can only remain secondary because suffering is not included in the model. It is only included on an analogical basis or is in-cluded as an indicator. We have already mentioned analogous references to suffering with regard to conceptions of suffering *of* the social body (see 1 in figure 1.1). Let us now focus instead on the versions in which suffering functions as an indicator.

Just as public health reports today sometimes consider suffering an 'indi-cator of precarity',[120] so it can be conceived of more generally as an indicator of social malfunction. In this case, social criticism does not really have a bearing on suffering itself, but rather on the social problems of which it is the indicator and which can be focused on as such without express reference to suffering. To speak of suffering as an indicator is certainly already to include it as an effect in the model, but for it to be truly included, it would further be necessary for a theory to trace the processes that lead from malfunctions to the suffering of individuals. Though this theory is external to a theory of social functioning, it may, however, be associated with it. In this case, the model not only deals with social dysfunction (suffering *of* the social body) and suffering that is the indicator of this (suffering *in* the social body), but also with social suffering itself. Durkheim in *Suicide* tries somehow to deal with these three subjects at once; he adds a consideration of feedback from suffering on the actions of individuals, and so, in a way, on the social context.

As long as a medical, psychological or psychosocial theory is not associated with it, the sociological model leads to a diagnosis that is not really about social suffering, even if social suffering can be included in it as an indicator and as an aggravating factor in social dysfunction. In such a model, if the diagnosis is accompanied by treatment, the proposed actions will focus on social dysfunction itself rather than the social suffering, and though the causes of the latter are affected by the required social transformation, the actions are not demanded by the fact of suffering. As an illustration of such a disjunction of social pathology and suffering, let us refer to the issue of social suffering that pervades the output of social economy in the first half of the nineteenth century in France.

In the writings of Buret, the revelation of suffering caused by poverty serves to describe a socially caused disease and to define its treatment, as shown in this passage from the introduction to *De la misère des classes laborieuses en Angleterre et en France*: 'The worry which today attacks the civilised nations has reached the level of dread: it seems that a sinister presentiment is warning them that they will soon have to submit to some terrible remedy so as not to die. Happily, economic ills can be cured by a peaceful treatment, above all in France, and only a little wisdom will be needed to avoid revolution, that perilous cure from which we are still sick'.[121] The suffering of individuals is only considered here insofar as it teaches us something about the general state of the social order that calls for remedies. According to the model of normative presuppositions of the social context, the relationship of social pathologies and suffering is just as external. The concept of suffering plays no decisive role in Goffman's thought, and though it is welcome in Honneth's, this is mainly because Honneth combines a sociological and an anthropological model of social pathology. Let us now see in what the latter consists.

As part of the anthropological model (third column of table 1.1), the diagnosis of social pathologies is based on standards that define normal human life, by which we must understand what gives human life its value and allows it to maintain itself in nondegraded forms. This model is characterized by a reference to human nature (or rather human existence as 'second nature') and to the idea that as human existence as such is socially instituted, social contexts have the capacity to produce denaturing effects on it. It can take two different forms according to whether the standards are located at the collective level or at the individual level. We can refer to the *Kulturkritik* of the late nineteenth century to illustrate the first option.

For authors such as Nietzsche, Weber, Tönnies and Simmel, the value of human existence depends indeed on those social variables that can be called 'culture' and produce specific 'types of humanity'. Transformations of culture are, in this sense, liable to produce pathological orientations. Nietzsche, for example, certainly develops a critique of social conditions when pronouncing a historical diagnosis of decadence, whose historical causes he seeks in a theory of nihilism and resentment, and when he mentions 'the philosopher as doctor of civilisation'.[122]

But we can also formulate a conception of social pathologies by focusing on the conditions for self-realization that each individual can demand. This is the route Honneth takes when making social relations conditions for a positive relationship with oneself and basing his conception of social pathologies on a 'formal concept of the good life'.[123] Through a closer reading of such incommensurable writers as Nietzsche and Honneth, we come to understand that the reasons leading them to describe the deformation of human existence in terms of 'pathologies' are diverse. It is either in a philosophy of life (or of the 'will to power'), as in Nietzsche, or in a desire to use the formal resources of the idea of social pathology (the diagnosis-aetiology-therapy conjunction), as in Honneth, that the deepest motivations of a reference to disease must be sought.

In the anthropological model, the link with the concept of suffering also remains external. This model can indeed do without any reference to suffering, and it can also refer to it in a purely metaphorical sense (the term 'suffering' designating in this case the 'discontent in civilization' itself, a connotation which Freud's title plays with without, however, adopting it) or as a simple indicator of social pathology (the status that references to 'social suffering' are given in the works of Honneth, who always seems to conceive of them as 'suffering in the social'). In both cases, social suffering plays no decisive role in social diagnosis, in aetiology or in the objectives of the proposed social transformations. The contingent nature of the association of such a model with the idea of suffering is shown from a contrary position by Nietzsche, who argues that suffering is an indicator of health and claims that the excesses of civilization are responsible for its assignment to the category of negative values.[124] In Honneth himself, the idea of social pathology refers to two types of distorted life which can be characterized respectively by the terms 'false' and 'unbearable'.[125] The first category seems to refer to the classic critique of consumer society, a society where it is the search for pleasure that alienates and not suffering that is pathological, a society that is also said to have managed to decrease the suffering associated with poverty. Only the second category, the 'unbearable', can give a decisive function to suffering in social criticism.

Only a model that we will call 'medical' (in the broad sense of a reference to health) gives suffering a decisive role (second column of table 1.1). Then social suffering can be understood in the sense of collective suffering (public health) or in the sense of social suffering (taking into account the social dimension of severe subjective harm that is not necessarily pathological). Three features distinguish the two approaches: the conjunction of diagnosis-aetiology-therapy, the concept of suffering and the meaning of the reference to health.

The way in which, in the 1920s, an author such as A. Grotjahn defined public health (which he called 'public hygiene') allows us to determine more accurately the nature of the *narrowly* medical model of social pathology. In the introduction to his classic work, specifically entitled *Soziale Pathologie*, the concept of social pathology serves to define the specific point of view of sociomedical investigations[126] and the type of joint diagnostic and therapeutic approaches associated with them.[127] Grotjahn begins by noting that the study of diseases from a social perspective involves raising them to the status of a collective variable through statistical methods, but then adds that the statistical point of view is not enough. First, in fact, sociomedical surveys must explain why a specific disease can take different forms depending on the social and cultural contexts. Second, they must engage in an analysis of the aetiological factors and social effects of disease.[128] Only in this way are they likely to determine to what extent diseases can be given strictly medical treatment responses and to what extent they call for a transformation of the social contexts in which they arise. In this model, suffering does not play a decisive role; the analysis relates instead to degeneration, morbidity and mortality.

What is meant here by social pathology? It is striking that in Grotjahn, the idea of social pathology is a *method of analysis* of a disease more than a genuine social diagnosis. Disease is not considered a component of certain social experiences, but as a reality *sui generis*, defined by medicine; all that is needed is to explain its factors and effects using auxiliary sciences such as statistics, sociology and economics.[129] Based on these methods of diagnosing an illness and tracing its aetiology, treatment focuses on disease, not strictly speaking on society, and only when medical therapy is insufficient is recourse to social transformations justified.

This model is narrowly medical for two reasons. First, it proposes to recode suffering (in terms of disease) by retaining of it only what fits into the grid of a predetermined nosography. Second, after having stripped suffering of its social context, it relies on independent theories developed by the social sciences about other epistemic objects to reintroduce from the side the social factors of suffering and so focus on forms of social therapy that are called upon to supplement the medical profession when it finds itself failing in its fundamental tasks. By contrast, a medical model in the broadest sense is characterized at once by the broader definition of suffering and by taking suffering as inseparable from its context, its dynamics and its social effects— two characteristics which form part of the problems of *social suffering* in the proper sense.

At the heart of the divergence between a narrowly medical model of social pathology and a model of social pathology focusing on social suffering in what we defined earlier as the proper sense of this notion, there is also the question of the standard for establishing a diagnosis: health. There is a world of difference here between the criteria of public health, whether they are limited to a negative definition of health in terms of degeneration, morbidity and mortality, or admit a positive definition of health (such as a 'state of complete well-being' following the definition proposed by the WHO[130]), on the one hand, and an expanded and negative model of health in which health is defined from the perspective of its relation with suffering, on the other hand.

In this second perspective, the idea of health continues to define a normative orientation, which social criticism may try to take over, but it is no
longer possible to frame the standard of health in terms of a set of predefined
criteria (mortality, disease, degeneration). It is rather by a clinical examination and ethnography of suffering that the nature and the meaning of suffering must be explored, a clinical examination and an ethnography themselves
informed by a sociological focus on social forms that structure the social
contexts of suffering and the experience of it, and by a metapsychological
emphasis on the psychological dynamics of suffering.

When the concept of health is understood in the sense of this negative
definition, it relies on a distinction between normal and abnormal suffering,
and immediately the problem arises of the status of this distinction. Specific
to negative definitions of health is the designation of health not as a state
(absence of pain), but as a goal and the object of a struggle in which suffering
appears both as a sign of failure in pursuit of the goal and as that against
which the individual struggles. Health is thus conceived as an always precarious balance and a victory, which must be continually reaffirmed, over a set
of disorders and dysfunctions. What is true of health in general is true of
mental health in particular, and this makes sense of the fact that Freud makes
heavy use of the vocabulary of struggle (conflict, repression, resistance, defence) and work (the work of dreaming, the work of grieving) in his metapsychology.[131] The normative dimension this negative definition of mental
health assumes that it is possible to integrate suffering in a subjectivation
process that does not harm subjectivity. Health thus ceases to be defined as
the other of disease and the field of abnormal suffering extends beyond that
of pathology.

Because such a link between suffering and health is not based on a set of
properties characterizing positive health, as in the case of the definitions of
positive mental health, criticism of social pathologies does not result in the
project of bringing the largest possible number of people to a state of well-
being defined by a set of medical and social standards. A conception of
negative mental health in terms of suffering refers only to the ideal of a
reduction of pathogenic or pathological disorders and a conception of social
pathology that is inspired by it criticizes the social conditions that either
produce a suffering that is intrinsically difficult to appropriate or make an
obstacle to the subjective processes that enable appropriate suffering subjectively.

From the perspective of political theory, the defence of such a medical model of social criticism that has bearing on suffering presents a twofold challenge: first, to elaborate the interdisciplinary dimension implied by the overlapping of philosophical problems (how can we justify a social criticism from the perspective of health?), sociological problems (what are the social factors which produce suffering and can they be transformed?) and psychological problems (is it possible to identify social factors of suffering understood in the proper sense of the term?), and second, to justify the use of such a model of social criticism rather than more classic and less problematic models. The method that will be implemented to address these issues draws its inspiration from the tradition of critical theory known as the Frankfurt School.

THE PERSPECTIVE OF CRITICAL THEORY

In the early 1930s, Horkheimer gave a definition of the tasks of critical theory that remains fruitful in general and particularly suited to the treatment

Table 1.1. Types of criticism of social pathology

	Sociological model	Medical model	Anthropological model
Criteria for social pathology	Social normality (organicism or functionalism; normative presuppositions of social life)	Health of individuals	Definition of human nature
Status of suffering	• suffering as a metaphor *or* • suffering as an indicator (*or* • suffering as cause and effect)	• subject (of public health policy) *or* • *cause and effect of specific social processes*	• suffering as a metaphor *or* • suffering as an indicator (*or* • suffering as cause and effect)
Meaning of the term 'social suffering'	suffering of the social body, collective suffering or social suffering	• collective suffering (public health) *or* • social suffering	suffering of the social body, collective suffering or social suffering

of the problem of social suffering. Three main features distinguish critical theory and traditional theory.[132]

First, a critical theory must combine in its approach philosophy (a philosophical formulation of a model of social criticism and an explanation of its normative presuppositions), sociology (a study of social causes which produce and reproduce the existing social order) and psychology (a study of forms of internalization of the existing social order and adaptation to it).

Second, in order to be able to formulate a comprehensive critique of the social order, the theory has to resist the fragmentation of society into isolated epistemic objects by separate social sciences and adopt a broad, though not encyclopaedic, perspective. It must adopt an interdisciplinary organizational structure that connects the various specialized fields through an explanation of global social structures—a form of explanation Horkheimer sought in Marx's critique of political economy before Adorno relied on a model in which social philosophy is viewed as the self-reflection of the social sciences.[133]

Third, critical theory must determine not only how the model of social criticism applies to the present order, but also what social interests it expresses and the social conditions that make it possible (in this sense it is *at the same time* a critical sociology and a sociology of criticism[134]), and how this social criticism can help to transform society.

The fact that the issue of social suffering designates both a new aspect of the social question and a type of blocking of the dynamic of emancipation which require the development of a new model of social criticism, the fact that this issue is being explored by different disciplines that adopt complementary points of view, the fact that it gives rise to controversies in which political and epistemological issues are deeply intertwined, all make critical theory an appropriate theoretical framework.[135]

NOTES

1. To mention only publications from 2004 and 2005: D. Fassin, *Des maux indicibles. Sociologie des lieux d'écoute* (Paris: La Découverte, 2004); J. Furtos and Ch. Laval, ed., *La santé mentale en actes. De la clinique au politique* (Toulouse: Erès, 2005); J. Ion et al., ed., *Travail social et souffrance psychique* (Paris: Dunod, 2005); M. Joubert and Cl. Louzoun, ed., *Répondre à la souffrance sociale* (Toulouse: Erès, 2005); *Cahiers de Recherches sociologiques*, no. 41–42 (2005): 'Nouveau malaise dans la civilisation. Regards sociologiques sur la santé mentale, la souffrance psychique et la psychologisation' (edited by M. Otero).

2. Fassin, *Des maux indicibles*.

3. Joubert and Louzoum, *Répondre à la souffrance sociale*; Furtos and Laval, *La santé mentale en actes.*

4. Ion et al., *Travail social et souffrance psychique.*

5. Ch. Laval and E. Renault, 'La santé mentale: une préoccupation partagée, des enjeux controversés', in Furtos and Laval, *La santé mentale en actes.*

6. G. Devereux, *From Anxiety to Method in the Behavioural Sciences* (The Hague: Mouton and Co., 1967), 31.

7. Although psychology has been trying, since becoming an autonomous discipline, to confront this limitation, these attempts remain marginalized and controversial. An example of an effort at placing such attempts at the heart of psychology is supplied by Politzer; see the texts collected in *Critique of the Foundations of Psychology* (Pittsburgh: Duquesne University Press, 1994).

8. P. Lazarfeld, M. Jahoda, and A. Zeisel, *Marienthal: The Sociography of an Unemployed Community* (Chicago: Aldine-Atnerton, 1971), 2.

9. For a synthesis of the different approaches to suffering in the domain of medical anthropology, see I. Willkinson, *Suffering: A Sociological Introduction* (Cambridge: Polity Press, 2005), 4–6, 16–45.

10. This is the viewpoint defended by H. Dreitzel in the only systematic and in-depth work which sociology has dedicated to this subject (see H. P. Dreitzel, *Die Gesellschaftlichen Leiden und das Leiden an der Gesellschaft. Vorstudien zu einer Pathologie des Rollenverhaltens* [Stuttgart: Ferdinand Enke Verlag, 1972], 17). The notion of 'role distance' has been elaborated by E. Goffman.

11. This criticism is developed notably in V. Das, 'Subaltern as Perspective', *Subaltern Studies*, vol. 6 (1989): 310–25, and G. Pandey, 'In Defense of the Fragment: Writing about Hindu-Muslim Riots in India Today', *Representations*, Vol. 37 (Winter, 1992): 27–55.

12. As A. Kleinman has noted, the social sciences' exclusion of psychological and medical issues lead them 'to render social life trivial and decorative in such a way that the sentence of death which we all know in advance that we are under and the real dangers of daily life that we confront—from ordinary accidents to structural violence, by way of the millions of little disruptions which pose risks for human beings—are systematically denied or distorted by them' ('Santé et stigmate. Note sur le danger, l'expérience morale et les sciences sociales de la santé', *Actes de la recherche en sciences sociales*, no. 143 [June 2002]: 97).

13. See, for example, P. Babin, *SDF, l'obscénité du malheur* (Toulouse: Erès, 2004).

14. On this point, see A. Kleinman, V. Das, and M. Lock, ed., *Social Suffering* (Berkeley: University of California Press, 1997), introduction.

15. E. C. Hughes, *Men and Their Work* (London: The Free Press of Glencoe Collier-Macmillan Limited, 1958), 43.

16. On the relationship between language and social cooperation, see G. H. Mead, *Mind, Self and Society* (Chicago: University of Chicago Press, 1934), chap. 2.

17. P. Bourdieu, *The Weight of the World: Social Suffering in Contemporary Society* (Cambridge: Polity Press, 1999), 600–601: 'We have all heard of struggles over inheritances or conflicts with the neighbours, about educational difficulties or office rivalries, and we apprehend these through perceptual categories which, by reducing the personal to the impersonal and the unique drama to human interest story, allow us in a way to economise on thought, on motion, in short on understanding. . . . The immediate half-understanding based on a distracted and routinised attention discourages the effort needed to break through the screen of clichés behind which each of us lives and which we use to express both the minor problems and major ordeals of our lives'.

18. For a defence of this position, see I. Wilkinson, *Suffering: A Sociological Introduction* (Cambridge: Polity Press, 2004).

19. Fassin, *Des maux indicibles.*

20. Devereux, *From Anxiety to Method.*

21. T. W. Adorno, 'On Subject and Object', in *Catchwords: Critical Models 2* (New York: Columbia University Press, 2005), 245–58.

22. J. Guillaumin, 'Pour une méthodologie générale des recherches sur les crises', in *Crises, ruptures et dépassements*, ed. R. Kaes et al. (Paris: Dunod, 1997), 223: 'the psychological gaze is *first of all* called forth by disturbances of interpersonal relationships'.

23. P. Jamoulle, *La débrouille des familles. Récits de vie traversée par les drogues et les conduites à risque* (Bruxelles: De Boeck, 2002).

24. See D. Fassin and R. Rechtmann, *L'empire du traumatisme. Enquête sur la condition de victime* (Paris: Flammarion, 2007).

25. The term is taken up by M. Jaeger. See his synthesis of the debate on 'medicalization' in *L'articulation du sanitaire et du social. Travail social et psychiatrie* (Paris: Dunod, 2006), 43–56. For a similar argument concerning the debate on 'victimization', see J. A. Zamora, *Enfrentarse a la crisis desde la perspectiva de las víctimas* (Madris: Foessa, 2014).

26. We could say the same of the effects of social violence. A. Kleinman and R. Dejarlais have written on this subject: 'The ethnographic perspective considers those who suffer the traumatising consequences of political violence as a category of "social sufferers" and not as patients or victims' ('Ni patients ni victimes. Pour une ethnographie de la violence sociale', *Actes de la recherche en sciences sociales*, no. 104 [September 1994]: 62).

27. V. de Gaulejac, *Les Sources de la honte* (Paris: Desclée de Brouwer, 1996); S. Paugam, *La disqualification sociale* (Paris: PUF, 1991).

28. On the concept of invisibility and struggles for visibility, see O. Voirol, 'Visibilité et invisibilité: une introduction', *Réseaux*, no. 129–130 (2005): 9–36.

29. Bourdieu, *The Weight of the World*, introduction and conclusion.

30. V. Das, 'Language and Body: Transaction in the Construction of Pain', in *Social Suffering*, ed. Kleinman, Das, and Lock, 67–92.

31. G. Spivak, 'Can the Subaltern Speak?', in *Marxism and the Interpretation of Culture*, ed. C. Nelson and L. Grossberg (Urbana: University of Illinois Press, 1988), 271–313.

32. See, for example, P. Molinier, *Les enjeux psychiques du travail* (Paris: Payot, 2006), 194–219.

33. A. Farge, J.-F. Laé, P. Cingolani, and F. Magloire, *Sans visages. L'impossible regard sur le pauvre* (Paris: Bayard, 2004).

34. This is, according to H. Arendt, one of the specific characteristics of the 'social question' as it appears in the modern era; on this point, see *On Revolution* (London: Penguin Books, 1990), chap. 1.

35. See E. Renault, 'L'idéologie comme legitimation et comme description', *Actuel Marx*, no. 43 (2008): 80–95.

36. Jaeger, *L'articulation du sanitaire et du social*, 55.

37. Ch. Dejours, 'Aliénation et clinique du travail', *Actuel Marx*, no. 39 (2006): 123–44.

38. Wilkinson, *Suffering*, 79–83.

39. On the general increase of suicide in France since 1975, which indicates 'serious contradictions between the demands of social life and the fate of individuals', see Ch. Baudelot and R. Establet, *Suicide. L'envers de notre monde* (Paris: Seuil, 2006), 242.

40. See, for example, S. Sengupta, 'On India's Desparing Farms, a Plague of Suicide', *New York Times*, September 19, 2006.

41. N. Sheper-Hughes, 'Mourir en silence. La violence ordinaire d'une ville brésilienne', *Actes de la recherche en sciences sociales*, no. 104 (September 1994): 70.

42. A. Kleinman and J. Kleinman, 'The Appeal of Experience; The Dismay of Image: Cultural Appropriation of Suffering in Our Time', in *Social Suffering*, ed. Kleinman, Das, and Lock, 1–24.

43. N. Scheper-Hughes, 'The Primacy of the Ethical: Proposition for a Militant Anthropology', *Current Anthropology* 36, no. 3 (1995): 415–17. For a synthesis of the debates on the media representation of suffering, see Willkinson, *Suffering*, 136–56.

44. N. Scheper-Hughes, 'Small Wars and Invisible Genocides', *Social Science and Medicine* 43, no. 3 (1996): 888–900.

45. Nancy Scheper-Hughes presents her work in anthropology as an effort aimed at 'discovering and drawing attention to hitherto unrecognised shapes and spaces of gratuitous and useless social suffering. . . . The paradox is that they are not distant nor hidden from sight: quite the reverse. As Wittgenstein remarked, the things which are the most difficult to perceive are often those which are before our eyes, and thus taken as self-evident' (ibid., 889).

46. Arendt, *On Revolution*, 222–23.

47. On this point, see, for example, D. Arnold, 'Gramsci and Peasant Subalternity in India', in *Mapping Subaltern Studies and the Postcolonial*, ed. V. Chaturvadi (London: Verso, 2000).

48. E. Faue, *Community of Suffering and Struggle: Women, Men and the Labor Movement in Minneapolis, 1915–1945* (Chapel Hill: University of North Carolina Press, 1991).

49. My thanks to Sylvette Uzan Chomat for having drawn my attention to this point.

50. On this subject, H. Joas, *The Creativity of Action* (Chicago: University of Chicago Press, 1996), chap. 3.

51. On this subject, see, for example, G. Deleuze and F. Guattari, *Milles plateaux. Capitalisme et schizophrénie* (Paris: Minuit, 1980).

52. On this point, see N. Loraux, *Les mères en deuil* (Paris: Seuil, 1990).

53. M. Ramphele, 'Political Widowhood in South Africa: The Embodiment of Ambiguity', in *Social Suffering*, ed. Kleinman, Das, and Lock, 99–118.

54. On these different points, see Das, 'Language and Body', and 'The Act of Witnessing: Violence, Poisonous Knowledge, and Subjectivity', in *Violence and Subjectivity*, ed. V. Das, A. Kleinman, and M. Ramphele (Berkeley: University of California Press, 2000), 205–25.

55. We are speaking here of a co-construction in order to emphasize that not only are the people concerned making an effort to express their suffering even when the cultural means to do this are lacking, but that furthermore one of the aims of this effort is precisely to win recognition of the social dimension of suffering. Summing up her study of the discourse of protest of Guatemalan peasant women who had lost their husbands during the civil war, Linda Green emphasizes in this way the advantages of a social suffering framework: 'These women experienced headaches, gastritis, stomach ulcers, weakness, diarrhea, irritability, insomnia, and weak blood, illnesses usually termed posttraumatic stress disorders. They also experienced "folk" illnesses such as *nervios* (nerves), *susto* (fright), and *pena* (pain, grief, sorrow). To categorize their suffering simply as a manifestation of a clinical syndrome or as a culture-bound construction of reality dehistoricises and dehumanises the lived experiences of these women. The widows themselves attributed a political cause to their bodily distress and pinpointed the onset of their physical problems to the events that surrounded the death or disappearance of their husbands' (L. Green, 'Lived Lives and Social Suffering: Problems and Concerns in Medical Anthropology', *Medical Anthropology Quarterly* 12, no. 1 [1998]: 5).

56. See E. Renault, 'A Critical Theory of Social Suffering', *Critical Horizons* 11, no. 2 (2010): 221–41.

57. W. B. Gallie, 'Essentially Contested Concepts', *Proceedings of the Aristotelian Society, 56 (1955–6)*, reprinted in W. B. Gallie, *Philosophy and the Historical Understanding* (New York: Schocken Books, 1968).

58. On the manner of theoretical treatment of these essentially contested concepts, see E. Renault, *L'Expérience de l'injustice* (Paris: La Découverte, 2004), 18–27.

59. Devereux, *De l'angoisse à la méthode*, 77.

60. Bourgois, *In Search for Respect*; D. Lepoutre, *Cœur de banlieue: Codes, rites, et langages* (Paris: Odile Jacob, 1997); P. Jamoulle, *La débrouille des familles* (Louvain: De Boeck, 2000); E. Hermant, *Clinique de l'infortune. La psychothérapie à l'épreuve de la détresse sociale* (Paris: Seuil, 2004); D. Zeneidi, *Les SDF et la ville. Géographie du savoir-survivre* (Paris: Bréal, 2002); P. Declerck, *Les naufragés* (Paris: Plon, 2001).

61. Jamoulle, *La débrouille des familles*, 29–30. On the more general question of how the anthropology of situations characterized by marginality cannot avoid accepting being affected by its subject matter, see more generally J. Favret-Saada, *Les mots, la mort, les sorts* (Paris: Gallimard, 1977). These methodological criticisms have given rise to certain critiques of the method put in place by Bourdieu and his collaborators in *The Weight of the World*. While Bourdieu emphasizes the importance of familiarity between the investigator and the investigation, the objection has been raised to this that only a relational distance allows the researcher to bring to light the tacit knowledge that forms the heart of the social experience, but which forms part of convictions that remain unexpressed by those who share the same social experience (S. Engler, 'Bourdieus soziologisches Denken und Verstehen', *Mitteilungen des Instituts für Sozialforschung* [2002]: 83–96). Though this methodological option is appropriate from a general point of view, it does not seem applicable to the experiences of poverty and social marginality because these are characterized by the general reluctance of individuals experiencing them to share their experiences without establishing a relationship of trust, either because they spontaneously perceive the researcher as an individual representing a world in conflict with their own (Fravret-Saada, *Les mots, la mort, les sorts*), or because the violence of their relationship with the outside world forbids them to step outside a range of limited and constraining roles (for example, relationship to a client, relationship to a police officer, relationship to a social worker, in the case of undocumented prostitutes (J.-M Chaumont, *Traite et prostitution en débat [Bruxelles, 1880–2003]. Matériaux pour une comédie sociologique.* Louvain: Université catholique de Louvain, Diffusion universitaire Ciaco, 2004]) or else because they are too destabilized to be able to offer their life story without taking precautions (Jamoulle, *La débrouille des familles*). This methodological option provides another example of the inadequacy of an epistemology of the human sciences that forgets the fact that the observer is observed and that this fact profoundly influences the content of the observation.

62. Let us specify that in proposing the unification of these meanings, we do not seek to establish by 'philosophical decree' the subject of the study of social suffering, but to specify the conditions necessary to overcome the obstacles just mentioned and the nature of the linguistic usages which make it possible to integrate a reference to social suffering into social criticism.

63. The legitimacy of such a distinction can be contested in various ways (for a synthesis of the arguments developed against this distinction, see Willkinson, *Suffering*, chap. 2). We can note that pain is always felt as part of a specific subjective experience and that it is impossible to distinguish its physiological from its psychological component. We can add that all suffering tends to be experienced in a bodily way. Nonetheless, the concept of masochism indicates that certain pains can be experienced as pleasure. Furthermore, there are numerous examples of pains which are not experienced as suffering: let us consider the example of a normal martial arts training session in which pain is experienced as an aspect of a task and not as subjective harm. I do not think it necessary or even pertinent to interpret this type of situation as linked to

the mobilization of defences against suffering; it is rather when a specific pain linked for instance to a blow is experienced as dangerous by the instinct of self-preservation or as a breaking in of the outside world upon bodily privacy that pain will be prolonged into suffering and will involve the mobilization of psychological defences (which obviously does not answer the question of subjective investment in this type of practice).

64. On these points, see S. Freud, 'Instincts and Their Vicissitudes', in *The Standard Edition of the Complete Psychological Works of Sigmund Freud* (London: The Hogarth Press, 1961), 14. On Freudian affect theory, see A. Green, *The Fabric of Affect in Psychoanalytic Discourse* (London: Routledge, 1999).

65. See, for example, F. Nietzsche, *Thus Spake Zarathustra*, 'On the Blessed Isles'. In *Beyond Good and Evil*, he writes that 'it almost determines the order of *rank how* deeply men can suffer' (para. 270). But in *The Gay Science* (book 5, para. 370), he does distinguish between two types of suffering: that caused by an excess of life (health) and that caused by its weakness.

66. A. Schopenhauer, *The World as Will and Representation*, para. 56–59.

67. On this point, see Kleinman, Das, and Lock, *Social Suffering*, introduction; A. Kleinman, 'The Violences of Everyday Life. The Multiples Forms and Dynamics of Social Violence', in *Violence and Subjectivity*, ed. Das, Kleinman, and Ramphele.

68. Positive definitions of mental health refer to norms of well-being, while negative definitions of mental health only characterize health as the ideal of a reduction of different forms of ill-being.

69. S. Freud, *Civilisation and Its Discontents*, in *The Standard Edition of the Complete Psychological Works of Sigmund Freud*, 64–145.

70. P. V. Lilienfeld, *La pathologie sociale* (Paris: Giard & Briére, 1896).

71. F. Müller-Lyer, *Soziologie des Leidens* (München: Albert Langen, 1914).

72. These two objections relate to a definition of suffering that is called social according to the model of collective suffering and that can be illustrated in the light of public health. But they do not relate to public health as such, which is only mentioned here as an illustration of social suffering.

73. Dreitzel, *Die Gesellschaftlichen Leiden und das Leiden an der Gesellschaft*, 9 sq. Fromm's work *The Sane Society* (New York: Rinehart & Company, 1955) is characteristic of this kind of process. Advanced capitalist society should, according to him, be described as sick because its social structures are responsible for the neurotic disturbances of its members. According to Dreitzel's reading, which is doubtless debatable, Fromm builds the idea of such a social causality on an amphibiological use of the concept of alienation, supposed sometimes to designate psychological disorders themselves, sometimes the structures of society themselves. Furthermore, because the concept of anomie has often been considered the concept of a suffering *of* the social body (Dreitzel, *Die Gesellschaftlichen Leiden und das Leiden an der Gesellschaft*, chap. 2), theories of anomie can themselves also lead to explanations of suffering *in* the social body by suffering *of* the social body. This is the case when suffering that is experienced, even expressed in interviews, is placed in relation to different forms of disorder of collective representations (collapse of horizons of expectations, as in C. Honegger and M. Rychner, ed., *Das Ende der Gemütlichkeit. Strukturelles Unglück und mentales Leid in der Schweitz* [Zürich: Limmat Verlag, 1998] or to the social structure itself [structural misalignment of individuals in relation to their roles, as in Dreitzel, *Die Gesellschaftlichen Leiden und das Leiden an der Gesellschaft*, chap. 5]) which are conceived of explicitly as theories of suffering in the social context and of suffering caused by the social context. But theories of social anomie can also be used independently of any reference to a suffering *of* the social body.

74. On this point, see the synthesis in R. Bastide, *Sociologie des maladies mentales* (Paris: Flammarion, 1965).

75. For an analysis of this Freudian claim, see N. Elias, 'Freud's Concept of Society and Beyond It', in *The Collected Works of Norbert Elias* (Dublin: UCD Press, 2014), 18:13–52. For an exploration of social suffering from this point of view, see I. Kaes, 'Réalité psychique et souffrance dans les institutions', in *L'institution et les institutions*, ed. Kaës R. et al. (Paris: Dunod, 2002), 1–46, and 'Souffrance et psychopathologie des liens institués', in *Souffrance et psychopathologie des liens institutionnels* (Paris: Dunod, 1996), 1–47.

76. G. Devereux, *Essais d'ethnopsychiatrie générale* (Paris: Gallimard, 1977).

77. L. Le Guillant, *Le drame humain du travail. Essais de psychopathologie du travail* (Toulouse: Erès, 2006).

78. N. Elias, *The Civilising Process: Sociogenetic and Psychogenetic Investigations*, revised edition (Oxford: Blackwell, 2000).

79. In France, research programmes on the social construction of suffering are being conducted mainly by authors such as D. Fassin and A. Ehrenberg.

80. Kleinman, Das, and Lock, *Social Suffering*; Das, Kleinman, and Ramphele, *Violence and Subjectivity*; V. Das, A. Kleinman, M. Lock, M. Ramphele, and P. Reynolds, ed., *Remaking the World: Violence, Social Suffering and Recovery* (Berkeley: University of California Press, 2001). This programme of research into 'social suffering' in fact brings together approaches from medical anthropology as well as from the ethnography of suffering, two disciplines whose borders are in any case porous; on this, see Willkinson, *Suffering*, 4–7, 79–108.

81. Kleinman and Kleinman, 'The Appeal of Experience; The Dismay of Images', 2: 'We can speak of suffering as a social experience in at least two ways . . . : 1) Collective modes of experience shape individual perceptions and expressions. These collective modes are visible patterns of how to undergo troubles, and they are taught and learned . . . , 2) Social interactions enter into an illness experience (for example, a family dealing with the dementia of a member with Alzheimer's disease). . . . As these examples suggest, relationships and interactions take part, sometimes a central part, in the experience of suffering. Both aspects of social experience—its collective mode and intersubjective processes—can be shown to be reshaped by the distinctive cultural meanings of time and place'.

82. Dreizel, *Die Gesellschaftlichen Leiden und das Leiden an der Gesellschaft.*

83. This type of position can be attributed to Bourdieu, although he proposes a theory of *both* structural (social forms) *and* dynamic (social transformation) of the misalignment of habitus.

84. This type of position could be compared with Simmel's sociology of poverty and Goffman's stigmatization theory, although neither of these gives a major role to the idea of suffering.

85. Freud's account of what we termed 'abnormal suffering' in *Civilisation and Its Discontents* provides an illustration.

86. Honegger and Rychner, *Das Ende der Gemütlichkeit. Strukturelles Unglücks und mentales Leid in der Schweitz.*

87. Kleinman and Dejarlais, 'Ni patients ni victimes'; Das et al., *Remaking the World.*

88. On the concept of 'career', see E. Goffman, *Asylum: Essays on the Social Situation of Mental Patients and Other Inmates* (New Brunswick: Aldine Transaction, 2007), 125 et seq., and H. S. Becker, *Studies in the Sociology of Deviance* (New York: The Free Press, 1991), 19 et seq.

89. F. Schütze, 'Verlaufskurven des Erleidens als Forschungsgegenstand der interpretativen Soziologie', in *Erziehungswissenschaftliche Biographieforschung*, ed. H. H. Krüger and W. Marotzki (Opladen: Leske +Brudrich, 1995), 205–37. See also G. Riemann and F. Schütze,

"'Trajectory" as a Basic Theoretical Concept for Analysing Suffering and Disorderly Social Processes', in *Social Organization and Social Process: Essays in Honor of Anselm Strauss*, ed. D. R. Maines (New York: de Gruyter, 1991), 333–57.

90. On this subject, see M. Legrand, *L'approche biographique. Théorie, clinique* (Paris: Hommes et perspectives/Desclée de Brouwer, 1993). For an example of life history analysis, jointly inspired by Bourdieu and Politzer, see M. Legrand, *Le sujet alcoolique: essai de psychologie dramatique* (Paris: Desclée de Brouwer, 1997).

91. Kleinman and Dejarlais, 'Ni patients, ni victimes', 62: 'Trauma is the link between the social and the psycho-biological phenomena which are at the foundation of the human experience'.

92. From sociology inspired by Bourdieu, for example, there is insistence on the fact that the theory of habitus cannot fulfil its explanatory function (and explaining 'social suffering' is one of its objectives) without developing a 'psychological sociology' (B. Lahire, *L'Homme pluriel* [Paris: Nathan, 1998]). From the psychology of work, there is insistence on the necessity of transforming clinical psychology into a social science (D. Lhuilier, *Cliniques du travail* [Toulouse: Érès, 2006]). From psychoanalysis, there is insistence on the fact that, insofar as this discipline studies a psychofamilial self isolated by the treatment apparatus, it is incapable of recognizing everything in psychological functioning that depends on external reality and that it should therefore be completed by a sociopsychoanalysis (G. Mendel, 'Psychanalyse et sociopsychanalyse', *Sociopsychanalyse*, no. 3 [1973]: 13–62). Among the many attempts to bridge the gap between sociology and psychology, one could also mention Elias's project of historicizing and dynamizing Freud's concepts ('Freud's Concept of Society and Beyond It'). Clinical sociology (V. Gauléjac and S. Roy, *Sociologie clinique* [Paris: Hommes et perspectives/Desclée de Brouwer, 1993]) or socioanalysis (Legrand, *L'approche biographique*, 45: 'Socioanalysis must construct itself at once with and against sociology') are also attempting to establish themselves as a discipline synthesizing psychological and sociological approaches. Ethnopsychiatry and clinical studies of work and exclusion offer other examples of synthetic approaches.

93. In this sense, any theory resulting from suffering leads to a critique of antinaturalism; on this, see S. Haber, *Critique de l'anti-naturalisme* (Paris: PUF, 2006).

94. E. C. Hughes emphasized in this way the importance of 'errors' in our social experience of work, adding 'in finding out how mistakes are handled, one must get at the fundamental psychological and social devices by which people are able to carry on through time, to live with others and with themselves' (*Men and Their Work*, 46).

95. On this theme, see G. Mendel, *L'acte est une aventure* (Paris: La Découverte, 1992).

96. A pitfall which some believe is illustrated in clinical sociology insofar as it may concentrate on areas where psychological elements and the social context are not distinguished from one another, areas designated by the terms 'social imagination' or 'family story' (V. de Gauléjac, *L'Histoire en héritage, roman familial et trajectoire sociale* [Paris: Desclée de Brouwer, 1999]; *La société malade de la gestion* [Paris: Seuil, 2005]), where clinical sociology does not bring the social context into play except as an accentuating factor in psychological conflicts (V. De Gauléjac and I. Taboada Léonetti, *La Lutte des places. Insertion et désinsertion* [Paris: Desclée de Brouwer, 1994]). This type of critique is developed notably by G. Mendel (*La Société n'est pas une famille* [Paris: La Découverte, 1992], 229–33). For a response emphasizing that clinical sociology rather seeks to combine a Freudian apparatus with a Bourdieusian approach to social pathways, see Legrand, *L'Approche biographique*, 48–92.

97. P. Bourdieu, *Masculine Domination* (Cambridge: Polity Press, 2001), 54–55: 'The materialist theory of the economy of symbolic goods . . . [seeks to give] its place in theory to the objectivity of the subjective experience of relations of domination'.

98. S. Freud, 'An Outline of Psychoanalysis', *Standard Edition*, 23:195.

99. Ch. Dejours, *Travail, usure mentale* (Paris: Bayard, 2000). See also *Psychopathology of Work: Clinical Observations* (London: Karnac Books, 2015).

100. Declerck, *Les naufragés*.

101. Becker, *Outsiders*, 19–41. N. Elias has pointed out that the lack of processual thinking in sociology also results in a problematic divide between history and sociology; see 'Towards a Theory of Social Processes', *The British Journal of Sociology* 48, no. 3 (1997): 355–83. For a defence of processual approaches to critical theory, see also E. Renault, 'Critical Theory and Processual Social Ontology', *Journal of Social Ontology* 2, no. 1 (2016), https://www.degruyter.com/view/j/jso.2016.2.issue-1/jso-2015-0013/jso-2015-0013.xml.

102. P. Bourdieu admits that habituses 'are constructed over the course of a specific history' (*The Logic of Practice* [Cambridge: Polity Press, 1990]) and that in this sense, an individual habitus is always different from a class habitus. But he then reduces it to a 'variant' of class habitus (101–2). For a critical discussion of the Bourdieusian theory of social trajectories, see Legrand, *L'approche biographique*, 48–54, 57–59.

103. D. Lagache, *L'Unité de la psychologie: psychologie expérimentale et psychologie clinique* (Paris: PUF, 1983).

104. On this point, see Legrand, *L'approche biographique*, 171–76.

105. On this point, see, for example, D. Zeneidi, 'Femmes SDF', *Le Passant Ordinaire*, no. 27 (2000): 7.

106. On this aspect, see, for example, M. Grenier-Peze, 'Un cas de violence au travail', in *Conjurer la Violence. Travail, Violence, Santé*, ed. Ch. Dejours (Paris: Payot, 2007), 226–39. For another example of the psychological repercussions of domination in which the problem is that an immigrant woman is forced to be a cog in the wheel of racial domination, see Lise Gaignard, 'Violence et travail. Essai sur les figures psychopathologiques de la culpabilité objective', in *Conjurer la Violence*, ed. Ch. Dejours, 151–71.

107. We could give plenty of other examples of the impossibility of giving a satisfactory analysis of social suffering without following it up to its macrosocial conditions. We could also demonstrate how the intersection of class, racial and gender domination specifically plays out in situations of extreme poverty such as that of Haitian peasants, where women's suffering is increased by the near impossibility of feeding their children and their specific vulnerability to AIDs (P. Farmer, 'On Suffering and Structural Violence. A View From Below', in *Social Suffering*, ed. Kleinman, Das, and Lock, 261–84).

108. See, for example, J.-R. Guérin, 'La médecine sociale et la médecine socialiste', *Gazette médicale de Paris*, March 18, 1848.

109. For a development of this type of analysis, see I. Wallerstein, *Unthinking Social Science: The Limits of Nineteenth Century Paradigms* (Cambridge: Polity Press, 1991).

110. A. Honneth, 'Pathologies of the Social: The Past and Present of Social Philosophy', in *Handbook of Critical Theory*, ed. D. M. Rasmussen (Oxford: Blackwell, 1996), 369–98. The idea of 'social diagnosis' comes from Vico, and the criticism of social pathology was developed in many ways by the philosophies of history of the eighteenth and nineteenth centuries; see E. Renault, *Connaître ce qui est. Enquête sur le présentisme hégélien* (Paris: Vrin, 2015).

111. Which could also, furthermore, be called a 'crisis'. For a rejection of the criticism of social pathology based on these doubts, see J. Habermas, *Legitimation Crisis* (Malden: Polity Press, 1988), chap. 1.

112. Which would return to a generalization of the exhaustive procedure proposed for example by Dreitzel with regard to sociology (*Die Gesellschaftlichen Leiden und das Leiden an der Gesellschaft*, chap. 2).

113. With all the reservations called for by the status of *Leçons de sociologie*: it is only a collection of notes not intended for publication.

114. E. Durkheim, *Leçons de sociologie. Physique des mœurs et du droit* (Paris: PUF, 1950), 16.

115. Ibid., 17.

116. Ibid., 19.

117. In the framework of Parsons's functionalism, we can also consider all dysfunctional phenomena pathological, letting ourselves be guided by the idea that phenomena that prevent or put in danger the reproduction of the social system are pathological. For a critique of these ideas, see, for example, Becker, *Outsider*, 7–8.

118. Honneth, 'Pathologies of the social'.

119. Goffman, *Asylum*, 171 et seq.

120. See, for example, the 'Rapport final du groupe de travail DGS relatif à l'évolution des métiers en santé mentale, avril 2002. Groupe de travail relatif à l'évolution des métiers en santé mentale: recommandations relatives aux modalités de la prise en charge de la souffrance psychique jusqu'au "trouble mentale caractérisé"'.

121. E. Buret, *De la Misère des classes laborieuses en Angleterre et en France: de la nature de la misère, de son existence, de ses effets, de ses causes, et de l'insuffisance des remèdes qu'on lui a opposés jusqu'ici, avec les moyens propres à en affranchir les soc iétés* (Paris: Paulin, 1840), 40.

122. F. Nietzsche, *Writings of the Early Notebooks* (Cambridge: Cambridge University Press, 2009).

123. Honneth, 'Pathologies of the Social'.

124. See paragraphs 22 and 225 of *Beyond Good and Evil*, in which Nietszche denounces the feminine side of pity for suffering and criticizes socialists for wanting to abolish it: 'You want, if possible—and there is not a more foolish "if possible"—to do away with suffering; and we?—it really seems that we would rather have it increased and made worse than it has ever been! . . . The discipline of suffering, of great suffering—know ye not that it is only this discipline that has produced all the elevations of humanity hitherto?' (para. 225).

125. A. Honneth, 'The Possibility of a Disclosing Critique of Society: The Dialectic of Enlightenment in Light of Current Debates in Social Criticism', *Constellations* 7, no. 1 (2000): 116–27.

126. A. Grotjahn, *Soziale Pathologie. Versuch einer Lehre von den sozialen Beziehungen der menschlichen Krankheiten als Grundlage der sozialen Medizin und der sozialen Hygiene* (Berlin: Springer, 1923), 12: 'There is no reason why we should need to give up the term "social pathology", which is so well adapted to the scientific study of the social characteristics of human illnesses'.

127. Ibid., 9.

128. Social factors affect in various ways the emergence and development of disease: '1. Social relationships produce or favour pathological states. 2. Social relationships are the bearers of the conditions of illness. 3. Social relationships are the occasion for appearance of pathological illnesses. 4. Social relationships influence the course of illness' (ibid., 18). But disease acts in turn upon social relations: 'States of illness are not only conditioned in their appearance and their course by social relationships, but also influence in their turn social states' (ibid., 18).

129. Ibid., 8.

130. See the WHO's definition: 'Health is a state of complete physical, mental and social well-being and not merely the absence of disease or infirmity. The enjoyment of the highest attainable standard of health is one of the fundamental rights of every human being without distinction of race, religion, political belief, economic or social condition' (http://www.who.int).

131. On these points, see notably Ch. Dejours, 'Construire sa santé', in *Les risques du travail*, ed. B. Cassou (Paris: La Découverte, 1985), and 'Problématiser la santé en ergonomie et en médecine du travail', *Le travail humain* 59, no. 1 (1994): 1–16.

132. M. Horkheimer, 'Traditional and Critical Theory', in *Critical Theory: Essays* (New York: Continuum, 2002), 188–52.

133. T. W. Adorno, *Philosophische Elemente einer Theorie der Gesellschaft* (Frankfurt am Main: Suhrkamp, 2008). On Adorno's conceptions of social theory, see E. Renault, 'Adorno: de la philosophie sociale à la théorie sociale', *Recherches sur la philosophie et le langage*, no. 28 (2012): 229–58.

134. On this point, see E. Renault, *Marx et l'idée de critique* (Paris: PUF, 1995).

135. See E. Renault, 'A Critical Theory of Social Suffering', for further development.

Chapter Two

A Political Vocabulary

In spite of all this, the English middle class, especially the manufacturing class, which is enriched directly by means of the poverty of the workers, persists in ignoring this poverty. This class, feeling itself the mighty representative class of the nation, is ashamed to lay the sore spot of England bare before the eyes of the world; will not confess, even to itself, that the workers are in distress, because it, the property-holding, manufacturing class, must bear the moral responsibility for this distress. Hence the scornful smile which intelligent Englishmen . . . assume when any one begins to speak of the condition of the working class; hence the utter ignorance on the part of the middle class of everything which concerns the workers . . . ; hence the miracle that the English have as yet no single book upon the condition of their workers, although they have been examining and mending the old state of things no one knows how many years.

—F. Engels, *The Condition of the Working Class in England.*

The political language of modernity developed under the pressure of two decisive events. The first was the French Revolution, a rupture organized around the concepts of freedom and equality and around the paradoxical conjunction of the two in the idea of citizenship.[1] The second was the discovery of the social question and the politicization of work and of property that it implied, which gave rise not only to political alternatives as fundamental as those of socialism and liberalism, but also to the set of projects which, from social economy to solidarism, were to lead to the ideological founding of the welfare state, which is currently being dismantled.[2]

The violence involved in the discovery of the social question and the depth of the change in visions of society and politics that it implied is prominently attested to by literary documents, such as the works of Dickens and Hugo, by the first inquiries into working conditions undertaken by doctors or philanthropists or, again, by foundational texts of socialism such as Engels's *The Condition of the Working Class in England.* It was the very reality of new forms of poverty and domination produced by industrial society that constituted the principal subject of these works and their political intention was precisely to bring to light this reality hidden beneath the principles of liberal society. It is not surprising that, to this end, these authors do not hesitate to describe the suffering of the poor and exploited, even to make a political argument out of it. This type of social criticism can be considered an immanent critique of liberalism.

By setting up the individual as a fact and as a value, liberalism was opening the way to a recognition of the affective and sentient materiality of the subject who bears this individuality, at the same time as it closed off this possibility by identifying the subject with a disembodied individual will. In one and the same shift, it proceeded to an invisibilization (in the form of denial and euphemization) of the lived experience of domination and poverty and also made possible criticism of this invisibilization in the language of suffering. This language certainly has a determinate historicity. But far from having made its entry into politics during the last two decades, as is some-times claimed, this language is specific to political modernity. It is partly linked to liberalism and is at the heart of one of the main political divisions of the past two centuries: the opposition of liberalism and socialism.

A specific feature of the term 'suffering' is that it can be used to articulate the unbearable. In this descriptive usage, it makes possible the telling of stories that are all the more polemical because the idea of suffering expresses something that we always wish to flee from ourselves and of which we wish to avoid, as far as possible, being spectators. This polemical connotation gives a directly political value to descriptions of social reality in terms of suffering. But as soon as it is applied to individuals who are experiencing it, this type of description can also serve as a moral interpellation: to say 'I am suffering' or 'they are suffering' amounts to saying 'you must help me' or 'you must all help them'. More directly than a collective responsibility, it is the individual responsibility of the people at whom the discourse of suffering is directed that is at issue when the interpellation seems to focus on the distress of an individual whose salvation depends entirely on the actions of another. Further, the term 'suffering' always runs the risk of making people think that the principal reality of the problem is in the lived experience of individuals more than in the social contexts where they are formed. The political focus of descriptive uses of the term seems, therefore, triply undermined by its pragmatic value: by a risk of moralization, by a risk of victimization and by a risk of psychologization.[3]

All political concepts are 'essentially contested' in the sense that different political alternatives within which which they can be mobilized are inscribed in them. This applies likewise to the concept of suffering, crisscrossed by the conflict between liberalism and socialism, torn between critical uses and moral or psychologizing neutralization. This concept can be understood in a polemical sense which rests upon its descriptive and demystifying value for a discursive consensus founded upon the invisibilization of certain social experiences. But it can also be mobilized in such a way that this type of criticism is countered simply with calls for individual responsibility, help for victims, even care for disorders of subjectivity. Whereas with regard to other contested concepts, the political conflict is theoretically prolonged by attempts at producing the 'correct definition' of the concepts (for example, the liberal definition of equality versus the socialist definition), a radical mistrust is directed towards the place of the concept of suffering in our political vocabulary. Marked by victimization and moralization, psychologization and medicalization, it supposedly has no rightful place in a political vocabulary and its use is supposedly always motivated by attempts at depoliticization; it should therefore, the claim goes, be expurgated from social criticism.

The concept of suffering certainly does not have the political importance of the concepts of equality, freedom, domination, democracy, justice, but to discard it remains, nonetheless, untenable. On the one hand, to discard it would be to fail to take into account the historical importance of the political uses of the language of suffering, the motivation for which was to contribute to the politicization of phenomena identified as infrapoliticial within the discursive consensus of liberalism. On the other hand, it would write off all the efforts to defuse the risks of the neutralization of a critique couched in terms of suffering through moralization and psychologization. If, then, discarding the notion results in an impasse, it only remains to attempt to confront theoretically the political aporias which pervade the concept of suffering.

The aim of this chapter is to contribute to this effort by establishing, on the historical terrain, that the term 'suffering' does indeed belong in the political vocabulary of modernity and by identifying a certain number of typical critical uses of the term 'suffering'. There are in fact two different

questions which seem to have sustained the use of the concept: that of penury
(1) and that of the type of subordination specific to the capitalist work relationship (2). Each of these social situations gives rise to a specific type of
reference to suffering, which can equally well be mobilized for the criticism
of other social situations (3).

This chapter offers reflections related to the history of political uses of
suffering. History and social sciences have dealt with this question from two
main points of view. Following the work of Hannah Arendt, a whole series of
works attempted to study the way in which a politics of pity has contributed
to the politicization of suffering since the eighteenth century. In Rousseau,
Robespierre or Saint-Just, pity for suffering is the key to a revolutionary
humanism. It is at the same time the sign of unity of the human race and the
source of a duty to eliminate inequality between people as far as possible.[4]
Different works have since attempted to study the metamorphoses of pity,
from its origins to the contemporary mediatization of suffering and to humanitarian policies.[5] But there are plenty of other modes of politicizing
suffering, and those which seem decisive in the era of the emergence of the
social question[6] do not deal with the suffering of others—that of the *sans-
culottes* whom free men claim to represent politically, or that which is observed at a distance and which creates ambiguous moral obligations—as
much as with suffering that gives rise to a sharing of experience and to
political demands.

The study of the social construction of modes of expression of suffering is
the second classical point of view on the political history of suffering. From
this perspective, we can speculate about the manner in which collective
representations of suffering go hand in hand with institutionalized political
responses and bring about certain ways of narrativizing suffering: 'Each era
reveals and stages a drama in the form of a question concerning the causes of
the ills of this life—why do good people suffer?—and carefully chooses a
possible way to deal with it politically, having put the humiliation to which it
is subjected on trial'.[7] Though this type of approach has proven fruitful, for
example, in accounting for the way in which the formalization of narratives
of suffering in the juridical arena accompanies developments in law, its
disadvantage is that it reduces the question of the expression of suffering to
that of a 'complaint.'

A complaint is a demand that an individual situation be taken into account
by the whole of the community. It therefore presupposes a consensual logic
which makes the whole community the recipient of a narrative, as well as an

acceptance of the legitimate forms for expressing suffering.[8] Suffering does, however, have other grammars. First, pathological suffering does not always find a means of expressing itself in instituted social frameworks, and it can then produce social groups seeking alternative forms of expression. Halbwachs has explained that the formation of communities of the sick can be explained in this way[9] and we could add that the effort to express suffering has led to the formation of communities making demands (organizations fighting cancer, organizations of users of psychiatric hospitals, political movements such as Act Up [AIDS Coalition to Unleash Power], communities that may even be revolutionary[10]).

That nonpathological suffering also has the capacity to cause profound upsets in the 'images of the world' is what Max Weber emphasized when he explained that the revolutionary powers of the religions of salvation and deliverance come from their response to the suffering of the subaltern classes.[11] Moreover, the political uses of suffering sometimes serve to give a name to social conflicts, and in this case they are frequently based upon a refusal of legitimated modes of expression of suffering and an attempt to construct new ones (the conflict with the Christian way of narrating misery and poverty is, for example, one of the challenges to socialism in the nineteenth century). Max Weber also suggests that the discrediting of Christianity and the rise of socialism originated in the incapacity of the former to give credible responses to the multiplication of workers' sufferings.[12]

Suffering cannot be reduced to a simple passive experience that would either have to remain silent (as in the figure of Bartleby) or would be forced to adopt socially validated scripts to represent one's misfortune (as in the figure of Job). Such a dichotomy inevitably leads to the conclusion that only suffering that remains unexpressed is truly subversive.[13] Felt or observed suffering produces practical effects (of adaptation and refusal) and cognitive effects (it makes us see things differently, possibly through demystification); these effects have a political potential. When suffering produces political effects, these do not proceed only from the activation of institutional responses to grievances, but also from efforts directed at social transformation. These efforts sometimes lead to the rejection of the legitimated ways of expressing suffering, even to attempts to devise new ones or to transform institutional responses to grievances.

It is in search of this type of political usage that we will now examine some episodes in the history of suffering.

SUFFERING AND POVERTY

The description of the effects of misery and poverty calls up almost naturally a reference to suffering. If this evidence is rarely recognized, it is without doubt partly due to a discreditation of misery and poverty as politically pertinent terms. This discreditation takes two forms. The first has to do with the prejudice which would claim that misery is an icon of the social question and that the time for it has passed now that we are in late capitalism, which, because it bestows well-being on the greater part of the populace, supposedly reorients questioning towards the issue of the democratic progress that is still possible and the issue of a more equitable distribution of wealth. This is a prejudice whose ethnocentrism is all too manifest in view of the severe poverty that has never been eradicated in the countries on the periphery[14] and that neoliberalism contributes nothing to eliminating because, on the contrary, it expands it in unprecedented ways.[15]

A second form of discreditation has to do not with the reality of poverty and misery but with their connotations. These notions bring up the idea of stripping bare, of a lack which places individuals described in these terms as passive and powerless, like victims who have given up on taking an active part in the resolution of their problems. In support of these prejudices there is often put forward the idea that it would be impossible to describe oneself at once as 'suffering' and as an active political subject, an idea which can be articulated in various ways. It is said that individuals who are victims of injustice do not describe themselves in terms of suffering when they revolt against domination and injustice and that it is always to defuse their demands that such descriptions are imposed upon them. It is also said that it is only when the sole justice possible is by way of a reparation (not a transformation), and the reparation cannot be obtained by the action of the people concerned, that they eventually make a political argument of suffering. At the heart of such arguments is the imputation of a link between descriptions in terms of suffering and victimization. But though these arguments may be plausible and even attractive from the simply speculative point of view, they do not withstand historical analysis. Modern and contemporary political history offers numerous examples of combative and contestatory uses of the term 'suffering'. Let us begin with the case of 'the suffering army'.

The years 1843–1844 left a deep mark on the history of Haiti. In a troubled moment which saw the fall of a lifelong president after a twenty-five-year reign, the partition of the island and the accession to power of the first black president (not 'man of colour', that is, mixed race, as before), there arose two revolutionary movements which, in a certain way, bear witness to the pendulum movement which leads from victorious political revolution to social revolution (or rather to the failure of a social revolution).

In 1843, following the government's constant trampling on the Constitution and its refusal to accept the consequences of the opposition's electoral victory, an insurrectionary movement led by the liberal bourgeoisie arose beginning in the southeast of the island. Constituted as a 'people's army', the opposition needed to rapidly obtain the departure of President Boyer and to attempt to reform power in a liberal and democratic direction. According to Henri Pauleus-Sannon, author of a comprehensive work on this historical episode, this political undertaking remains the boldest in the whole nineteenth-century history of Haiti: 'It seems to us that the Revolution of 1843 was at once the most significant, the most coherent and the most generous attempt which has been made among us to establish this freedom'.[16]

The new forces in power were rapidly confronted with several major difficulties, such as the conflict with the Spanish part of the island, and internal disputes within the victorious party. Soon a peasant insurrection would arise from the same southeastern area; it would contribute to ending the revolutionary interregnum in favour of a new president who, presented as a man of consensus, was above all the embodiment of conservatism and continuity. If we are to believe Henri Pauleus-Sannon, the 'revolt of the pikes' (*'révolte des piquets'*), the peasant movement headed by little known leaders, was used as a tool by adversaries of the revolution.[17] But according to Paul Moral, we should instead see it as the expression of a relatively autonomous movement, both in terms of its political slogans and in its social base.

The social context of the 1843 revolution is complex. Various social factors came into play: a conflict between the black and mixed-race elements of the postcolonial aristocracy, a conflict between the heirs of colonial exploitation and the small farmers (whose property titles were more often rested on appropriation, carried out during independence, than on law), a perpetuation of a slavery-like capitalism on the large estates and finally the agrarian crisis of the years 1840–1848.[18] While the principal actors of the 1843 revolution belonged to different parts of the bourgeoisie, the 'revolt of the pikes' was the act of poor peasants and must be considered as belonging to the continuity of local movements which, 'from 1836–1837 . . . were developing in opposition to the harsh operation of the large estates'.[19] As

Henri Pauléus-Sannon himself emphasizes, the 'revolt of the pikes' also had its own political content: 'After the moral revolution which had just occurred one year previously, and which was the work of a sizeable portion of the bourgeoisie, there appeared the material revolution, with quasi-socialist tendencies, carried out by men of the people who appeared with the more or less vague intention of making themselves a place in the sun of democratic equality'.[20]

If this historical episode holds interest for us, it is because the chief actors in what observers called the '*révolte des piquets*', 'piquets' being the pikes that were the peasants' only weapons, called themselves the 'suffering army'. There is little documentation on the 'suffering army', but enough to establish that the expression was indeed used within the army itself, and notably by its leaders, including the 'commander in chief' Jean-Jacques Acaau. Doubtless the reference to suffering can be explained in part by the living memory of slavery, which Du Bois for example showed had had a profound effect on the collective identity of the American black diasporas, contributing to an engraving of suffering into the heart of popular culture.[21] Doubtless it also drew its particular force in the Haitian context from the perpetuation of many of the social structures of slavery despite their official abolition. But its meaning must be sought in a more specific social and political conjuncture. The official assessments that have been preserved indicate that the Acaau army's motto was 'equality–freedom' and that it issued its judgements 'in the name of the suffering people'.[22] Henri Pauléus-Sannon maintains that the insurgents gave themselves this name by analogy with the 1843 insurrection, which called itself the 'people's army'.[23] The term 'suffering army' thus made it possible to designate a specific social actor: not the people in general, which the bourgeoisie claimed to represent, but the suffering people. The name has a double meaning: not only did the insurgents designate themselves as suffering subjects, they also used the term 'suffering' to distinguish themselves from the liberals struggling for the respect of private and political rights in the name of the people.[24]

Is it possible to further specify the meaning of a reference to suffering? It has sometimes been emphasized that the leaders had a mysterious character, particularly Acaau, 'former police lieutenant', whose attire leaves no doubt as to the poverty and the type of peasantry that he represented: 'He was dressed in a straw hat full of holes, a torn jacket, a pair of trousers in the same state, long oversleeves, pistols hanging from his belt and sapattes'.[25] Whatever may have been Acaau's confusion and ignorance, it seems that, for him, the idea of suffering had a quite precise political content, linked to the situation of a poverty which he attempted to bring to light and which, in its reality, gave sufficient legitimacy to an insurrectional movement.

The view proclaimed after the conquest of the city of Cayes doubtless gives sufficient proof of this: 'What did the farmer have to say to whom the Revolution had promised a reduction in foreign merchandise and an increase in the value of his goods? He said he had been tricked, and to add insult to injury, the constitution which ordains all rights and duties had received the ultimate high-handed insult in the courtyard of the very place where the Constitutional Assembly was deliberating. The population of the countryside, awakened from its slumber, murmured of its misery and resolved to work to win its rights'.[26] A strange proclamation which seems to indicate that it is not only necessary for misery to attain a certain level, but also for the poor to be cheated in order for them to decide to speak of their poverty. Or rather to murmur of it, because beginning to murmur is enough! Enough for what? To set in motion a process of legitimization of insurrection, a process of socialization that brings poor peasants out of their isolation to form a coalition for a collective struggle—unless Acaau is instead suggesting that the reality of misery can never be completely voiced, only referred to.

From the few scraps of the history of the suffering army which have been conserved, three conclusions can apparently be drawn. The first concerns the specificity of references to suffering in the modern era. The political discourse of modernity is mainly centred on the law, an operator that permits us to distinguish between legitimate and illegitimate political demands. Political liberalism, having initially excluded the possibility that the question of well-being and suffering may be a matter for the law to deal with, has led to a sort of political invisibilization of the problems linked to the reality of poverty and misery. In the context of a liberal revolution, a reference to suffering thus takes on a double political value: it criticizes an unbearable political reality (the unbearable aspects of the experience of poverty and misery) which, for this same reason, deserves to be transformed. But, equally, it criticizes the fact that the unbearable has been passed over in silence in the name of universal rights. In the speeches of Acaau, the language of suffering criticizes the state of 'deception' in which the poor peasantry is kept and demands that people begin at least to murmur the reality of suffering.

In this sense, his 'suffering army' is very different to the first 'suffering army' known to history, the term also designating one of the Norman peasant revolts of the seventeenth century.[27] What 'suffering army' meant in this case and by whom the term was used is still more difficult to know precisely. Let us suppose that suffering meant at that time 'to suffer from hunger' and that the term limited itself to conveying the legitimate demand to have enough to eat. Doubtless the legitimate demands linked to the reproduction of life and to an existence free from the fear of suffering hunger and distress are again present in the demands of Acaau and his troops. But added to them is another critical dimension, here consciously used, which gives modern use of references to suffering their specific nature: in the modern period, descriptions of suffering can produce effects of demystification. Doubtless modern societies need in general, and not only in Haiti, a form of demystification of their normative principles to bring to light their own social pathologies;[28] references to suffering notably can eminently fulfil this purpose.

The example of the '*révolte des piquets*' allows us moreover to show that the description of experienced suffering can also be a reason to act. Here is a first political illustration of the dynamic of suffering, of its productivity: the term 'suffering' does not only designate that which, in the experience of poverty and misery, is unbearable, but also that which can lead the individuals who experience it to denounce and struggle against poverty and misery.[29] The very idea of suffering has solidarity with demands, at least inchoate ones; it implies a sort of implicit social criticism.[30]

The experience of suffering is an experience of the unbearable. Therefore it has the power to bring about processes of refusal of the unbearable, processes which are at once practical and cognitive. In the practical register are included adaptation, flight or struggle. Like pain, suffering can lead to anger, even rage—a rage which has long figured among political concepts and which has found itself granted a new currency by movements such as Act Up. In the cognitive register are included the effects of the mobilization of psychic defences intended to attenuate suffering, but also the construction of forms of expression and representation and the invention of solutions to transform its causes, and doubtless also demystification (of which it can be noted in particular that it accompanies the majority of traumatic experiences, in the form of a disillusioned gaze brought to bear on the world where the trauma has occurred). Suffering can thus undeniably play the role of a motive for political struggles (in a practical refusal of the unbearable) and of an aim (in a plan to struggle against its social causes). It is also a principle of legitimation of these struggles.

A third lesson: it seems that the discourse of suffering also draws part of its political weight from the opportunity that it offers for sharing a negative social experience and, in this way, contributing to the construction of a collective subject. The term 'suffering' also designates the components of the experiences of poverty and misery which can be shared in 'communities of suffering'. The argument by which Marx explains the powerlessness of the peasantry is well known: 'The small peasant proprietors form an immense mass, members of which live in the same situation but do not enter into manifold relations with each other. Their method of operation isolates them instead of bring them into mutual intercourse. . . . Each individual peasant family is almost self-sufficient; it directly produces the greater part of its own consumption and obtains its means of life more through exchange with nature than through intercourse with society. . . . In so far as these peasant proprietors are merely connected on a local basis, and the identity of their interests fails to produce a feeling of community, national links, or a political organisation, they do not form a class. . . . They cannot represent themselves; they must be represented'.[31]

It would be more than anachronistic to project the Marxist analysis of the French small peasantry onto the postcolonial Haitian peasantry: the perpetuation of the plantation system, the variety of modes of ownership of land, the liveliness of the culture of runaway slaves and many other factors ensure that the situations are indeed incomparable. We can nevertheless conclude that the poor Haitian peasantry, like all posttraditional peasantries subject to the principle of the individual ownership of land, was characterized by a certain isolation, perhaps reinforced by the difference between the living conditions of peasants employed in the plantation system and those of small landowners. When Acaau writes, 'The population of the countryside, awakened from its slumber, murmured of its misery and resolved to work to win its rights', does this not suggest that the simple fact of making public the suffering characteristic of poverty has made it possible, if not to break this isolation, at least to share an experience on the basis of which collective demands can be formulated?[32]

Critics of the discourse of suffering most often content themselves with analysing the political effects of this discourse either on people outside the group concerned (compassion) or on the group concerned, but when the discourse is held by people other than this group's members (psychologization). What are the effects produced on the members of the group by a discourse of suffering that they hold themselves? Suffering individualizes and isolates, at least in the first instance, even when it is caused by collective events (such as wars or traumatic catastrophes) or by global social phenomena (such as an economic crisis or the collapse of industries that structure the social life of an entire region). When suffering refers to socially produced misery, the description of suffering as a collective reality linked to a determined context can be a powerful vector of the struggle against isolation and of a shift towards collective mobilization.

The struggles of the unemployed provide an example of this, as the social isolation of unemployed people is even more paradigmatic than that of the peasant. Confronted with their own failure in finding work, at the very same time as they are subjected to formal and informal injunctions to reintegrate themselves into society, the unemployed almost inevitably come to assign to themselves the responsibility for their own situation and to interiorize a negative identity which is accompanied by different forms of suffering. Isolation and internalization of shame constitute obstacles to collective mobilization that may seem insurmountable. And yet we saw in the France of the 1990s quite powerful movements of the unemployed developing on the basis of the work of organizations which contributed to enabling a sharing of the negative experiences of unemployment and a collective representation of the social injustice that they constitute.[33] The description of suffering brought about by a social world is far from necessarily locking us into the position of powerless victims: it constitutes on the contrary a possible springboard for demands made in the name of suffering.[34]

SOCIALIST CRITICISM

If the political uses of the term 'suffering' are so varied and widespread, how can we explain the fact that they are so spontaneously associated with depoliticization? Replying to this question requires us to consider more closely the decisive episode in the construction of modern political language that was the discovery of the social question in the middle of the nineteenth century in Europe.

That the destitution of the working population was reaching unbearable levels and that it was accompanied by extreme suffering while industry and wealth were booming is not really in dispute: even though the liberal camp of that time tends to pass over the problem in silence or exclude it from the list of questions worthy of political attention, there are within its own ranks observers to realize that the problem and the controversy has to do above all with the causes and remedies of this new poverty. The liberal response consists, in one of its most typical versions, in maintaining that this poverty is in part an inevitable fact and in part a phenomenon explicable by the perverse effects of a system of public charity to which it is preferable to substitute private generosity.[35] The socialist discourse, for its part, consists in emphasizing that there is a link between this poverty and the organization of society, in refusing all solutions which come from public or private charity and in promoting a social transformation (through the association of scholars and industrialists, national workshops intended to guarantee work, the redistribution of wealth in favour of the poor, the self-negation of the proletariat as a subordinated class, etc.).

In such a context, it may appear that description in terms of suffering fits better into the liberal than the socialist position. Does it not make it possible to confine the proletariat in the role of victims who must wait for the bourgeoisie to come to their aid, while excluding poverty from the domain of specifically political questions in order to transfer it to our individual responsibility when faced with the suffering of others (Tocqueville's private charity)? Inversely, should socialism not pass over in silence individual suffering in order to emphasize the genuine social dimension of poverty and demand responses in a political language that does not allow itself to be contaminated by the rationales of assistance and charity? In support of this fairly classic interpretation, the authority of Marx and Engels is sometimes appealed to, as they are reputed to have fought against the very idea of the 'social question' and all the moralizing versions of social criticism for these reasons.[36] These common ideas miss the mark as much with respect to the purpose of references to suffering in primitive socialism as with regard to their role in the work of Marx and Engels.

In France, what marked the irruption of the social question onto the public stage was the revolutionary days of July 1830 and the first uprising of the *Canuts* (the Lyon silk workers) in November 1832.[37] To aid in identifying some of the socialist references to suffering, the texts published in *L'Écho de la fabrique*,[38] the first workers' journal in France and probably in the world, provide indispensable documentation.[39] And the proximity that will be observed between the uses of suffering in this journal and in the work of Marx and Engels will confirm that it offers us a unique tool with which to unearth the meaning and the general value that references to suffering were granted in the socialist thought of the years 1830–1840, a period when the working class was becoming aware of a commonality of interest[40] and began to develop its own specific discourse.[41]

Founded one month before the 1831 uprising (the first issue is dated October 30, 1831) by workers and publicists, this *Journal des chefs d'ateliers et des ouvriers en soie* appeared weekly until the second uprising of 1834. Describing itself as the organ of the Lyonnais working class, it had a triple goal: making known the reality of the workers' poverty, denouncing the 'merchants' (*'négociants'*) (who represented the manufacturers and nego-tiated the piece rates with the workers)[42] and contributing to the improve-ment of the physical and moral condition of the working class, as well as to its cooperative organization. The prospectus announcing the creation of the first workers' journal in France is written in these terms: 'Human beings destined to such a laborious life should at least have the certainty that further advantage will not taken of their misery to make it still worse. . . . Until today with no defence against the intrigues of commerce, exposed to the brutalities, the crying injustices of certain merchants . . . these unfortunates have chosen to use publicity for the defence of their rights. Through it they aim to make known with precision and frankness to a population of more than 150,000 souls, of which they form the greater part, the cause of the general malaise from which this same populations suffers'.

L'*Écho* stands in the tradition of efforts made by the workers following the July Revolution of 1830 to develop an awareness of their own situation and a voice.[43] Public description of suffering is part of such efforts. It would be tedious to bring up the innumerable references to 'the state of immisera-tion and suffering in which the lowest classes of society are sunk' (no. 46), to the 'hideous and immoral wound of poverty' (no. 32), to 'the frightful mis-ery' into which the workers are sinking (no. 2). Constantly, the different aspects of the social question are brought up: low pay, uncertainty about future work and its payment, difficulty in maintaining a sense of one's own dignity and giving one's children a good education, housing problems, food and water problems, health problems, and it is always indissociably in the registers of rights, dignity and suffering. That the vocabulary of suffering belongs to the political language of socialism is an obvious fact which bursts into the daylight when one reads L'*Écho*.

For the purpose of specifying the different political uses of the theme of suffering, and the reasons that can lead to its marginalization, it also offers unexpected archival resources because in the course of three years, which mark the editorial succession of Chastaing to Vidal, then his removal in 1833, there appear three political lines which involve different types of rela-tionships to suffering.[44] Under the direction of Vidal, the journal's founder, the question of suffering is omnipresent. The Saint Simonian reference to the rational organization of production predominates, the general orientation being that of mutualism and the defence of the Lyon model, notably of the role of 'Labour Courts' (*Conseils de Prud'hommes*). Under his stewardship, the disclosure of suffering fulfils a dual purpose: that of a cry of alarm in the face of the disorganization of society and the destitution resulting from it and that of a denunciation of the excesses of the industrial bourgeoisie.

After Vidal's death, the journal was run by Chastaing, who gave it a more radical orientation, at once political (clearly republican) and more social (affirming a demand for social equality). The democratic demand and the theme of social equality led to new purpose being given to the description of suffering. Again, a dual purpose: on the one hand, discrediting the social order that produces suffering and, on the other, underlining the irreducibility of class conflict and legitimizing the self-organization of the working class. But it is almost paradoxical that, under his editorship, the theme of suffering remains just as present as before,[45] while all the factors which would explain its disappearance after his removal were already in play. First, an objective factor: the end of the crisis which followed the first uprising and of the deterioration of the living conditions which it brought. Next, an ideological factor, having to do with the conjunction of republicanism and a theoretical and practical Fourierism. Description of the experience and the particular context of exploitation and poverty becomes less urgent as soon as the emancipation brought by republican law is expected. The analysis of living conditions takes on a lesser importance when it is through the Fourierist theory of the ideal society that an effort is made to give republicanism its social complement. The practical Fourierism of mutualists also played a role as an orientation towards social experimentation rather than towards conflict, on the one hand, and towards experimentation guided by the goal of pleasure in work rather than by the description of suffering at work, on the other hand. If the theme of suffering remained fundamental in Chastaing's view, it was for its polemic and critical focus, in other words as a result of the radical orientation that he was attempting to give the journal and that would cost him his editorial post. In the third period of *L'Écho*, that of a reorientation towards a mutualism more concerned with defending and reforming the system of collective manufacture and its modes of democratic collaboration among workers, merchants and manufacturers, the description of suffering would no longer be in question.[46]

Certainly, Vidal was already proposing various stagings of the class struggle. He relentlessly denounced the contempt in which workers were held and the continuous humiliation they had to endure. The description of workers' suffering forms part of this type of criticism. Evidence for this, for example, is the ironic contrast of the dancing of the rich and the suffering of the poor: 'We do not wish to believe the statement by the *Courrier de Lyon*, which says that *for the wealthy to dance is to give back to the working class.* Well then! yes, dear sirs, dance! dance! and dance again! How much good that does for the unfortunate who has no bread, and those refreshments which are so abundant at the ball, may they soften the breast of the unfortunate worn out by suffering. The music was delicious . . . and the worker gave forth a death rattle on his bed of sorrows' (no. 15). But in essence, the purpose of these descriptions is to show that due to the recognition in law of the equal dignity of citizens and the central social function fulfilled by workers, such contempt is no longer possible. Vidal denounces in particular those who knowingly ignore suffering, which is a sign of contempt for human dignity, as in this tale where it is the fear of the poor's illnesses that leads merchants to construct inhumane conditions ('the cage'[47]) that they reserve for their workers when the time comes to pay them: 'Cholera, it is said, has already brought us improvements, and as the proverb says, it is an ill wind that blows nobody any good. Also, several merchants have had the *cages* of their workshops enlarged; others have made them more healthy by the circulation of air, and it is even said that some have placed, in these formerly insalubrious spaces, jars of lime chloride. You may percieve however nature of the empire of fear! philosophers, sing the praises of morality, it is a good thing no doubt; men of compassion, sing the praises of philosophy, it too is good, but all this is nothing in comparison to fear' (no. 24).

But Vidal's objective was to promote an organization between the poor and the moneyed classes which would be to the advantage of all[48] because 'the social organisation needs rich men and poor men, that is to say proletarians and men of property, and these are two indispensable classes, whose interests are linked. . . . The industrialist is a free man, he is the equal of the banker, of the businessman; he who thinks otherwise misses the mark by four centuries' (no. 22); in more moderate terms, the prospectus spoke 'of establishing a balance which, without slighting the general interest of the bosses of factories, would bring about an improvement in the fate of those who depend upon them'. The struggle against abuses, which constituted one of the principal goals of the review during its first two years (in the context of the reform

of the Labour Courts), participates in this political strategy aiming at a reform meeting the well-understood interests of each of the parties. And it will
be noticed that here again, in a context in which the Labour Courts (*Conseils
de Prud'hommes*) produced a jurisprudence that was often problematic in
light of substantive laws, without, however, being able to rely exclusively on
custom, which is often in need of reform, the argument from suffering makes
it possible to legitimate demands that could not be based on an argument
defining abuses as the violation of custom or of private and commercial
law.[49]

The date of 'reconciliation' was thought to be close ('the days of a full
reconciliation are not far away' [no. 12]) and, in efforts made to reach it,
references to suffering played a dual role. First, the function they fulfilled is
to legitimate workers' demands. Nothing, indeed, authorizes keeping certain
individuals in conditions of suffering: 'Man, to whichever class he belongs,
is not born to languish forever in a state of suffering, but to have a part in the
bounty granted to us on this earth by the mighty Being who rules us' (no. 12).
Moreover, the workers saw themselves that their suffering justified their
demands because they had become aware of their dignity; as Chastaing
wrote, 'The peoples wish to reach the Promised Land of well-being, they
have too much light not to be ashamed of the rags of poverty' (no. 36).

On the other hand, the term 'suffering' is used for its force of interpellation. By emphasizing the suffering specific to the general condition of the
canuts and to the particular abuses in which the merchants engaged, Vidal
and his collaborators exhort the latter to face up to their responsibilities and
to participate actively in the resolution of the problems rather than seeking to
profit from them. The strategy used to this end is not only to exhibit the
scandal constituted by the very fact of destitution, it is also to make morally
unbearable to the bourgeoisie the responsibility that they carry. Speaking of
L'Écho de la fabrique, Vidal says that 'each page makes blush those who
speculate upon their [the workers'] misery' and then illustrates this theme by
a fable in which the workers' rare hours of sleep bring them rest while the
rich man finds himself pursued during his sleeping hours by his conscience:
'For him sleep becomes a torture; his hand has refused to succour the unfortunate! . . . All is overthrown; a dream shows him the being whom he has
humiliated at the pinnacle of grandeur, and himself subject to a proletarian
who now has power over the destiny of the proud man, for whom the poor
man was less than the lackey who wore his livery. What a frightful
dream! . . . Scarcely has it ended when an even more painful one follows it.

The rich man has committed a selfish act during the day, his iron hand has not belied his heart; it has lowered the wage of a husband and father; it has taken from him half his children's bread; but Heaven avenges the poor, and the selfish man is oppressed even in his sleep; he believes he has lost all, fortune and grandeur; all is a prey to those whom he long treated as helots; it is on them that his fate will now depend. Oh! what a terrible dream. . . . A cold sweat runs down this brow which has never blushed, because decency never dwellt in the soul of the cruel man' (no. 23). A text by Bouvery expanded even more clearly what could be called the strategy of shame: 'From now on, our task is to show how absurd and how injust is the way good and ill are shared out in society, as it has been made for us. It is to make our adversaries understand how to what extent their system is derisory and cruel to us, how hateful and ridiculous are the sophisms which inspire their selfishness, so that by making them blush, we may force them to carry out themselves the reforms that our position demands' (no. 43).

For Chastaing, a workers' organization remains the chief political objective, but it is no longer conceived so much according to a Saint Simonian model of the association of scientists and industrialists, but rather as an ideal of social equality (no. 30–34), attributed either to the 'levellers' (no. 30) or to Fourier (no. 44, 60). The priority of social over political reforms, as well as the reality of class antagonism, is more clearly affirmed. References to suffering have the purpose of bringing to light the reality of destitution and the seriousness of its concrete effects, of presenting it as a social pathology that it is useless to conceal: 'Will the doctor cure the patient by denying the illness? . . . Oh! the time has come, all of society must inquire about the obscure tears of the indigent'.[50] Thus suffering is no longer presented solely as a moral scandal, but also as an injustice: 'Let us be truthful: the proletarian is the one who has the most to suffer from this tax [the indirect tax]. It makes the working man's life too expensive; because of it, this working man *can no longer live by his work*, unless his salary increases in proportion. Oh! see how unjust this tax is, it crushes the indigent, it brushes past the well-off man, it spares the rich man' (no. 23).

Reconsidered in terms of injustice, references to suffering maintain their purpose of legitimation and interpellation, but their meaning changes in line with the new political goals: they tend to be reformulated according to the logic of the 'alarm' and the social emergency. Chastaing depicts the extent of the workers' suffering to the Lyonnais bourgeoisie, no longer only to make it perceive the well-foundedness of the proletarians' demands and become aware of its share of responsibility, but also to make it perceive a threat. The rationale is no longer that of a call to reconciliation but of the description of a situation of social emergency which calls for solutions as pressing as they are radical, which, in a certain way, justify violent mobilization.

Twice, Chastaing raises an 'alarm cry'. In no. 36, the article entitled 'Cri d'alarme' sets itself the task of considering the following question: 'What man knows today how to prevent the people from dying of hunger, industry from expiring of exhaustion, the social order from collapsing under riots?' It continues in this way: 'Will we spend a long time asking this question? For on its solution depends the future of the human race, for there is the wound that must be healed. From all sides a cry of alarm goes up. A patriotic and orator who has a great future (Garnier-Pagès) declared on the rostrum: It is not opinion that assembles the riot, it is misery which pushes people to revolt. When one considers society from this point of view, political rights only have a relative interest; they appear only in the background. . . . The proletariat must disappear, and with it the riot will cease'. In the lead article in no. 42, again from Chastaing's pen, the subject is revisited: 'Defender of the working class, the Echo, an ever-vigilant sentinel, raises the cry of alarm repeated by a thousand voices'. Even though Chastaing, in the same article, continues to maintain that 'the worker demands that the merchant fraternise with him', the theme of a situation of social emergency and the idea of revolt being justified by destitution provide a new syntax of suffering, split between two differentiated audiences.

On the one hand, the discourse of suffering is no longer essentially intended to justify and motivate reforms in the eyes of the bourgeoisie, but to identify them as the principal agents of the conflict, or as the enemies: 'To you, happy citizens surrounded by fortune and power.—To you who are moved only by ambition or cupidity.—To you who, indifferent to the ills of your fellow-men, let your useless life slip away in sweet quietude.—I want to disturb your souls, arouse there remorse and fear.—I want to place there the invisible larva which must become a gnawing worm.—Be attentive! before your eyes will pass in succession the various tableaux where the miseries of the proletariat are outlined.—My gallery is far from being exhausted, each day supplies a page for this history of the people.—I shall engrave every page: what do I care for your anger! I have already offered to your annoyed eyes Demangeaot or the proletarian dying of hunger, Vichard or the soldier reduced to begging, Blois or the indigent old man; today I will show you Mitaine or the proletarian in prison. . . . Let the anathema hurled at society surprise no one any longer! let people be surprised, on the contrary, that, with so many ruinous elements, it can still subsist. O proletarians, you are admirable for your forbearance in bearing your ills' (no. 3).

On the other hand, the discourse of suffering is no longer addressed only to society, responsible for the extent of an unbearable poverty, but also has the goal of justifying protest action in the eyes of the workers themselves. It is no doubt possible to reconcile with this political logic the idea, expressed in no. 43 by Bouvery, that it is for the workers themselves to describe their suffering and their needs. The author seems to insist on the motivating role that his description can fill in the constitution of the proletariat as a political force: 'See where we are! more unfortunate, I boldly declare, than we were before '89, for on the one hand we have done nothing to relieve our misery, and on the other, our feelings have been made a thousand times sharper by the destruction, under I know not what pretext of the dignity of man, everything we once used to hide their bitterness from ourselves. It is time for such a state of affairs to cease, we must urgently take another direction, we must walk the road of material improvements, and it is for us, the proletariat, who suffer the most under the existing order, to proclaim our needs, to demand that they be lessened, by virtue of our right to live. We must walk down this road with calm and moderation . . . but also with perseverance and firmness . . . ; above all let us be capable of defending our own interests, and let us no longer trust those ambitious intriguers who, behind the mask of apostles of humanity, seek only to make use of us as instruments in their rise'.

In the writings of Bouvery, who nonetheless defends political positions specific to mutualism, the logic of emergency is accompanied again by the suggestion that destitution confers a right to revolt, and in the following text, we are not far from finding the idea that the absolute destitution of the poor, by harming their 'right to demand' not only the satisfaction of 'basic needs', but also 'a little above the minimum', gives them an absolute claim on society: 'The upshot of all that I have previously said is that a horrible malaise is tormenting society; that this malaise has its source in the precarious state of the workers who, as they become enlightened, perceive that their existence is threatened more and more every day by competition, the introduction of machines and egotism, and take action to push away the nightmare which is crushing them; that it is urgent, indispensable, to provide a remedy as soon as possible for the ills of this class of men who are significant because of their usefulness and the injustice of which they have been victims ever since creation, and redoubtable because of their numbers and their disdain for life' (no. 48).

But it is true that, from the start of the period of Chastaing's editorship, *L'Écho de la fabrique* tends to give an ever smaller place to the description of suffering, and this tendency would only become more marked after his removal. On reading *L'Écho*, it does not seem, therefore, that the marginalization of the lexicon of suffering specific to primitive socialism can be explained by the development towards a socialism that is more political (more aware of its objectives and more oriented towards strategic questions) or more materialistic (more aware of its class interests and of the power of social antagonisms). Contrary to what one might assume, it can be explained rather by the dual dissemination of republican demands and Fourierist ideas. When social equality is once again subordinated to political equality, it no longer seems so necessary to describe situations of ordinary injustice and unsatisfied demands: the description of inequalities tends to be reiterated in a universal language rather than in terms of particular lived experiences. And even when social theory is seen as the means of criticizing the abstraction of republicanism and completing political emancipation through social emancipation, the result is that social emancipation is thought in terms of the principles of the social organization of the future and not in terms of the experience of the present.[51]

It is tempting to put forward the following hypothesis: in the lexicon of early socialism, the vocabulary of suffering is central, and in the history of the workers' movement, it is not Marxism which was the first to contribute to its marginalization, but rather republicanism and certain uses of what was later called 'utopian socialism'. The uses of the term 'suffering' in the work of Engels and Marx must therefore be reexamined. Far from discrediting the vocabulary of suffering, it appears in fact that they recognized its full legitimacy—perhaps it should even be said that they were reacting against utopian marginalization and republican discreditation. This remark applies to the early Marx and Engels as much as to the late Marx and Engels. Let us begin with the young Engels and the young Marx.

In the writings of Engels and of Marx, socialism and communism are interpreted as historical reactions to the concrete conditions of existence of the working class, and the 'realistic' point of view that they would always pit against attempts to base revolutionary programmes on juridical or moral foundations can be explained by the conviction that political objectives must be defined on the basis of practical and theoretical efforts to surmount the difficulties of life in current social conditions.

The importance of a description of the way in which these conditions of life and work were experienced by the working class appears clearly from the first lines of the preface to *The Condition of the Working Class in England*: 'The condition of the working class is the real basis and point of departure of all social movements of the present because it is the highest and most unconcealed pinnacle of the social misery existing in our day. French and German working-class Communism are its direct, Fourierism and English Socialism, as well as the Communism of the German-educated bourgeoisie, are its indirect products. A knowledge of proletarian conditions is absolutely necessary to be able to provide solid ground for socialist theories, on the one hand, and for judgments about their right to exist, on the other; and to put an end to all sentimental dreams and fancies pro and con'. [52] A description of the workers' misery thus has a triple polemical use: against the liberalism that passes it over in silence ('have they ever paid any serious attention to your sufferings?' [53]), against philanthropic solutions which never manage to take the measure of a structural problem (the entire book demonstrates this), but also against the versions of socialism and of communism which tend to lose sight of the reality of destitution in favour of republican abstractions and utopian constructions.

When he describes the reality of living conditions, Engels does not hesitate to resort to the vocabulary of suffering. We can even note that he considers this vocabulary fitting for his dedication of the book to workers, and his witness to the sharing of the experience described: 'Working men, to you I dedicate a work, in which I have tried to lay before my German Countrymen a faithful picture of your condition, of your sufferings and struggles, of your hopes and prospects. I have lived long enough amidst you to know something about your circumstances; I have devoted to their knowledge my most serious attention, I have studied the various official and non-official documents as far as I was able to get hold of them—I have not been satisfied with this, I wanted more than a mere *abstract* knowledge of my subject, I wanted to see you in your own homes, to observe you in your everyday life, to chat with you on your condition and grievances, to witness your struggles against the social and political power of your oppressors'. [54] It will be noticed that, in these lines, suffering is not distinguished from social and political struggle: the description of suffering serves the struggle. The oppositions that could have been seen as consubstantial with socialism are no more at work in

Engels's writings than in *L'Écho de la fabrique*. The comparison can be pushed further. It is striking, for example, to find in the work of the young Marx the 'strategy of shame' whose importance we have seen in one article of Vidal, combined with certain elements of the strategy of the 'alarm cry', whose role has been described by Chastaing. In the text from 1843–1844 titled 'A Contribution to the Critique of Hegel's Philosophy of Right. Introduction', Marx's aim is to depict the misery of the current situation in the most sombre light, to 'shame' the bourgeoisie, while at the same time 'giving courage' to the proletariat: '[Criticism] must set out to depict the stifling pressure which all the different spheres of society exercise on one another, the universal but apathetic ill-feeling and the narrowness of vision which both acknowledges and misconstrues itself. . . . The important thing is not to permit the Germans a single moment of self-deception or resignation. The actual burden must be made even more burdensome by creating an awareness of it. The humiliation must be increased by making it public. Each sphere of German society must be depicted as the *partie honteuse* of that society and these petrified conditions must be made to dance by having their own tune sung to them! The people must be put in *terror* of themselves in order to give them courage. In this way a pressing need of the German nation will be fulfilled, and the needs of nations are in the ultimate causes of their satisfaction'.[55]

Similarly, suffering in the work of the young Marx fulfils a purpose of legitimation analogous to that Chastaing and Bouvery give to it. We are familiar with the idea that the possibility of a social revolution depended entirely upon the alliance between 'suffering humanity that thinks' (the proletariat won over to socialist ideas) and 'thinking humanity that is oppressed' (revolutionary philosophers).[56] We would be mistaken in reducing this statement to a simple philosophical play on words and to a metaphysical conception of suffering and of the proletariat. It is founded rather on a common use of the term 'suffering' to designate the reality of poverty as a motivational and demystifying force: here suffering appears not solely as the origin of revolt, but also as the process from which socialist ideas emerge.

Marx contents himself with adding that absolute sufferings carry in themselves an absolute critique of the world which produced them and the revolutionary demand of a world based on the antithetical principle of respect for humanity: the 'positive possibility of emancipation' lies in 'the formation of a . . . sphere which has a universal character because of its universal suffering . . . which is, in a word, the *total loss* of humanity and which can therefore redeem itself only through the *total redemption of humanity*. This dissolution of society as a particular class is the *proletariat*.[57] It is the suffering engendered by poverty that is in question here, and as in the quoted passages of Chastaing and Bouvery, also a poverty that grants a right over society, a right all the more legitimate because this poverty is established by a new social organization based on collectively assumed political choices: 'For the proletariat is not formed by *natural* poverty but by *artificially produced* poverty; it is formed not from the mass of people mechanically oppressed by the weight of society, but from the mass of people resulting from society's *acute disintegration*, and in particular from the dissolution of the middle class'.[58]

Though Marx and Engels were already concerned in the mid-1840s with showing that these living conditions could be explained by the deep dynamics of capitalism, they were not yet in possession of the principles of their materialist conception of history. And one might assume that the developmemt of their theories led them to localize the origin of political conflicts in macrosocial dynamics (the proletariat's dawning awareness of its social purpose and its interests) or economic ones (the contradiction between productive forces and social relationships) which can without risk be focused upon independently of analysis of the conditions of life and of work. If this were the case, it would be difficult to understand the constancy of the positive judgements of Marx (and of Engels himself) on the book that Engels dedicated in 1845 to the living conditions of English workers.

A reading of *Capital* permits us furthermore to find new, deeper analyses of the concrete ways in which capitalist exploitation is experienced. The reality of the expropriation of peasants is broadly described in the chapters on so-called primitive accumulation. The demonstration of a tendency to absolute pauperization and the analysis of the reserve army of capital are accompanied by a chapter describing the concrete forms of workers' suffering (it takes up themes developed by Engels, basing them on updated sources). As for the analyses of the transformation of manufacture into large-scale industry and the theory of wage labour, they are supported by detailed descriptions of conditions of work and their global effect on workers' individual and collective existence. It is moreover striking that the only place where social and political struggles are analysed in *Capital* immediately follows the description of the effects of overexploitation.[59] Struggles for the reduction of the work day are thus addressed as struggles against the effects of working conditions in such a way that we could say that, in *Capital*, class struggles are only explicitly dealt with as struggles against suffering.

Thirteen years after the publication of the first edition of *Capital*, Marx would give a final proof of his interest in the question of the living conditions of the proletariat, writing the questionnaire for a 'Workers' Enquiry' (1880) for the *Revue Socialiste*. It is the workers' living conditions as a whole that Marx was trying to identify in asking questions about working conditions, accidents, the length of the working day, remuneration of work and 'physical and moral' health,[60] as well as about the capacity of workers to make demands oriented towards social transformation. As suggested by Leda Leal Ferreira, the range of questions is the sign of an attempt to access the concrete experience of the worker considered in all its dimensions, a task as useful as it is difficult to reconcile with the disciplinary fragmentation and the specialization specific to the contemporary social sciences.[61]

Marx emphasizes the interest both scientific and political of the task in terms which take up again themes we have already encountered: 'The blackguardly features of capitalist exploitation which were exposed by the official investigation organised by the English government, and the legislation which was necessitated there as a result of these revelations (legal limitation of the working day to 10 hours, the law concerning female and child labour, etc.), have forced the French bourgeoisie to tremble even more before the dangers which an impartial and systematic investigation might represent. In the hope that maybe we shall induce a republican government to follow the example of the monarchical government of England, by likewise organizing a far-reaching investigation into the facts and crimes of capitalist exploitation, we shall attempt to initiate an inquiry of this kind with those poor resources which are at our disposal. We hope to meet in this work with the support of all workers in town and country who understand that they alone can describe with full knowledge the misfortunes from which they suffer, and that only they, and not saviours sent by Providence, can energetically apply the healing remedies for the social ills to which they are a prey. We also rely upon socialists of all schools who, being wishful for social reform, must wish for an exact and positive knowledge of the conditions in which the working class—the class to whom the future belongs—works and moves'.[62]

In the first forms of socialism, it is the criticism of living conditions which constitutes the act of denunciation of industrial society and 'organization' is the remedy envisaged in the struggle against isolation, precarity and dependence engendered by the competition between workers and the disorganization of production. Though it tends to take on a secondary importance in *L'Écho*, it is noticeable, for example, that, in the *Atelier*, the principal workers' journal of the 1840s, dominated by a Saint Simonism radicalized under the influence of Buchez, a large number of articles are dedicated to 'inquiries' on conditions of life.[63]

In the work of Marx and Engels, capitalism also remains the target of a criticism based on effects, where suffering plays a determining role. And in a context where, at the heart of the workers' movement, the ideological struggle was absorbed by political, strategical and programmatic questions, to the detriment of the analysis of the experience of destitution, Marx emphasized until the end that description of the conditions of life and work is fundamental: it is upon a description of the effects of poverty and domination that a criticism of capitalism must be founded, and not upon narrowly politicial, moral or juridical demands; it is in these effects that the springboards and motivations of revolutionary action are found, springboards and motivations which define the point of view from which political questions should be posed.

If the analysis of these effects is thus a fundamental task of the first forms of socialism, it is true that it does not constitute the specific task of Marxism. For Marxism has in fact the specific goal of making explicit the general social framework within which the drama experienced by the proletariat unfolds, a general social framework reconstructed through analysis of the social dynamics which may be able to overcome capitalism. This analysis identifies the structural contradictions which, on the one hand, make this overcoming possible, and on the other hand, make it possible to sketch out the forms that the future could take. But in trying to retain only the heart of Marxism, Marx's successors forgot many elements which contributed to the strength and efficacity of Marx critique of capitalism.[64]

CAPITALISM AND SUFFERING

Not only does the social question give a novel purpose to the political language of suffering, but the very existence of capitalism gives an unprecedented form to suffering. Suffering produced by the long-term failure to meet fundamental needs always accompanies poverty, and poverty did not have to wait for capitalism to come into existence. But the major social transformations brought about by capitalism saw the appearance of a new form of suffering, as much quantitatively as qualitatively.

First of all, quantitatively. The first years of the nineteenth century were marked by this disturbing paradox: in the countries where wealth increased the most, the number of individuals who must make do with quantities of food insufficient for their biological needs and live in conditions of total squalor also increased exponentially. This is what Tocqueville himself recognizes in his first essay on pauperism: 'The countries which seem to be most impoverished are those which in reality account for the fewest indigents, and among the peoples most admired for their opulence, one part of the population is forced to rely on the alms of the other in order to live. Cross the English countryside and you will think yourself transported into the Eden of modern civilisation. . . . Now look more closely at the villages; examine the parish registers, and you will discover with indescribable astonishment that one sixth of the inhabitants of this flourishing kingdom live at the expense of public charity. . . . The average number of indigents in France . . . is one pauper to twenty inhabitants. But immense differences are observable between the different parts of the kingdom. The department of the Nord, which is certainly the richest, the most populous, and the most advanced from all points of view, reckons close to a sixth of its population for whom charity is necessary. In the Creuse, the poorest and least industrial of all our departments, there is only one indigent to every fifty-eight inhabitants'.[65]

It is certainly possible to limit ourselves to highlighting the percentage of those who were dependent upon charity. But the problem is rather that the level of wages and insecurity of employment led to a chronic failure to meet the most fundamental needs as well as to degrading housing conditions. In *The Condition of the Working Class in England*, Engels illustrates the chronic undernourishment of the proletariat by the nonnegligeable number of deaths from hunger in the big cities, and he emphasizes the poor quality of the food which was reserved for them, citing the convictions of the merchants who were profiting from poverty.[66] In *Capital*, twenty years later, Marx would again count the deaths from hunger, and he would denounce rotten or adulterated food, still a current question. He would also cite the studies of public health establishing that a large part of the working population was not receiving the minimum nutritional requirements.[67]

Engels cites the numerous reports deploring the inhumanity of the housing conditions reserved for the immense majority of the working population. Let us content ourselves with reporting some numbers: in the working-class area of Manchester called 'Little Ireland', the sanitation police noted 'a single privy for 380 persons in Parliament Street' and reported that 'often the inspectors found, in a single house, two families in two rooms. All slept in one, and used the other as a kitchen and dining-room in common. Often more than one family lived in a single damp cellar, in whose pestilent atmosphere twelve to sixteen persons were crowded together', (the total population living in cellars in the urban area being estimated at 40,000 or 50,000).[68]

Capital would cite the medical reports of its time, which were astonishingly similar, including that by Bell, doctor for the poor in Bradford, considered only the third most squalid city of the time: 'Vincent Street, Green Aire Place, and the Leys include 223 houses having 1,450 inhabitants, 435 beds, and 36 privies. . . . The beds—and in that term I include any roll of dirty old rags, or an armful of shavings—have an average of 3.3 persons to each, many have 5 and 6 persons to each, and some people, I am told, are absolutely without beds; they sleep in their ordinary clothes, on the bare boards. . . . I need scarcely add that many of these dwellings are dark, damp, dirty, stinking holes, utterly unfit for human habitation'.[69]

Capitalism was accompanied by a massive production of situations of extreme failure to meet needs which, before it, characterized only periods of crisis (epidemics, wars, droughts and famines); under capitalism this suffering became the normal condition of a great part of the population, a new situation which led to the coinage of the neologism 'pauperism'.[70] But to the quantitative aggregation of suffering linked to the failure to meet fundamental needs were added specific forms of suffering.

A first specific factor in suffering is connected with the type of domination built into the capitalist work relation. The relationship of subordination implied by the wage relation requires not only that the worker carry out prescribed activities and surrender the product of his work, but also that he accept submitting his activity to the logic of valorization of capital. In this subordination, it is the whole of the body that is mobilized in the experience of a constraint which weighed, at the beginning of industrial capitalism, on almost the whole of daily existence. In this way, capitalism created a form of suffering through an incorporation of constraint which was not part of the work of either peasants or craftsmen.[71]

Committed to describing the concrete effects of work situations, *L'Écho de la fabrique* did not fail to mention the concrete forms of this process of incorporation of constraint: 'The excess of work, by capturing the worker, by attaching him to a job where all the parts of his body are continually moving, is harmful to health; and according to the statements of the best-known doctors of our city, three-quarters of the illnesses of factory workers are due to this cause. An eighteen-hour working day on Jacquard looms, which are normally painful to move, where the stomach pressed against the roller receives the kick-back of the flap, prevents digestion, disposes to irritation, is primary cause of lethargic illnesses. Doctors declare that they can only cure these illnesses with sleep, a change of situation and a good diet. Let us now make the comparison: if the working man's ordinary duties destroy his health, what becomes of him who is forced to work day and night for a week, and not to stop his work until his strength abandons him and sleep conquers him? Who, not even troubling to lie down on a bed, for fear of resting too much, sleeps on the job, and soon wakes trembling, because sleep, in that position, is as painful as work. How many do we not see who, after such excesses, fall ill, and remain so for a month before being able to take up work again; others go to the hospice, and do not return. How many times have we seen mothers in tears, having lost their children, whose docility towards the merchants and fear of having no more work forced to make themselves captive for ten nights at a stretch, and thus to be the involuntary cause of their death' (no. 17).

Of course, this text features the specific characteristics of the system of collective manufacture, where the work day is not fixed by any limit, where, furthermore, incorporation involves self-constraint; it nonetheless expresses in an almost pure form the tendency to total mobilization of the body which characterizes capitalism as long as its dynamics are not hindered. It has furthermore the merit of emphasizing that the incorporation of constraint accompanies the interiorization of domination, a compliance due to the situation of dependency in which, for their survival, waged workers are placed in relation to the employer. This interiorization is itself the cause of suffering when workers know that all of their efforts will not permit them to obtain enough money to meet their minimum expenses and that, at their employers' mercy, they must sometimes accept conditions which should be unacceptable. Suffering experienced in the body can thus be accompanied by resignation to a constraint experienced as unavoidable: 'Today, many weavers are so downcast that they only continue to work at this profession because it is morally impossible for them to change it' (no. 45).

A second factor specific to the suffering induced by capitalism is the dissolution of traditional bonds of solidarity which make it possible collectively to confront the vagaries and difficulties of existence, social bonds which allow us to find support in others in the face of hardship. The emergence of capitalism was accompanied by a profound alteration of the forms of social organization and by a recasting of social relationships in favour of the demands of the valorization of capital. Nothing guarantees that social transformations instigated by capitalism are compatible with the maintenance of the social supports of existence. Manifestly, capitalism started by destroying these before the welfare state was brought into existence in an attempt to reestablish them, and all signs lead us to believe that capitalism is again beginning its undermining work in the age of neoliberalism.[72]

Concerning suffering which is no longer explained so much by domination (via constraint) as by disaffiliation there is also much discussion in *L'Écho de la fabrique*. The belief that industrial society was leading to destruction of the social supports of existence is what the first forms of socialism had in view in their criticism of 'egoism' and 'competition'. In *L'Écho*, these criticisms are sometimes accompanied by the observation that the disappearance of forms of protective social organization involves a greater vulnerability to suffering. This is the argument of a text already quoted, in which Bouvery seems to be referring to the end of workers' guilds and the banning of professional organizations: 'Look at where we are! more unfortunate, I boldly declare, than we were before '89, for on the one hand we have done nothing to relieve our misery, and on the other, our feelings have been made a thousand times more acute by the destruction under I know not what pretext of the dignity of man everything which up until now we had used to hide their bitterness from ourselves' (no. 43). And it is the same Bouvery who would depict isolation and the difficulty of envisaging a future for oneself, in a word precarity, as the source of suffering, in another text already quoted: 'The upshot of all that I have previously said is that a horrible malaise is tormenting society; that this malaise has its source in the precarious state of the workers who, as they become enlightened, perceive that their existence is threatened more and more every day by competition, the introduction of machines and egotism, and take action to push away the nightmare which is crushing them' (no. 48).

If it is possible to mount a denunciation of capitalism based on suffering, then, this is due to three different processes: a process of social polarization which tends to keep a considerable mass of society in poverty, a process of mobilization of bodies and interiorization of constraint (two processes which point to specific forms of institutionalization of class domination) and a process of social upheaval whose aims are not always compatible with maintaining the social supports of existence (a process referring us back to the logic of disaffiliation). These three processes engender suffering and, insofar as they affect the same people, they must be considered as the different factors in a single experience of suffering. In the nineteenth century, they seemed generally to produce their effects in conjunction, but nothing prevents them from separating and, in fact, they have been able to produce independent effects. Each of these three processes specifies both a specific genesis and a specific definition of social suffering.

On the one hand, the suffering caused by a lasting failure to meet fundamental needs is a social suffering when society is responsible for this failure to meet needs. This is the case, for example, when society condemns individuals to a wage which barely permits them to survive and which is so irregular that it is impossible to escape for any length of time from the horizon of the struggle for survival. In the minds of Marx and Engels, this suffering constitutes the normal state of the condition of a waged worker. The history of the twentieth century has proven that this was not the case and today it is mainly in certain zones of societies on the periphery of the world economy and in certain enclaves of poverty in the centre that such suffering is found. Sometimes this poverty can be explained by overexploitation, as in the case of the populations employed in the plantations of the Brazilian northeast, who kill their children en masse in order to be able to survive, [73] or again in the case of Indian peasants affected by suicide epidemics. [74] But in zones of social exclusion such as slums, [75] the population seems instead to be left to itself, in such a way that the prevailing poverty cannot be explained by overexploitation or by the necessity of a reserve army for capital, even if a part of the populations concerned is also subject to overexploitation.

If it is solely the description of the failure to meet fundamental needs in extreme social situations such as slums that is at issue, we could ask ourselves what the vocabulary of suffering brings when the reality of lack of provision draws attention to an economic problem that the vocabulary of needs seems sufficient to designate. But can we content ourselves with describing the living conditions in these zones of intense destitution by means of an indeterminate reference to a failure to meet fundamental needs? It is clear, of course, that these living conditions are also characterized by violence and by phenomena of habituation to situations ordinarily judged 'inhuman' by all those who recount them; a violence and dehumanization which both also cause new forms of suffering. Certainly, we could also take the view that the categories of violence and of 'inhuman life' suffice to describe the other dimensions of the phenomenon. But the simple combination of references to needs, to violence and to dehumanization can take account neither of the ways in which these different elements are experienced as indissociable by the inhabitants of the slums, nor of the intertwining of social and psychological dynamics which structure the drama lived through by those who experience such living conditions.

It is clear that categories are lacking to describe these situations. Observers are tempted to make use of the Marxist category of the 'lumpenproletariat' or the Arendtian notion of 'loneliness',[76] but each turns out to be as unsatisfactory as the other. The idea of the lumpenproletariat places at the centre of the analysis the link between great poverty and criminal activity without explaining the link between misery and violence. As for 'loneliness', it reduces dehumanization to the loss of a common world without taking into account either the psychological dynamics of adaptation to the unbearable or its range of social effects. A problematization in terms of social suffering permits us to address these lacunae. The idea of a dynamic dimension of suffering, which can bring about either a destructive or—at the least—an incapacitating adaptation to the unbearable, or a violent reaction, has here a genuine heuristic power.[77]

From this suffering due to the long-term failure to meet fundamental needs, we have distinguished two other types of suffering: on the one hand, that which originates in the constraints exercised on bodies and minds, and, on the other hand, that which originates in the weakening of social resources that allow people to confront the difficulties of existence. The idea of social suffering therefore includes both the positive meaning of the social production of specific constraints and the negative meaning of the absence of social resources with which to confront them. All the signs are that these forms of suffering continue to characterize capitalist societies in general, to varying degrees and in differing ways. Constraints do not originate only in the way in which class domination is expressed in the work relationship, but also in the symbolic and instutional forms of class and race domination, as well as different types of epistemic violence produced by particular institutions. The processes of social disaffiliation can, for their part, reveal themselves in different ways (destructuring of traditional societies, destruction of affiliations with the town or neighbourhood, atomization of work collectives, reduced family solidarity, etc.).

Everything seems likewise to indicate that the combination of the mobilization of individuals by capital and of the precarization of their existence is taking on new forms. On the one hand, mobilization at work today seems to target minds as much as at bodies. On the other hand, flexibilization of work and individualization of social relations make the precarization of society appear as a qualitatively new problem.

The vocabulary of suffering seems particularly suited to giving an account of this double transformation. Because the new constraints of work have a specific bearing on subjectivity, the question of the mode of interiorization and of experience of these constraints becomes absolutely determinant, as witnessed to by the emergence of the arduousness of working conditions and the suicides that this causes as a matter of public concern. The vocabulary of suffering also allows us to take account of the unbearable aspect of the experience of precarity and exclusion in societies where fundamental needs are, however, met for the majority. Decisive factors in such a case are the weakening of intersubjective resources allowing people to confront ordinary forms of domination (class, gender and race) as well as the appearance of new forms of epistemic violence, leading to new forms of relation to oneself (the identity conflict caused by the paradoxical injunctions of neomanagement, the negative identity of the unemployed or the homeless for example).

If the 'social question of subjectivity',[78] as it is emerging today, has the features of the global slum, of new forms of subjective constraint at work and of processes of disaffiliation making ordinary domination more difficult to bear, then the problematic of social suffering can claim a triple political pertinence. It allows the description of central elements of these three phenomena. It is in this general context that current controversies concerning suffering ought to be examined. They clearly originate in one of those 'returns to the things themselves' in which social criticism, every now and again, turns away from the abstractions of political theory and towards the description of concrete forms of poverty, domination and social injustice.

NOTES

1. E. Balibar, *Citizenship* (Cambridge: Polity Press, 2015).

2. R. Castel, *From Manual Workers to Wage Laborers: Transformation of the Social Question* (London: Transaction Publishers, 2003).

3. We can furthermore find in Victor Hugo's *Les Misérables* an illustration of these different stages. On the one hand, there is the will to describe the raw reality of a suffering that we would prefer not to see: three times Jean Valjean tries to make his interlocuters understand the reality of the misery experienced in poverty, three times they react with incomprehension. On the other hand, there is a statement that celebrates the way in which individuals can ransom themselves from the depths of immiseration and whose implications doubtless do not go much further than fine sentiments.

4. On this point, see Arendt, *On Revolution*, chap. 2; 'On Humanity in Dark Times: Thoughts about Lessing', in *Men in Dark Times* (New York: Houghton Mifflin Harcourt, 1968), 3–31.

5. See, for example, L. Boltanski, *La souffrance à distance* (Paris: Métailié, 1993).

6. At least if we understand this concept in its historical sense, which goes back to the social and political conjuncture particular to the nineteenth century, and in a retrospective sense, as in Arendt, who understands by it a politicization of poverty which she sees as going back to the eighteenth cenury (*On Revolution*, chap. 2).

7. J.-F. Laé, *L'instance de la plainte. Une histoire politique et juridique de la souffrance* (Paris: Descartes and Cie, 1996), 13.

8. Ibid., 14: 'The appearance of a complaint is bound up with a politics which can remedy it, it even draws strength from this in order to invert itself into a political numbness'.

9. M. Halbwachs, *The Causes of Suicide* (London: Routledge and Kegan Paul, 1978), 273: 'illness, whatever it may be, makes the patient who is stricken with it conspicuous. Especially when they are suffering greatly, patients are somewhat misunderstood. That is why, in sanatoria and spas, they seek each other out and form small unique societies on the basis upon a mutual comprehension of their ills'.

10. Spk, *Turn Illness into a Weapon* (Frankfurt: PF/SPK, 1995), with a preface by J.-P. Sartre; see also 'The Communist Manifesto for the Third Millennium', http://www.spkpfh.de/GENOZIDengl.html.

11. See M. Weber, 'The Social Psychology of World Religions' [1916], in *From Max Weber: Essays in Sociology* (New York: Oxford University Press, 1946, 1970), 267–301.

12. Ibid., 275–76: 'The rational need for a theodicy of suffering and of dying death had extremely strong effects. As a matter of fact, this need has molded important traits of such religions as Hinduism, Zoroastrism, and Judaism and, to a certain extent, Paulinian and later Christianity. Even as late as 1906, when a large number of proletarians were asked the reasons for their lack of religious faith, a mere minority among a considerable number of proletarians have as reasons for their disbelief in Christianity conclusions derived from modern theories of natural sciences. The majority, however, referred to the "injustice" of the order of this world—to be sure, essentially because they believed in a revolutionary compensation in this world'.

13. As in Laé, *L'instance de la plainte*, fitting with the Deleuzian interpretatation of the same Bartleby (G. Deleuze, *Critique et clinique* [Paris: Minuit, 1993], chap. 10).

14. For a critique of the way in which dominant contemporary political philosophy reproduces this prejudice, see, for example, E. Dussel, *Beyond Philosophy: Ethics, History, Marxism and Liberation Theology* (Lanham: Rowman & Littlefield, 2003).

15. On the explosion of desperate poverty in the countries on the periphery, see notably M. Davis, *Planet of Slums* (London: Verso, 2006).

16. H. Pauléus-Sannon, *Essai historique sur la Révolution de 1843* (Cayes: Imprimerie de Bonnefil, 1905), ii.

17. Ibid., 128–29.

18. On all these points, see P. Moral, *Le paysan haïtie: étude sur la vie rurale en Haïti* (Paris: G. P. Maisonneuve and Larose, 1961), 27–45.

19. Ibid., 42.

20. Pauléus-Sannon, *Essai historique sur la Révolution de 1843*, 135.

21. See particularly the analysis of 'sorrow songs' in W. E. B. Du Bois, *The Souls of Black Folk* (Chicago: A. C. McClurg and Co., 1903), chap. 14.

22. These documents can be found preserved in T. Madiou, *Histoire d'Haïti* (Port-au-Prince: H. Deschamps, 1991), 131 et seq.

23. Pauléus-Sannon, *Essai historique sur la Révolution de 1843*, 128–29.

24. Whereas, for Arendt, making the people a political subject rests on a principle of pity for the suffering of the destitute, the reference to suffering serves here to criticize the fiction of the people. History is decidedly less simple than its grand speculative reconstructions.

25. Madiou, *Histoire d'Haïti*, 133. Sapattes are a type of leather sandal.

26. Ibid., 134.

27. The revolt of the Barefooted launched in Caen on the first of August 1639 was led by someone called Bras-Nus ('Bare Arms') claiming the rank of colonel in the suffering army; he ended broken on the wheel.

28. As suggested by Honneth, 'The Possibility of a Disclosing Critique of Society'.

29. On the productivity of suffering, see the interpretation of the 'Book of Job' by A. Negri, *Job. La force de l'esclave* (Paris: Bayard, 2002), totally opposed to that proposed by J.-F. Laé.

30. In a certain way, this idea can already be found in Freud, when he claims that the suffering of the melancholic originates 'from a mental constellation of revolt' (Freud, 'Mourning and Melancholia', in *The Standard Edition of the Complete Psychological Works of Sigmund Freud*, 14:248). This idea will be developed later by Adorno: see on this subject A. Honneth, 'Eine Physiognomie der kapitalistischen Lebensform. Skizz der Gessellschaftstheorie Adornos', in *Pathologien der Vernunft* (Frankfurt/Main: Suhrkamp, 2007), 70–92.

31. K. Marx, 'The Eighteenth Brumaire of Louis Bonaparte', in *Surveys from Exile* (London: Verso, 2010), 238–39.

32. We also find confirmation in the contemporary era that a self-description in terms of suffering can go hand in hand with an engagement in struggle. Is it not indeed one of the most distinguishing characteristics of Act Up to have, in one and the same movement, sought to bring AIDs out of invisibilization in showing the reality of the suffering of the persons infected and otherwise concerned and to have affirmed their 'rage' against all the measures of discrimination striking the minorities concerned in the first instance by the virus? Does not described suffering appear here as one of the elements of legitimation of struggle, as an explicit foundation for rage? It is also worth noting that far from neutralizing a political question through moralization and medicalization, the political use of a discourse of suffering allows struggle against the injustice that is the invisibilization of sickness, as well as against all attemps to neutralize the associated political problems by purely compassionate or medical responses.

33. See, for example, D. Demazière and M.-F. Pignoni, *Chômeurs: du silence à la révolte* (Paris: Hachette, 1998).

34. There are moreover forms of collective demand which are based explicitly on the sharing of a social experience described in terms of suffering. A wholly remarkable illustration of this is offered by the community of 'those affected by the terrorist attacks of the 1st of March' (*Asociacion 11-M afectados del Terorismo*) in Spain. This organization, which brings together victims of the 2004 train bombing in Madrid and families and friends of these victims, chooses to give itself the name of 'afectados' rather than that of 'victims' for various reasons. On the one hand, the term 'victim' illustrates a stance of demand oriented towards simple reparation (by the police and judicial system notably), whereas the group wished to pose broader political questions and participate in the debate on Spain's involvement in the second Iraq war. On the other hand, the issue of victimhood leads to enclosing the individuals concerned in the two public icons of silent sorrow and the sorrow of the spectacle, whereas the organization wished on the contrary to fight against the making of the attacks into a media spectacle while at the same time refusing their political instrumentalization and refusing all others the right to speak in the name of their sorrow. Finally, the logic of victimhood leads to a view in which only victims and their close family can be seen as legitimate complainants, whereas these collective events such as terrorist attacks affect a much bigger group of individuals and social relationships. By presenting suffering as a condition, the *Afectados* emphasize the legitimative/critical

power of lived suffering and the mobilizing force of its description and they situate the political dimension of suffering in the distortions of the relationship to the world that it causes: it is indeed the fact itself of being affected, of having suffered something which transforms our relationship to others and to the outside world, and not only of a more or less irremediable loss, which is presented by the members of this collective as the purview of their political commitment. By inventing this new political language and by thus limiting the pertinence of the schema of the victim, the collective would attract the virulent hostility of the organization of ETA victims, a powerful supporter of the conservative *Partido Popular*.

35. A. De Tocqueville, *Memoir on Pauperism* (New York: Ivan R. Dee, 1997).

36. See Marx's article, 'Critical Notes on the Article: "The King of Prussia and Social Reform. By a Prussian"', in *Early Writings* (London: Penguin, 1973), 401–19. On the meaning of this critique, see E. Renault, *Marx et la philosophie* (Paris: PUF, 2014), chap. 3.

37. For an introduction to the social and political context of the first workers' publications in the early 1830s, see A. Dewerpe, *Le monde du travail en France, 1800–1950* (Paris: A. Colin, 1998), 53–59.

38. Now available in a digital version at http://echo-fabrique.ens-lsh.fr/.

39. For an overall introduction to *L'Écho de la fabrique*, see L. Frobert, ed., *L'Écho de la Fabrique. Naissance de la presse ouvrière à Lyon, 1831–1834* (Lyon: Ens éditions, 2010). On its political context, see F. Rude, *Les révoltes des canuts (1831–1834)*, new edition (Paris: La Découverte, 2007).

40. E. P. Thompson, *The Making of the English Working Class* (Harmondsworth: Penguin, 1984).

41. On the emergence of workers' discourse in this period, see J. Rancière and A. Faure, ed., *La parole ouvrière* (Paris: UGE, 1976).

42. The Lyon system is a system of 'collective manufacture'; see on this subject Alain Cottereau, 'The Fate of Collective Manufactures in the Industrial World: The Silk Industries of Lyon and London 1800–1850', in *World of Possibilities: Flexibility and Mass Production in Western Industrialisation*, ed. C. F. Sabel and J. Zeitlin (Cambridge: Cambridge University Press, 1997), 75–152.

43. On the way in which the topic of workers' discourse is treated in *L'Écho*, see notably the texts on the charivaris of April 1, 1832, and April 15, 1832.

44. For a description of these three periods, see Frobert, *L'Économie de la Fabrique*.

45. See the tables in 'Misères prolétaires': 'We will continue thus to assemble the most salient features of the history of the proletariat, which our previous articles scarcely began to sketch. May our readers not be repelled if we are obliged to draw their gaze to all the places where the heart of a sensitive man must feel a natural distaste. It is on the benches of the courts of assizes, of the correctional police, in hospitals, and everywhere that humanity suffers that a page of this history is sketched out. As faithful historians, we must write this history in tears; for the life of the proletarian can be summed up in these three words: *Birth, suffering and death*. Misery presides over his birth, and as his inseparable companion, does not abandon him until his death, save for certain very rare exceptions' (no. 7).

46. I have developed these arguments and those that follow in E. Renault, 'Mépris et souffrance dans l'Écho de la Fabrique', in *L'Écho de la Fabrique*, ed. Frobert, 87–110.

47. For a description of the humiliations linked to the cage, see the denunciation of the 'abuse of payment on a fixed date' by Falconnet: 'Finally there comes the day for which all have sighed: all arrive early at the blessed *cage*, from where, after having languished for two or three hours, thirty men pressed against one another, stifled with heat and boredom, see the approach of the teller who, measuring with a self-important eye the number of those making a demand, says, muttering between his teeth, the *menagerie* is certainly full, and then replies to

the request of each one: I do apologise, but I can only give you half of what you are owed' (no. 22).

48. The utopian texts that he named 'Rêveries' bear witness to this: 'If I were a merchant, I would hav no *cage*, where the humiliated worker is shut up like an *Ourang-Outang*, and only sees his master through the bars. I would not want to leave him standing for hours at a stretch; there would be a cushioned bench around my house' (no. 12); 'If I were a merchant, I would want to leave my house only during the hours of rest; and there, receiving my workers myself, I would prove to them that I believe in equality, and that it is not a little gold or a suit of Sedan cloth that separates one member of the human race from another. If I were a merchant, I would not wait for cholera before I removed the *cage* from my shop, and my workers would wait their turn in a spacious, clean and airy apartment; I would not want them to be pressed one against another like sardines; these poor devils deserve to be better treated, whatever certain financiers of modern origin may say. . . . If I were a merchant, I would not want my workers to display their poverty when they came to claim what was due to them. I would make them go one by one to the teller, and I would want the teller to treat the worker who had the misfortune to ask for only ten francs as well as he who asked for two hundred' (no. 26).

49. On the specificity of the production of law in the Labour Courts, see A. Cottereau, 'Droit et bon droit. Un droit des ouvriers instauré puis invincé par le droit du travail', *Annales. Histoire, Sciences Sociales*, no. 6 (2002): 1521–57. On the defence of the system of regulation by *L'Echo de la Fabrique*, see L. Frobert, *Les Canuts ou la démocratie turbulente. Lyon, 1831–1834* (Paris: Tallandier, 2009), 56–66.

50. M. Chastaing, 'Économie sociale. De l'émeute des chiffonniers' (no. 25).

51. On the presence of republicanism and its critique in *L'Écho*, see Frobert, *L'Économie de la fabrique*. On the presence of Fourierism, see J. Beecher, 'Le Fouriérisme des canuts', in *L'Écho de la fabrique*, ed. Frobert, 111–40.

52. F. Engels, *The Condition of the Working Class in England* [1845] (London: Penguin, 2009), 32.

53. Ibid., 28.

54. Ibid., 27.

55. K. Marx, 'A Contribution to the Critique of Hegel's Philosophy of Right : Introduction', in *Early Writings*, 246–47.

56. K. Marx, *Letter to Ruge*, May 1843, in *The Letters of Karl Marx* (Englewood Cliffs, NJ: Prentice-Hall, 1979), 29.

57. Marx, 'A Contribution to the Critique of Hegel's Philosophy of Right: Introduction', 256.

58. Ibid.

59. On this point as on the role granted to suffering and acting bodies in *Capital*, see E. Renault and S. Haber, 'Une analyse marxiste des corps?', *Actuel Marx*, no. 41 (2007).

60. K. Marx, *Workers' Questionnaire*, Collected Works, Vol. 24 (London: Lawrence & Wishart, 2010), 334. Which is the general physical, intellectual and moral condition of working-men and working-women in your branch of trade?

61. L. Ferreira, 'À propos de l'Enquête ouvrière de Karl Marx (1880)', *Travailler*, no. 12 (2004): 15–20.

62. Marx, *A Workers' Inquiry*, 22.

63. For an overview of workers' enquiries in France as a whole, see M. Perrot, *Enquêtes sur la condition ouvrière en France au 19e siècle* (Paris: Hachette, 1972).

64. This is doubtless because Marxism, in the first stage of its development, in the work of Kautsky, Labriola and Plekhanov, set itself the principal task of producing syntheses of its specific orientations which it was led to neglect by the issue of social suffering. But if this issue

appears today so far from the heart of Marxism, it is doubtless even more because of later political and social developments which reduced it from a reflection on the causes and failures of the workers' movement to the elaboration of a discourse of method formulated principally by philosophers in universities (on this subject, see P. Anderson, *Considerations on Western Marxism* [London: New Left Books, 1976]). Marxism thus continued its development towards doctrinaire socialism and '*Kathedersozialismus*', two theoretical orientations that were the target of Marx and Engels's constant hostility. Nevertheless, social experience was not entirely forgotten in the development of Western Marxism because it plays a decisive role in Gramsci, Mao and *Socialisme et Barbarie*, for instance; see E. Renault, 'Marxism, Politics and Social Experience', in *Karl Marx: Perspektiven der Gesellschaftskritik*, ed. R. Jaeggi and D. Loick (Berlin: Akademie Verlag, 2013), 285–95.

65. Tocqueville, *Memoir on Pauperism*, 7–9.

66. Engels, *The Condition of the Working Class in England*, 61–62, 107–17.

67. K. Marx, *Capital*, vol. 1 (London: Penguin, 1990), chap. 25, sec. 1–2.

68. Engels, *The Condition of the Working Class in England*, 102–7.

69. Marx, *Capital*, chap. 25, sec. 2.

70. Beginning in the 1820s, the term 'pauperism' designated a state of destitution that had become chronic; its first attested usage in France dates from 1823; on this question, see Perrot, *Les enquêtes ouvrières*, 10–11.

71. Suffering which could only be compared to the suffering specific to enslaved labour, incomparably more serious.

72. Castel, *From Manual Workers to Wage Laborers*.

73. Nancy Sheper-Hughes ('Small Wars and Invisible Genocides') describes the way in which poor peasants in the northeast of Brazil make widespread use of techniques for the elimination of their infant children (the child mortality rate reaching 38 percent) in order to resist the state of malnutrition in which they are kept.

74. S. Sengupta, 'On India's Desparing Farms, a Plague of Suicide', *New York Times*, September 19, 2006.

75. With regard to the explosion of slums brought about by neoliberalism (a billion urban dwellers now live in them), there has been talk of a 'return to Dickens', with the further point that the explosion of slums has given an unprecedented significance to mass poverty: 'No one knows whether such gigantic concentrations of poverty are biologically or ecologically sustainable' (Davis, *Planet of Slums*, 5).

76. André Corten, *Diabolisation et mal politique. Haïti: misère, religion et politique* (Paris: Karthala, 2000).

77. We should note that the notion of 'malestar social', which is frequently used to describe slums (without seeming to designate more than a convenient label), and the perspective of 'social suffering' aim to describe this cycle of adaptation to destitution and violence, when they are used in the publications of the United Nations (*UN Habitat*); see http://www.unhabitat.org.

78. See Ch. Laval, *Des psychologues sur le front de l'insertion: souci clinique et question sociale* (Ramonville-Saint-Agne: Érès, 2009).

Chapter Three

Outlines of a Conceptualization

If history and sociology are dramatic sciences, they only study the broad frameworks of the environment in which the major dramatic events of each generation unfold, and the major themes whose variations are shown by these events. But dramatic events always have a quality in the here and now that neither history nor sociology can explain. . . . Similarly, political economy teaches us the economic conditions of crime, why in a bourgeois society there must necessarily be crime, but not why such and such an individual committed such and such a crime. There is a place for a discipline which studies dramatic events in their specific actuality and particularity.
—G. Politzer, *Les fondements de la psychologie*, 83

It took me a long time to grasp that refusal of the existential was a trap, that sociology constructed itself against the singular and the personal, the existential, and that this is one of the major causes of sociologists' inability to understand social suffering.
—P. Bourdieu, RMI talk, 1992; quoted by V. de Gaulejac, *Cahiers internationaux de sociologie*, 355

References to suffering currently pervade so many discourses that it has been said that the 'the topic of suffering saturates the social scene today'.[1] With its general social validity, the topic of suffering has in a certain sense established itself as a paradigm: initially the language of suffering prevailed as one of the legitimate forms of expression for painful emotions and the difficulties of experience; subsequently, the term 'suffering' has, it seems, become more than ever one of the keys to the reading of social inequalities, difficulties and forms of domination.

Important in everday discourse, the lexicon of suffering has in addition been given institutional validation in the field of the politics of health (the concept of suffering is in this instance defined by the terminological couplet 'psychological suffering/mental health') and in the field of social work (where instead use is made of the conceptual contrast 'suffering/empowerment dispositives'). As much in its shared uses as in its institutional uses, the term 'suffering' designates not only psychological difficulties, but also claims to describe their social contexts and consequences.

The emergence of this paradigm has been accompanied by a complex debate on the theoretical and political value of the theme of social suffering. A possible option is to suggest a global interpretation of the emergence of the paradigm. Drawing inspiration from Michel Foucault and from the comparative and genealogical methodology of a 'political anthropology of health', one has thus been able to identify the problematic of social suffering with a new episteme that is interdependent with a new face of biopower. This allows us to denounce at the same time a) shared discourse on suffering, b) institutional discourse and c) theorizations with a bearing on social suffering.[2] But although it seems a fertile approach to interpret the question of social suffering as a political topic sustained by social and cultural constructions, it is not certain that the generalizing methods of genealogy and of comparison are the methodological instruments best suited to producing a description of the meanings and concerns which today characterize the debates on social suffering.

As against the constructivist approaches which believe they can find an adequate explanation in a mode of producing and of justifying legitimate pronouncements, but also against the functionalist approaches which believe they can explain the genesis of a social norm through the function it fulfils in a determinate institutional context, it may be useful to recall the following two Weberian principles. A discourse can only acquire social validity if it satisfies psychological and social interests and, in a context of social confrontation, a new norm cannot acquire general validity unless certain groups manage to impose it on the rest of society.[3] It may also be useful to recall that once granted general social validity, a discourse still does not satisfy all social interests in the same way. If it becomes necessary to use it to give a legitimate expression to individual or collective expectations, to social difficulties or subjective harm, these are still not necessarily expressed adequately in this form, so that certain social groups may undertake to confer new uses on the discourse by modifying its meaning.[4]

Nothing entitles us, a priori, to attribute an undifferentiated meaning to references to suffering in everyday discourse. Furthermore, nothing justifies attributing the same meaning to their reformulation in institutional discourse and theoretical discourse. We have used the expression 'paradigm of suffering' to designate the general validity which the vision of society in terms of suffering seems to possess. But the term 'paradigm' itself (just as the Foucauldian notion of episteme and any approach in terms of an historical a priori) is always at risk of conveying a dual illusion. With such an illusion, agreement around the relevance of a valid schema at a given time period is accompanied by an agreement about its meaning and its legitimate uses, an illusion that the nature of this schema is not substantially modified by its investment in discursive practices as different as everyday discourse, institutional discourse and theoretical discourse. If it does not wish to be the victim of such illusions, the study of the genesis and the value of the problematic of social suffering must make an effort to isolate the different spaces of social validity of the discourse of suffering, while at the same time determining its concerns and its meanings, which are specific each time. The origins of the paradigm of social suffering are so complex that they would need an entire work of research combining the methods of the history of ideas, of the sociology of public problems, of the sociology of knowledge and of historical epistemology.[5] Whatever may be the results of such research, the question of the theoretical consistency of the problematic of social suffering remains open.

Is it possible to produce a concept that is sufficiently determinate for the reference to social suffering to go beyond appeals to the public and the discursive struggle against the invisibilization of the effects of domination, exclusion and poverty? Is it possible to produce a theory of the social conditions of suffering rigorous enough for the idea of social suffering to go further than a principled criticism of liberal affirmation according to which the origin of suffering is always, in the last analysis, individual? Is it possible to develop a theoretical model of social suffering that gives the idea of suffering a determinate role to play, while being based on a social theory and a credible psychology?

If these questions are rarely taken seriously, it is chiefly because the ideas of 'social suffering' and of 'social pathology' are not recognized as major notions in the history of the human sciences. They did, however, play a decisive role in the emergence of the human sciences. Their importance is negative, to begin with, because, on the one hand, the first social science, political economy, defended the autonomy of its subject by maintaining that there is no social origin of suffering and, on the other hand, the study by social medicine and social economy of the social conditions of destitution played a fundamental role both in the emergence of the methods of sociology[6] and in the affirmation of a social reality irreducible to economics.[7]

The importance is also positive insofar as it is impossible to retrace the history of the heroic episodes in the human sciences, those of their founding struggles, without concluding with a general reevaluation of the themes of social suffering and social pathologies. Indeed, to defend their autonomy and mark their hegemony over the social sciences, Durkheimian and Freudian theory were led to propose definitions and concepts of social suffering alternative to those of political economy and social medicine. It is not possible to analyse here the importance and the originality of the conception of social suffering involved in the concept of 'social pathology' proper to the work of Durkheim, or those of the notion of 'suffering of social origin' associated, in the work of Freud, with the problematic of the 'discontents of civilisation'.[8]

As we cannot restore all the richness and the complexity of a story which deserves to be unearthed in a detailed fashion, we will content ourselves with recalling that classical political economy rejected the idea of social causes of suffering and has by doing so fixed the theoretical framework of the first debates related to suffering as social pathology (1). We will then explain how social medicine, on the one hand, expanded to fill the spaces left empty by this social science and, on the other hand, challenged it by proposing alternative definitions and conceptions of social pathology and suffering. We will explain the limits of this approach in order to define by contrast the challenges that a pertinent theoretical conception of suffering must confront (2). We will then draw inspiration from different psychological and sociological theories so as to propose an approach to resolving the various aporia implied by the idea of social suffering[9] (3). Finally, we will undertake to measure the relevance of our model for conceptualizing social suffering by applying it to two theoretical wholes which develop the analysis of the suffering induced by social relationships: the 'clinical study of work' and the 'psychodynamics of work' on the one hand (4), and the clinical approaches to suffering linked to serious precarity on the other hand (5). In the one case as in the other, we will deal with a clash of paradigms and explanatory models more than with a unified theoretical field. The pertinence of our conception of social suffering will thus depend on its capacity to take account of these theoretical conflicts and their stakes. Insofar as the debate related to suffering at work and to

psychic suffering linked to exclusion is developed within different conceptual frameworks, we will propose a sort of theoretical translation intended to
make apparent the shared difficulties and concerns—even similarities—
masked by the differences of lexicon and subject matter.

NATURALIZATION, IMPUTATION OF RESPONSIBILITY AND EUPHEMIZATION

Unevenly distributed in society, social suffering seems to concern chiefly the
poorest layers of the population. Because suffering is desired by no one, the
simple fact of observing the suffering of those poorer than oneself cannot fail
to appear as a challenge to the social order from which the observers benefit,
as a questioning of the legitimacy of the life they lead. From this comes the
ideological and psychological issues with which the description and the theorization of different forms of suffering are surrounded.

   Suffering that is not pathological (not associated with an illness that appears in diagnostic manuals) already indicates to those who observe it that
individuals are not satisfied with the situation that they are experiencing and
that furthermore they are of the same humanity as the observers, a humanity
that is not content to suffer. As for pathological suffering, because illness is
among other things a social handicap, it brings with it a requirement for
differentiated treatment and a special form of attention on the part of the
other and, more generally, of the collectivity. Here again, suffering is a
demand, interpellation and questioning of those who benefit from inequality;
it subjects them to a demand to respond to the problem and to justify themselves.

   It is not surprising, then, that responses to the spectacle of suffering often
take the form of justification by legitimation or by invisibilization.[10] Because
socially dominant groups in a society generally have the capacity to make
their conception of the world appear as modes of general representation of
the social, it is not surprising that the forms of suffering linked to poverty
have been the target of powerful discourses of justification and that they have
been subject to different forms of invisibilization, either in the form of denial
of suffering in general and of its social origin in particular or in the form of
various euphemisms.

   Certainly, not all historical eras treated the poor in the same way. In the
eighteenth century, for example, at the point when processions of the impoverished were making their way across France and filling the hospitals,[11] the

response to poverty was arrest and detention. Denial includes the erasure of those who, no longer belonging to the social order, are carefully shut out of its spaces. At one stroke, poverty is subjected to moral condemnation and to denial born of its social dimension. A striking example of such moral condemnation taking the form of a denunciation of the morals of the impoverished is given by Lieutenant Guyot, in charge of repressing the mutinies in the Hôpital de Bicêtre. His letter reporting on the interview with a prisoner in 1769 contains these lines: 'I believed I would find some oppressed innocent, I looked for him and did not find him. My heart, which had softened at their fate, upon seeing them close up hardened, so to speak, by degrees, and despite myself, they appeared to me to be all more or less guilty. There are even, and I can say it without inhumanity, some who are not punished in proportion to their crime and whose existence in this frightful seclusion, however hard, even cruel, is a special grace'. Arlette Farge accompanies this text with the following commentary: 'What a marvellous text, not for judging by our own measure but for understanding that extraordinary interlacing, remorseless entanglement of commiseration, contempt, desire, longing for punishment'.[12] Ideological legitimation and psychological defence come together here in a euphemization of suffering and an imputation of responsibility which count among the constant traits of the modern discourse on poverty.

From the French Revolution onwards, the objective was no longer to erase poverty, but to reabsorb it. It was in this context that classical political economy launched the debate on the relationship between poverty and work.[13] Considered as an economic agent, the poor person is defined in the framework of a dual problematic: that of his or her type of economic activity (relationship to work and consumption) and that of the voluntary or involuntary nature of his or her poverty.

Most of the economists of the end of the eighteenth and the beginning of the nineteenth century distinguished between two major categories of the poor, according to whether individuals were capable of work or were prevented from working by age or infirmity. Malthus, for example, maintains that the second category of the poor can benefit from charity, while the first is only entitled to it in a very limited fashion because individual responsibility has a determining role in their case: 'We may perhaps take upon ourselves, with great caution, to mitigate the punishments which they are suffering from the laws of nature, but on no account to remove them entirely. They are deservedly at the bottom in the scale of society; and if we raise them from

this situation, we not only palpably defeat the end of benevolence, but com-
mit a most glaring injustice to those who are above them'.[14]

This type of discourse is still current, and if it certainly has a strange
sound today, this is because it connects two very different interpretations of
the worker: that of being mere labour power (an objectifying neutralization
of the problems experienced by the reduction of the impoverished to a quantity of physical strength[15]) and the opposing one, of having free will, which
makes individuals bear the full responsibility of the social situations they
must navigate (individuals who, consequently, deserve what they endure).
This second aspect expresses itself in the work of Malthus in the form of a
theory of the laziness and imprudence of the poor. Because poor people are
by nature loafers and reluctant to work, the suffering they experience is
ultimately the only way to make them work, in such a way as to constitute a
spur for the whole of society: 'Such a stimulus seems to be absolutely necessary to promote the happiness of the great mass of mankind'.[16] But the
irrationality of the poor is not only illustrated in their relation to work, as
emphasized by numerous economists who denounce irrational forms of consumption and sexual practices. Malthus thus mocks the irresponsible behaviour of the poor in the demographic sphere,[17] one sign among others of a
moral depravity which, in the eyes of the classic writers, bears a heavy
weight of responsibility for poverty.

Malthus offers an illustration of the different forms of euphemization of
suffering. Far from being a scandal, it fulfils a positive 'stimulus' function
for the whole of society, and ultimately is only a well-merited punishment, a
chastisement that the natural law reserves for the immoral behaviour of individuals. Malthus illustrates as well the two principal procedures with which
the human sciences can contest the social dimension of suffering: naturalization of suffering, tracing it back to individual nature (infirmity or youth,
natural inequalities with regard to the physical and intellectual capacities
required for work) or to the natural necessities which are built into in economic laws (temporary effects due to the introduction of machines, for example), and moralization of suffering, explaining it by the immoderated self-
will of the poor, even by their ill will (their choice of social assistance to the
detriment of work).

Certainly, we are dealing here with judgements that the human sciences
rarely take up as such on their own account, but Malthusian cynicism poses a
more general problem. Given that inequality with regard to suffering in society is a political question and that the human sciences hand down decrees on

subjects whose causes could be social, natural or purely individual, they are in fact led to defend political positions when they meet the question of suffering. Classical political economy offers the example of a consciously assumed defence of the liberal exclusion of suffering from the domain of questions that may raise a call for social change. Is it superfluous to recall that, in a discursive context marked by liberal ideology (under the sign today of neoliberalism), it is impossible to contest this kind of theoretical-political positioning as long as we exclude suffering as not belonging to the subject matter of the social sciences, as long as we reduce the experience of social suffering to a social construction?

The exclusion of the theme of social suffering by classical political economy immediately called forth oppositional discourses seeking to take responsibility theoretically for this aspect of social reality. Eugène Buret in particular sought to confront this discipline with the problem posed by the existence of a 'suffering and degraded population'.[18] To the definition of political economy as an abstract science of wealth, Buret opposes the requirements of a study of the totality of the social organism (or 'physiology of society'[19]) which comprises wealth as much as destitution and which understands the latter not only as an extreme degree of poverty, but also as 'morally felt poverty'.[20] Starting from the principle that products must be made for man and not man for products,[21] that work is not a merchandise like others but the very existence of the workers, it proposes enlarging the field of political economy by integrating into it the study of destitution and its consequences for 'life, health, morality':[22] 'When one considers scientifically capital and what is produced, one has only carried out half of the economic task: it remains to study the influence of production and distribution on the physical and moral condition of that great number that makes up the nations'.[23]

But there are plenty of different ways to deal theoretically with what political economy passes over in silence. For Buret, it is clear that the explanations that economists give of poverty are unsophisticated: they simply contend that 'poverty is explained by poverty'.[24] Certainly, the principles of modern society are good, but the manner in which political economy tries to put them into practice is not the right one. Poverty is the expression of a transitory disorder which cannot be overcome except by policies founded on a taking into account of the moral ends of social life.[25] Starting from the same premises, the social economy of the time would generally end up with more moderate conclusions.[26]

In the work of Villermé, for example, one of the main representatives of the French hygienist school of thought, the study of poverty settles in the spaces left unexplored by political economy without in any way raising questions about the latter. His *Tableau de l'état physique et moral des ouvriers* (1840) accumulates data related to the health and the living conditions of the working class. And though he sometimes gives striking descriptions of the deleterious effects of industrialization,[27] the work concludes by criticizing 'those who not only deny . . . the improvement [of the workers' conditions], but moreover represent to us industry and commerce, those two great springs of freedom, of well-being, of civilisation, as causes of poverty, brutalisation and all sorts of ills'.[28]

Starting from the correct principle that 'it is in an indirect, mediated fashion, or through the situation regarding nutrition, clothing, housing, fatigue, length of work, morals, etc. in which workers found themselves that occupations most often impact, for good or for ill, on their health or that of their families',[29] Villermé locates the determining conditions in factors exterior to the strictly economic organization of society. Ultimately, destitution and its harmful effects on health can be explained by the overcrowding of individuals in insanitary neighbourhoods and by the breakdown of morals. Responses to the social question thus suppose interventions in the extra-economic domains of urbanism (promotion of individual dwellings rather than the projects for large workers' housing complexes),[30] the promotion of responsibility (hence the defence of the system of bonuses)[31] and of solidarity (benevolent fund and provident fund).[32] We could say schematically that once suffering is understood as 'physical and moral poverty', it is always possible to emphasize the moral side of its causality to the detriment of its economic aspect. Villermé proceeds to do this.

In combination with the overvalution of moral causality, Villermé maintains that one aspect of destitution, its strictly economic component, is inevitable. This is an effort at neutralization of the explosive force of the social question, to which the conclusion of *Sur les cités ouvrières* is a transparent testimony: 'We must recall in closing: that everywhere where the population of workers amounts to a large number, it will never be possible to supply suitable housing to all those who make up that number. That the workers who earn the smallest salaries will always be reduced to staying in the cheapest housing, that is to say in uncomfortable, insufficient and unhygienic lodgings in dilapidated and poorly maintained houses: "Such is the fate of the poor in all countries; the force of circumstances, the harsh law of necessity wish it so"'.[33] The defence of the principles of political economy leads anew to naturalizing suffering, but only a part of it.

We see to what kind of conception of social pathologies classical political economy has led social economy. In the same way as the first is compatible with a model of social pathology which would take into account the suffering caused by social deregulations which have to do with failure to obey economic laws (see the explanation of crises by the institutional obstacles to the proper functioning of the market), the second elaborates a model of social pathology entirely founded on the distinction between a necessary and an accidental empoverishment.

It is certainly to such a definition of social pathology that Cherbuliez is referring in his *Études sur les causes de la misère, tant morale que physique, et sur les moyens d'y porter remède* (1853) when he prescribes the following treatment: 'Pushing back physical poverty to within its normal limits . . . when we have done this, we will have defeated pauperism; there will only remain the poor, that is to say a certain sum of accidental poverty'.[34] Social economy thus tends to promote a conception of social suffering in which suffering is described as 'physical and moral poverty' or else is explained by an accidental lack of social provision (worsening of housing conditions, demoralization, loss of social bonds) more than by social structures themselves. In the model of social pathology that it proposes, only suffering not required by economic laws is identified as abnormal.[35]

There are other ways of justifying a privileged social position when confronted with suffering and, to this end, medicine can substitute for political economy. The theories built on the opposition of good and bad fatigue supply an illustration of this. Since the eighteenth century, the history of discourses on fatigue, as much as that of the discussions concerning destitution, is deeply impregnated with bourgeois ideology. Over the course of the eighteenth century, a first problematic of bad fatigue was put in place. In 1733, Georges Cheyne published *The English Malady*, which explains that the way of life of the elites caused fatigue, obesity and a high suicide rate. During the same period, the article 'Work' from Diderot and Alembert's *Encyclopédie* maintained that 'man regards work as a trouble, and thus as the enemy of his rest, it is on the contrary the source of all his pleasures and the surest remedy for boredom'.

In the synthesis that he proposes of theories of 'bad fatigue' and that we follow here, Marc Loriol emphasizes that 'the bourgeois discourse on bad fatigue is a means of differentiating themselves first of all from the lazy and libertine aristocracy, then, from the nineteenth century onwards, from the working man with his supposedly depraved morals (alcoholism, unrestrained sexuality)'.[36] If it is possible to distinguish here between a good and a bad fatigue, this is because work is considered a source of health, and only morally condemnable forms of activity (those of the undeserving poor and the debauched rich) or inactivity (laziness of the nobility) would cause a pathological fatigue. In this line of argument, pathology is as it were a punishment of what is contrary to bourgeois morality.

But at the end of the nineteenth century, this use of the concept of 'bad fatigue' by the bourgeoisie as an instrument for denuncing the defects assumed to characterize other social groups was supplanted by another problematic. The idea of 'bad fatigue' was at that point used to give an account of the specific psychological difficulties of the new subclasses of the bourgeoisie. In *A Practical Treatise on Nervous Exhaustion* (1880), New York doctor Beard describes a pathology which he called neurasthenia, to account for a weakness of the nerves caused by the urban and industrial way of life of the American elites. Subsequently imported to Europe, the category of neurasthenia serves to designate a fatigue linked to the intellectual activities of the elites which, as such, must be taken seriously and given appropriate treatment. The idea of pathological fatigue no longer served to denounce, but on the contrary to justify a social group by demonstrating the psychological cost of its apparently privileged social position.

By comparison, the poor man is in fact to be envied because he lives from manual work which, causing a good fatigue, cannot produce pathological effects, but only natural effects of wear and tear linked to time. Thus doctor Proust (the father of the writer) claims that if there are few workers who present in his practice with neurasthenia, it is because 'working men do not use their brains'.[37] In France, it was only after health insurance was put into place for employees of industry and commerce (1928–1930) that it would become plain that the poor could also suffer from neurasthenia. Neurasthenia, then, lost its social prestige and was denounced more and more as a phantasm without medical reality: 'When working men can more widely access medicine, neurasthenia is no longer an illness, but laziness'.[38]

At the beginning of the twentieth century, the idea that intellectual work is more tiring than physical work was also developed in another form, that of the study of the psychophysiology of work. Following the work of Italian physiologist Angelo Mosso, *La fatigue intellectuelle et physique* (1895), a series of writings were produced aimed at augmenting work productivity while at the same time reducing the suffering caused by work.[39] The goal was to promote scientific management of the workforce by redefining tasks in line with the physiological capacities of the commodified labour force by proceeding to a process of selection for occupations that distributed work suited to the physiological capacities of manual workers and employees.

Here again, the different attempts to measure fatigue led to the idea that the expenditure of 'nervous energy' was absolutely determinant in all causes of fatigue, so that the pathologies of intellectual workers' fatigue were judged more serious than those of manual workers. There only remained one more threshold to cross to reach the idea that because the work of managing a business called for a higher energy expenditure, it should be better remunerated than manual work; a threshold crossed for example in the work of economist André Liesse, *Le travail au point de vue scientifique, industriel et social* (1899).

With the problematic of fatigue, we are no longer dealing so much with a denial of the social dimension of suffering (by naturalization or moralization) as a form of euphemization. To transcribe suffering as fatigue is not without consequences: fatigue comes neither under the heading of what is ethically or psychologically unbearable nor under the heading of what is pathological. Furthermore, because it belongs to organic functioning, it can be the subject of a functional approach and encourage the project of controlling it according to scientifically determined measures, at the same time as it seems to have only a fairly weak relation to the social environment. To say that a situation is unbearable is to pronounce a qualitative judgement with a strong contextual dimension and it is this type of judgement that always brings with it the idea of suffering when it is associated with the experience of domination and poverty. The quantitative problematic of fatigue allows one to respond to this type of critical reference to suffering by transposing it into a quantitative and decontextualized space, by transforming a judgement on an unbearable environment into a problem either of excessive demands on faculties or of a momentary mismatch between capacity and task. It is this logic that we still encounter today with the distinction between good and bad stress, with the problematic of the personal management of one's own fatigue, of the comparative strenuousness of careers, etc., problematics which neutralize the question of suffering at work.

In these discussions on fatigue there appears another important point for the current debate on social suffering: the denial of the psychological life of the poor. The elites demand the right to express their psychological problems, and medicine develops categories that satisfy this demand. This process is, so to speak, a constant of the nosographic categories developed with regard to fatigue, and this well before the emergence of capitalism, as M. Loriol shows, going back to the *acedia* of the monks of the Middle Ages and the melancholy of the court nobility: 'Most of the tags given to pathological fatigue—*acedia*, melancholy, neurasthenia, chronic fatigue syndrome—have always been associated, at least in the beginning, with privileged social categories'.[40] Subaltern social categories do not have the chance to cut medical nosography to the measure of their subjective difficulties, first of all, doubtless because the recognition of the problems linked to social subalternity is a more direct challenge to the social order; second, because they generally do not have the social and cultural resources to impose forms of public representation of their social experiences; and finally, because as a client base they are less profitable for doctors (and today for the pharmaceutical industry) and more culturally distant from the medical professions: 'Still today, is work-related stress not perceived as the special characteristic of management, despite the epidemiological and occupational health studies demonstrating precisely the opposite?'[41]

Categories like 'neurasthenia' do develop a definition of suffering by conceiving of it as fatigue and they do propose a social aetiology (the way of life of the elite). But when it comes to the fatigue of the poor, suffering is pushed back either onto natural wear and tear of the body or onto a technically deficient organization that calls for ergonomic remedies and better job selection (that is to say a matching of life history to function which also calls for technical responses): denial of the social dimension of a suffering which is supposedly explicable in terms of natural constraints, of technical mechanisms or of specific details of life history.

Neither political economy nor medicine are in question here as such. At most, we may suspect that the definition of their disciplinary boundaries involves a structural incapacity to deal adequately with the question of social suffering. These disciplines have contributed to the consolidation of a discourse on the social context in which the suffering of the dominated and deprived has no place. It was thus necessary to reserve a specific treatment for them, even though these two disciplines are not the only ones to serve as vehicles for this discourse. Anthropology, for example, has developed a theory of the culture of poverty which emphasizes the intergenerational dimension of problems and the transmission of violent and self-destructive values and behaviours.[42] It is clear that this type of discourse can claim a basis in truth, inasmuch as psychological disturbances, including those with a strong social dimension, cannot remain without effect on relationships between the generations; very often, it is even necessary to wait for the test of the passage of a generation before one can tell if the 'resilience' was illusory. The problem is not taking into account the intergenerational dimension of the question but the reification and overvaluation of this type of causality under the name of the 'culture of poverty'. In a unilateral way, we thus trace back social effects to a distant origin without relation to the current context, an origin on which collective actions can no longer get any grip. This culturalist short circuit also risks giving rise to forms of naturalization through imputation of responsibility (they are responsible for belonging to a culture which leads them to do what they do) and of euphemization through cultural relativization (they simply live in a culture which is different from ours).[43]

THE EMERGENCE OF SOCIAL MEDICINE

Because the question of mental health forms one of the centres of gravity of the current controversy over social suffering and social criticism cannot confer a decisive role on suffering unless it develops a medical model of social suffering, the link during the first half of the nineteenth century between social medicine and the social question deserves an attentive examination. Should we see in social medicine a discourse suitable for criticizing new social realities or, on the contrary, an instrument intended to institutionalize the new social order, as Foucault suggests?

Related to the historical context of its emergence, social medicine seems endowed with an undeniable subversive impact. From the beginning of the century, under the pressure of an industrialization as rapid as it was unregulated and of an uncontrolled explosion of the urban population, the health of the working class deteriorated suddenly and spectacularly: the child mortality rate as well as the general mortality rate of the population rose, the average height of the population shrank, the military authorities noted physical inferiority in young recruits from urban areas, workers were sometimes so worn out that they were dismissed at around the age of twenty, industrial workplaces produced an enormous number of what we would call work-related illnesses and accidents, while working-class neighbourhoods were centres of propagation for spectacular epidemics.[44]

In France as well as in Germany and in Great Britain, different types of enquiries into workers' lives had the aim of describing the destitution caused by new conditions of work and new forms of poverty; doctors were responsible for the most consistent contributions.[45] The sanitation reform movement which developed in Europe in the 1830s and 1840s dealt with the connections between poverty, illness and death. It conceived health in an overall perspective as a right of citizens, even though pervaded by many kinds of disagreement concerning the binding force of this right and the legitimate ways of honouring it. It is not insignificant that the end of the 1840s and the revolutions which shook Europe marked the culminating point of the political discussions related to the connection between health and poverty, with the publication of the magazine *Die medicinische Reform* by Virschow and Leubuscher in Germany (1848–1849), the editorial slant given by Jules Guérin to the *Gazette médicale de Paris* in 1848[46] and the passing of the first Public Health Act[47] in Britain, also in 1848.

The year 1848, then, is the date when a certain wing of the sanitary reform movement became radicalized, proposing a model of criticism of social pathology which took to task the very principles of liberal society in the name of health. In Germany, in the work of a doctor like Virschow, it becomes clear that the idea of sanitary reform was understood both as a reform of society and of medical practice: according to him, medicine should abandon its overly narrow definitions of illness and take account of social factors in those definitions.[48] Far from constituting only the development of a medical subdiscipline, as Foucault believed,[49] the idea of social medicine appeared at the time as a challenge posed from outside of medicine by society to doctors. We find the same subversive tone in the France of 1848. Thus the day after the February revolution, Guérin was hoping that a 'social revolution' would be an opportunity to redefine public health, which had been finally set free from the medical straitjacket and was thus in a position to fulfil its functions.[50] Social medicine, as he defined it, seeks to respond to a new type of sociopolitical demand which can be met neither by the liberal political institutions which are founded on denial of social suffering nor by classical medical institutions. He thus stated that social medicine 'provides the secret for the improvement of the impoverished classes' and that, more than anything else it can aid in social organization.[51] This is also what Virschow was suggesting when he defined doctors as the 'natural advocates of the poor': 'Doctors are the natural advocates of the poor and the social question, for the most part, falls within their competence'.[52]

If the socialist movement remained until 1848 relatively external to the public health movement,[53] and if the latter could up to this point be interpreted as stemming from a liberal biopolitical technology, the revolutionary events of 1848 would be the opportunity, in France and in Germany, for a quite radical change in perspective. The appearance of the social question as a major political problem made the vicious circle of illness and poverty a highly sensitive political subject, faced with which a doctor could scarcely avoid making a political judgement. In the upheaval of 1848 a new idea of health reform developed, one which is commonly associated with Germany because the medical reform movement emerged in this time of political effervescence, whereas, in France and England, it was born into more peaceful times. Virschow, Neumann and Leubuscher were its main figures, and we cannot help being struck by the proximity between the terms used in 1848 by the leaders of *Die Medicinische Reform* and those used by Guérin in the *Gazette médicale de Paris*. In these two critical analyses, dedicated to bringing the revolutionary spirit into public medicine, a conception of public health reform was forged which was characterized by a break both with the status of references to health in public policy and with the function granted by medicine to public health.

The neologisms used by these authors, 'public medicine' (*öffentliche Gesundheitspflege*) and 'social medicine', signify the break. When Virschow makes use of the term 'public medicine', it is to denounce the inadequacy of a medicine which contents itself with administrating health through the logics of the public health police and to demand the constitution of a true medicine of poverty.[54] When Guérin coins the neologism 'social medicine', it is within the framework of a criticism of the terms 'medical police', 'public hygiene' and 'legal medicine', which, on the one hand, express in his view the powerlessness and lack of daring of the medicine of the past with regard to the problems posed by the cycle of illness and poverty,[55] and, on the other hand, remain bound up with a narrowly administrative conception of public medicine, let us say of a conception of politics ruled by the model of the political rather than the social aspect of the 1848 Revolution (hence the opposition of 'political medicine' and 'social medicine').[56] In both cases, what is demanded is a break with the manner in which public health is administrated.

This first break is indissociable from a second, which concerns the disciplinary status of medicine itself. Guérin as well as Virschow state that it is impossible for the definition of its methods, subjects and tasks not to be affected by the general upheaval of society in the revolutions of 1848. The former is thus led to demand medicine to engage in a systematic study of the relationships between health and society,[57] the latter to develop a multicausal analysis of illness to take into account its social factors.[58] In the thought of both, a reorganization of the medical profession is furthermore deemed necessary, in order that the free for all of competition among doctors should cease and they be able to dedicate themselves to the political and social purpose imposed on them by events: 'Medical organisation is possible today with the character of revolutionary progress, but on condition of being achieved while respecting individual freedoms, and taking as the principal aim of medicine the interests of society, shaping it into SOCIAL MEDICINE'.[59]

These conceptions of public medicine and social medicine were obviously developed under the impact of the social question which, in their view, is indissociably that of the inhumanity of the new conditions of work and of the new forms of poverty associated with industrialization and urbanization. The link between their conceptions and the social question has to do first of all with the position of the doctor, situated as a frontline actor confronted daily with the reality of the effects of industrialization and the conditions of life specific to pauperization in the countryside and in towns: the doctor was confronted both with the political need to publicize the reality of injustice and with an awareness of the inadequacy of a purely medical response to the degradation of health and of existence.[60]

The link with the social question was also based on the conviction that medicine cannot remain neutral with regard to the way in which these forms of poverty raise anew the question of democracy. In the work of both Guérin and Virschow the demand is formulated for a medicine which acknowledges its political dimension and for doctors who unite the duties they owe as citizens and the responsibility they bear as doctors.[61] From this results an original conception of social medicine, which goes along with a model of social pathology irreducible to those of political economy and social economy. In their work, social medicine is simultaneously conceived of as a 'social science', as a diagnosis having to do with 'social pathologies' and as a reflection on 'social therapies'. It thus leads to a medical model of social pathology in which medical standards allow all the gravity of the social question to become apparent while at the same time demanding an assumption of political responsibility for these problems. This demand falls within the more general framework of the socialist questioning of the liberal order.

In the work of Guérin, the term 'social medicine' clearly has two meanings. In a first meaning, it designates a study of the interaction between health and society, an investigation of the social causes of health, morbidity and mortality, what we can call a sociology of health, while keeping in mind the initially unstable connotations of this notion.[62] But in 'social medicine', the adjective also has a more directly political meaning, as indicated for example by the following statement according to which 'social medicine, humanitarian medicine, is the key to the chief problems of our age'.[63] Jules Leroux, giving the first definition of socialism in 1834,[64] opposed it to individualism and thought that the synthesis of the two was the aim of a 'human science'[65] or of a 'social science'.[66] By 1845 he had come to the view that this synthesis belonged to a form of socialism.[67]

As Rosen emphasizes, it is with reference to this conception of the 'social', which highlighted the shortcomings of a liberal political order and criticized the claims of political economy to institute a spontaneous and autonomous order of cooperation, that Fourcaut coined the term 'social hygiene' in 1844, before Guérin invented 'social medicine' in 1848.[68] It was also in this sense that in Germany Salomon Neumann maintained in 1847 that 'medical science is at its heart private and in its essence a social science',[69] before Virschow and Leubuscher took up in their turn, in *Die medizinische Reform*, the definition of public medicine as a 'social science'. Not only was the term 'social medicine' coined during a determinate historical conjuncture, it was part of a chain of terminological innovations whose theoretical and political implications are clear.

Both an inquiry into the social conditions which cause the lives of individuals to lose all value for them and a demand that society restore to individuals the conditions of a life worth living, social medicine is, in the work of Guérin, a theory of 'social pathologies' and of their 'social treatment'.[70] It is striking that 'social pathology' is conceived as coming from a 'moral and psychological diagnosis' related to justice of society, its general organization and the role that work should play in it.[71] The concept of 'social therapy' makes explicit the directly practical dimension of such diagnoses: 'Societies perish like individuals! What remedies are fitted to preventing their decadence, to delaying their death? After the shocks, the convulsive illnesses that have shaken them, what means are suited to calming them?'[72]

Guérin emphasizes that the systematic study of the interactions between health and society does not presuppose any predefined social system and that, in this sense, social medicine must be distinguished from socialist medicine. But it is clear in his mind that the study of social pathologies can only demonstrate the correctness of socialism, as witness the last lines of the article dedicated to the distinction between these two medicines: 'To return to the distinction between . . . *social medicine and socialist medicine*, we declare that the one shall be eternally stable because it shall be eternally true, because it shall rest upon facts, abstraction made from systems; whereas the other, marching adventurously into space, exposes itself to the risk of falling into the void due to a lack of a basis and an aim. We do not mean by this that socialist medicine does not encompass a great number of just and high-minded points of view. The generous sentiments which animate it are on the contrary an inexhaustible source of truth. The whole point is to free them from the shadows in which they are shrouded'.[73]

Placed back into the context of terminological innovations—'socialism', 'sociology', 'social science', 'social hygiene' and 'social medicine'—Virschow's well-known formula loses much of its mystery: 'Medicine is a social science and politics is nothing but medicine writ large'.[74] At the historical moment of the social question, medicine must make itself a social science in the sense of a science wanting humanity to govern the relationship of individuals to society as a whole. If the social question is the most urgent political question and the greatest challenge posed to the idea of democracy, if furthermore the social question is above all the fact that the lives of many people are affected by so much suffering that they are barely worth living, politics can in effect be understood as an extension of the project of social medicine.

This conclusion is not valid for the public health reform movement in general, but it is for 'social medicine' understood in the historical sense of the term. Social medicine is in this sense the political return of the repressed, of the object of liberal denial. In 'social medicine' as it has historically existed, suffering is integrated into a model of 'social pathology' which does not end up in a justification of the social order by means of a theory of 'normal suffering', but rather in a general questioning of the organization of society. To do this, social medicine proceeds to the articulation of a medical diagnosis, to a sociological aetiology and to the demand for a social treatment, while criticizing the fantasy character of the social aetiology identified by social economy and the inadequacy of the treatments advocated by public health with regard to the ills it diagnoses.

Guérin thus defines social medicine as the joint study of 'social physiology', 'social pathology', 'social hygiene' and 'social treatment'.[75] The first describes the way in which people are able to cope with the social and legislative order; the second has to do with social and legislative orders which the 'constitution of peoples' renders unbearable, and the 'damaged organisation which results from this'; the third operates to 'spare peoples certain illnesses inherent in their constitution and their climate'; the last concerns the remedy of social pathologies. The idea of social pathology is associated in his work with the idea of a diagnosis to which public health can be the only therapeutic response. But in his view, diagnosis calls for social criticism because it denounces a social injustice, inequalities (with regard to health) whose factors are social. It calls for a treatment bearing on social factors whose transformation depends on political action.

We can understand, then, that in such conditions a sociomedical approach can claim a critical value. It is only if pathologies are diagnosed within the framework of a sociomedical aetiology and social causes render inadequate any purely preventive or curative medical response that the discourse on suffering comes under the remit of social criticism in the strict sense. We thus see that all the critical implications of social medicine are based on the social aetiology of health inequalities and on an intertwining of the two meanings of the word 'social': a criticism that is social by reason of its socialist (or humanitarian) orientation can only really be so by virtue of its sociological (or aetiological) point of view.

Hence a first limitation on this medical model of social pathologies: social medicine indeed runs up against the absence of a social theory that could compete against political economy. As one option, social medicine can content itself with using the force of statistical descriptions to formulate a social diagnosis as scientific as those which political economy claims, but in this case, as in the work of Villermé, it has to weaken the link between diagnosis and treatment and give up social criticism. The other option is to maintain, on the contrary, that the study of the social preconditions of the inequalities of health allows us to identify necessary social transformations, but it must then content itself with Virschow's generalities on the required transformation of the organization of work and of urban housing, on the right to work and medical care, on the necessity of more rational agricultural policies and of sanitation measures. Grotjahn, in particular, would take him to task for this: his social medicine does not have available social sciences which would allow it to constitute itself as a true theory of social pathology.[76]

The model of social pathology coined by 'social medicine' poses an even more general problem, which has to do with the approach to the social question using a nosographic grid that is defined a priori. Social diagnosis aims, certainly, at bringing to light the experience of poverty and exploitation with which doctors are in direct contact, and social medicine is thus part of the tradition of social writings which emphasize the extent of the suffering of the working classes and the gulf separating the experience of poverty from the theories of political economy. To be sure, the description of suffering in terms of degeneration, morbidity and morality allows us to make it seem abnormal, whereas political economy emphasizes on the contrary its positive contribution to normal social functioning. But sufferings that are strongly felt by those frontline actors, doctors, cannot be reduced to degeneration, morbidity and mortality. As a diagnostic tool addressing the reality of the experience of poverty, social medicine partly misses its aim. As a treatment, it accompanies the political demands that arise from the social question and it tries to put itself at their service. But in translating them into a heterogenous language, it undoes the link between social critique and lived experience, along with the specific demands that arise from this.

We are dealing here with the limits of the narrowly medical model of social pathology. When social suffering is described with medical concepts, the categorizations and methods which make it possible to trace the social genesis of disorders, above and beyond simple quantitative measures, are generally lacking. Moreover, in this model, suffering is reduced to pathological suffering, in such a way that a whole dimension of the subjective impact of poverty and exploitation is passed over in silence, as is the specifically polemical scope of the theme of suffering. In effect, whatever may be the intentions motivating the use of such a model of social pathology, it cannot really make suffering appear as a demand for redress sustained by the experience of an unbearable social reality (which is a different thing to the experience of an illness or the frequency of mortality and of degeneration). Thanks to social medicine, suffering does come back into view as social suffering, but what remains obscure is the nature of the social causes that produce it, and what remains underestimated is the whole of that part of the experience of poverty and exploitation which cannot be reduced to duly catalogued pathologies. There is a need for a broader and more differentiated conception of suffering and a more specific conception of the social and subjective factors in suffering, but also for a model capable of connecting in a coherent way these conceptions of suffering and their various factors in order to fill these gaps. We must now deal with the development of such a model.

Content and Dynamics of Suffering

In the first chapter, we spelled out the different possible meanings of the expression 'social suffering'. In order to move from semantic to conceptual analysis, we will begin by identifying different types of content of suffering. We will then take up the dynamic dimension of suffering. We must combine these static and dynamic distinctions to develop a complete and coherent conception of social suffering.

Content of Suffering

As a general rule, the term 'suffering' seems to designate the result of a long-term and unbearable nonsatisfaction of the 'needs of the self', whether this be due to the repression of tendencies rooted in these needs, to the conflict of these tendencies or to an unavailability of the objects of need or of the means of satisfying them. But there exist different kinds of needs of the self, and suffering takes on a different content according to whether it is the nonsatisfaction of this or that need which is at issue.

When we speak of a 'need of the self', we understand the notion of the 'self' (*le moi*) in an entirely general sense: we distinguish between the bodily self and the psychological self, this latter encompassing just as much the id and the superego as the 'ego' (*le moi*) in the technical sense Freud gives to this concept[77] (all of which we put in the category of the psychological self), as well as everything having to do with the constitution of the self in socialization (the social self). By needs of the self, we mean a totality of fundamental needs linked to the bodily, psychological and social parts of our existence, which define general tendencies oriented towards a search for satisfaction—tendencies having to do mainly with biological needs, with the principle of self-preservation, with drives and demands for recognition—and the psychological constraints linked to the ways in which these tendencies must be unified and symbolized so as not to imperil the unity of the self. The idea of a need aims to circumscribe the viewpoint of a social psychology making the individual the subject of needs which are not only economic or social but at once economic, social and psychological.[78] It is taken here in biological and psychological senses (which both presuppose a connection between a lack of the object of its satisfaction) and in a sense that could be called metapsychological,[79] which designates the structural constraints on the psychic inscription of the pursuit of needs and of the satisfaction of drives.

The concept of a need, and even its indeterminacy, is the key to a negative anthropology whose terms were set out by Marx. In the *Economic and Political Manuscripts of 1844*,[80] he defines man as a being of needs, thus emphasizing the finiteness constitutive of a being who depends on something other than him- or herself (outside objects, other beings, a society) to maintain his or her existence. The idea of negative anthropology designates a second type of constitutive lack: nothing defines the way in which fundamental needs must be satisfied. A need only establishes in this sense *tendencies* which can be put into action in different ways. This classic analysis must be completed by taking into account the fact that the psyche is defined by drives detached from bodily needs and by work aiming at unifying the tendencies that they establish and at finding stable compromises between their demands for satisfaction, social demands and the availability of their means of satisfaction. We have already noted that suffering cannot be conceived of as simple displeasure. It must rather be conceived of as a long-term lack of satisfaction of tendencies deriving from fundamental needs or drives, whether this stems from the unavailability of their objects or from the conflict of these tendencies.

Starting from the distinction between needs linked to the body (physical self), to the process of structuring an individual psyche (psychic self) and to the process of individualization through socialization (social self), we propose to distinguish between 'physical suffering', 'psychic suffering' and 'psychosocial suffering'.[81] Tendencies stemming from these different selves are intertwined in such a way that the different contents of suffering defined by these different tendencies cannot be conceived of as independent species, but only as distinct kinds.

In the chapter 1, we ruled out the use of the term 'suffering' to designate biological dysfunctions, while specifying that the idea of suffering covers specifically the way in which the self experiences these, as well as bodily harm and privation, and the way in which it invests its psychological sufferings in a bodily way, either in the form of somatization or as an element of interaction with others. It is in this sense that we refer now to a 'physical suffering' to account for the sufferings attributed to the body.

This physical suffering is not strictly psychological because it concerns a body that is eroticized, socially and culturally conditioned, equipped to bear without suffering a variable degree of pain, of privation and of violence. Some physical sufferings contain furthermore a dimension that is even more directly psychological, insofar as numerous psychological sufferings are ex-

Suffering

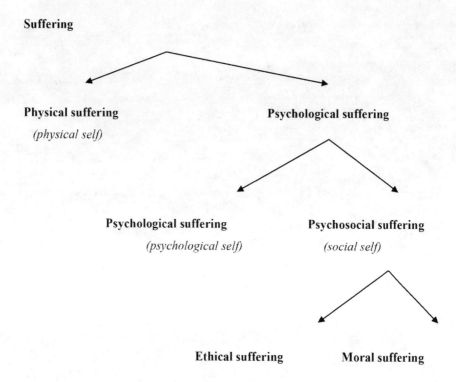

Physical suffering   Psychological suffering
(physical self)

Psychological suffering   Psychosocial suffering
(psychological self)   *(social self)*

Ethical suffering   Moral suffering

Figure 3.1.   Suffering.   Source: Author's own.

perienced through the intermediary of the body (somatization). [82] It could thus seem invalid to distinguish psychological suffering and bodily suffering. But not all psychological suffering is experienced by the body in the mode of suffering: certain psychological sufferings are accompanied by bodily insensitivity, others by an absenting from the body. These facts suffice to justify the distinction between bodily and psychological suffering.

Two types of psychological suffering can be distinguished: psychic suffering proper and psychosocial suffering. The first can be traced back to the self as psychic apparatus with a history dating from early childhood, the second to the self as the personal identity constructed during socialization. This distinction is advanced here in the light of a theory of the psychicl apparatus borrowed from Freud and from a social psychology inspired by Mead. It rests more precisely on the hypothesis that two complementary theorizations are in play here. The idea of the psychic self here covers not only fantasies, but also identifications and defences with which the individual psyche reacts to fundamental erotic and social events over the course of his or her existence. The idea of the social self designates for its part not so much the constitution of a second self through secondary (nonfamilial) socialization as a set of distinct processes of individuation depending on the logic of intersubjective adjustment, on intersubjective expectations and on the validation of the positive relationship to oneself. Here we are dealing with two perspectives on psychological life and not with the analysis of two distinct selves.[83]

By psychic suffering we understand a suffering which has its roots in the tensions which pervade the structures of the psychic apparatus: conflicts of the id with the ego and the superego, conflicts of the pleasure principle with the reality principle and conflicts between drives. These vectors of psychic suffering are concretized in experiences such as fear in the face of vulnerability, traumatic disruptions, object loss or unsatisfied drives. The role of anxiety in psychological economy, whether it be rooted in a schema of vulnerability when faced with the outside world and in the lack of unity of the drives, as in Freud, or in the distance between the symbolic and the real, as in Lacan, doubtless deserves to feature as one of the main sources of psychological suffering. Even though the idea of trauma has been contested in various ways over the history of psychoanalysis, it was never rejected by Freud, who recognized the existence of traumatic neuroses[84] and who integrated trauma into the aetiology of other neuroses as an occasional factor.[85] The repression of drives and object loss, with the conflicts linked to them, refer back for their part to the explanation of other forms of neurotic suffering.

These different sources of suffering can contribute in two ways to the aetiology of suffering: as factors directly causing fear, trauma, loss or psychological conflict or as indirect factors, when an event or a current social situation awakens a past trauma, fear, loss or conflict. A particular experience is transformed into suffering by the echo that it raises in the structures of an individual psyche. This particular experience can be an apparently innocuous event, but it can also be a direct factor in anxiety, a traumatizing event or a loss. The dynamic of psychological suffering depends on this complex interweaving, which Freud described using the concept of a 'complementary series', emphasizing that the aetiology of neuroses includes endogenous and exogenous factors varying in an inverse relationship to each other: the more the psychic structure is weakened, the milder the triggering factor can be; the more significant the effects of the exogenous factor, the more it is liable to cause an imbalance in the psychological structures.[86]

The expression 'psychosocial suffering' designates, by contrast, experiences in which individuals face social situations that go against a group of fundamental self-conceptions and habits which govern their relationship to themselves as well as their relationship to the world. Psychosocial suffering can be traced back to needs no longer anchored in the self as a psychic structure but in the self as a personal identity. As Mead demonstrated, the conditions of interaction and the adjustment of our expectations to those of others cause specific subjectivation effects. Social logics are embedded in individual psychology (they institute it as a 'self' and as a 'mind'[87]) by defining a group of relations to the self and the world which can lead to specific sufferings. It is particularly to the social psychology of stigmatization,[88] to the clinical sociology of shame[89] and to theories of recognition that we owe the development of the analysis of these specific forms of suffering.[90] They supply numerous arguments in favor of distinguishing 'psychic suffering' from 'psychosocial suffering'. Indeed, it is difficult to agree that ethical suffering linked to the experience of invisibilization, contempt, stigmatization or humiliation consists only of hidden transfers of anxiety or projections of hidden psychic harm.

The psychosocial approach takes into account different forms of suffering which can result in particular from a splitting or emptiness of identity and imprisonment in systems of social logic contrary to strong identifications and evaluations. Even more fundamentally, it is the positive relation to oneself (a sign of an intact identity and the condition of the projection of the self onto an horizon of autonomy and of self-realization) which can be put in question in interaction, for example in a confrontation with an institutionalized denial of recognition. When the absence of recognition no longer takes the form of a denigrating recognition, but rather that of invisibility, the image of the self can itself end up disappearing. The social interactions typical of life on the street provide an illustration of these two stages: that of an interiorized shame from which individuals will continue to suffer as long as they have not managed to escape the street[91] and that of a kind of disappearance of self-awareness, which is also accompanied by a kind of disappearance of the awareness of suffering: 'Pain, through not being heard or relieved, ends up not being perceived. . . . When there is no more neurological perception, there is no more self-awareness. But if there is no more self-awareness, neurological perception disappears also'.[92] If it is important to emphasize the existence of a specific psychosocial content of suffering, this is not only to designate the specific processes of suffering connected with the logics of interaction, but also and more generally to take into account this intersubjective dimension of suffering: it can only exist for as long as it can be the subject of demand capable of being heard. This explains the political and relational dimensions of the concept of suffering which we described in the previous chapters.

Among forms of psychosocial suffering, we propose a distinction between ethical suffering and moral suffering, returning to the classic philosophical distinction between ethics and morality which refers back respectively to questions of the good life and of the just life. The domain of ethics stems from a group of strong identifications and evaluations which constitute the coordinates in terms of which individuals confront the problem posed by their identity and starting from which they attempt to organize their life plans. The case of upward or downward social mobility, as well as problems of dual absence, characteristic of immigrant status,[93] or of double consciousness, charcteristic of the status of colonized person,[94] as also the different forms of exposure to social contempt, provide examples of ethical suffering. A second type of identity suffering brings into play ideas connected not with what individuals identify as the values and contexts which make up the value of existence, but with the principles to which all individuals must submit in their relationships with others. This is what could be called 'moral suffering', to indicate specific sufferings that individuals endure when they are led to do what they explicitly consider unjust or unworthy, immoral or perverse. Occupational psychology has given descriptions of this type of situation under the heading of 'acceptance of the dirty work'.[95]

Having been presented the content, let us try to specify the meaning of the distinction between the two forms of psychic suffering. Conceiving of the distinction between the psychic self and the social self as a distinction in perspective amounts to the attempt to combine psychoanalytic and psychosocial explanations of social suffering. There are thus two ways of contesting this distinction. The first consists in maintaining that psychoanalysis and social psychology are sufficient unto themselves or are incompatible in the explanation of suffering. The second is based on the idea that sociological orientations irreducible to social psychology manage to give better explanations of social suffering than social psychology can.

Against the first type of objection, we would like to briefly defend the hypothesis that Freudian social psychology and Meadian social psychology are complementary and gain from being joined together. It even seems that the psychosocial explanations proposed by Freud could be systematically completed by dealing with the subjectivation effects of socialization and interaction; both when they deal with social support in terms of vulnerability (*Hilflösigkeit*) and when they deal with a positive relationship with the self in terms of the ego ideal, they only retain one of the aspects of the problem. In effect, forms of social contempt have the power to cause by themselves forms of shame and, even if the experience of shame brings into play the individual's psychological investment (an original narcissism), it does not suffice to exhaust its reality. Freud's argument seems unconvincing when he reduces shame (or 'the intense feeling of guilt') to a simple 'social modification of neurotic anxiety'.[96] Furthermore, even when we admit that it is always a primitive vulnerability that comes to the fore when the intersubjective supports of existence collapse, we must recognize that these have a reality of their own which produces specific effects.

In the same way, the Freudian theory of the ego ideal allows us to take into account a group of identifications with individuals and groups whose importance in the analysis of suffering is unquestionable and which, in a certain way, are already distributed between the two schemata of the psychic self and the psychosocial self.[97] But the strong identifications and evaluations which derive from socialization cannot be reduced to primary and cultural identifications. Even if we conceded that socialization (in its secondary type) only produces secondary identifications that replay primary identifications, it would have to be acknowledged that socialization produces specific subjectivization effects which modify the action of the primary identifications.

The reformulation which Honneth has given to Mead's social psychology[98] inclines us to the view that the psychic approach must also always be combined with an analysis of psychic processes. On the one hand, we can point out that in order for expectations of recognition by others to matter for individuals, the individuals must have positive access to themselves and to others, access which is conditioned by fundamental psychic processes whose study is taken up by psychoanalysis.[99] On the other hand, we can regard recognitive expectations as replaying on another stage a primitive vulnerability and the primitive demands rooted in drives. And it must be added that the effects of the denial of recognition always weigh on identity through the intermediary of psychological defences. Contrary to what a unilateral use of theories of recognition might lead us to think, studies by social psychologists show that stigmatized individuals express higher self-esteem than nonstigmatized individuals![100] Whether we are considering the issue of recognition or of its effects, we must therefore conclude that the social self is based on the psychological self.

The second basic challenge to our typology is posed by the claim that the subject social psychology deals with (the social self) should be explained by concepts other than those to which it has recourse. The very idea of psychosocial suffering could thus be contested from the point of view of the Bourdieusian sociology of the habitus. It would then be affirmed that social existence is governed by habitus—that is, by incorporated social logics indissociable from a classification system and from a normative and strategic knowledge that remain preconscious—in relation to which the conscious sphere where the idea of identity belongs plays only a superficial role. If the concept of identity is undoubtedly not adequate to explain social behaviour, it is however difficult to concede that the strong evaluations of individuals and the other components of identity can remain without effect on behaviour and on the suffering that can be bound up with it. In a way, this type of objection rests on a narrow notion of personal identity in which it is conceived of as a principally cognitive relationship to the self. By contrast we are referring to the concept of a practical identity in which the cognitive relation to the self is indissociable from the evaluative relation to the self, which cannot be separated from a practical relation to the social environment. Rather than setting up identity and habitus in opposition to one another and taking the view that what is thought of under the concept of identity inadequately connotes what should be described in terms of habitus, a more convincing account considers identity to be inseparable from a set of cemented habits of the self, to which it nonetheless cannot be reduced by virtue of its evaluative dimension. [101]

The Bourdieusian explanation of social suffering confirms furthermore that it is not particularly easy to set up in opposition to one another the perspective of habitus and that of identity. In his *Méditations pascaliennes*, Bourdieu implicitly distinguishes normal from abnormal social suffering. In a sense, suffering belongs to the normal conditions of socialization insofar as, on the one hand, dispositions rest on an incorporation of the principles of social division and of forms of social subordination and, on the other hand, these dispositions are never perfectly adjusted to the totality of our interactions. [102] But there is also a type of abnormal social suffering which can no longer be explained by the general logic of the constitution of habitus and by an occasional mismatch with the environment of action, but by a conflict between habituses and by a structural mismatch with the conditions of action. [103]

Habituses have their own inertia, so that they may become permanently 'out of sync'. This can be explained by individual social trajectories (upward or downward social mobility) as well as by social developments (crisis situations or an overturning of the rules of a social domain). The inertia of the habitus can also explain that one and the same individual may incorporate contradictory practical and normative logics, this 'tearing apart' of habituses being explicable in its turn either by individual trajectories (when those who have moved between social classes interiorize the logics appropriate to the new social situations) or by collective processes (such as immigration, the precarization of work, mass unemployment affecting certain professions): 'It has been observed that to contradictory positions, which tend to exert structural "double binds" on their occupants, there often correspond destabilised habituses, torn by contradiction and internal division, generating suffering'.[104]

If we admit that the idea of personal identity only ever designates, for individuals, a group of practical problems to be resolved and that, in this sense, nothing requires the reduction of identity to the explicit self-definition of the self, split habituses fall within the problematic of psychosocial (or identity-related) suffering. If we admit, moreover, that a central issue of identity is the appropriation by the individual of his or her social action and its results (because an individual is always in his or her own eyes also what he or she does), the suffering caused by maladjusted habituses is also a form of psychosocial suffering.[105]

The distinctions that go to make up this sort of typology make it possible to specify the articulations of a conception of social suffering. The idea of social suffering becomes clearer when we understand that the social context acts directly upon each of these contents of suffering. First, different social factors may contribute to the production of the first type of content of suffering. Collective events such as wars or industrial disasters may be responsible for all sorts of bodily harm and intrusion. The economic organization of the production and distribution of wealth, as well as its crises, may be the direct source of serious privations. Specific social relationships within specific institutional frameworks, as well as the social structures of domination, may also be a factor that facilitates all kinds of violence and privation.

Second, the social context can come into play regarding the different forms of psychic suffering, whether this be via the intermediary of traumatic violence[106] or of social processes that lead to the dismantling of intersubjective relationships which check anxiety and protect against deprivation (the family or whatever may take its place).

Social contexts also seem able to impact on the psychic conflict itself, whether this be through the weight of prohibitions or through contradictory injunctions (either within an institution or between institutions). If we are to believe comparative epidemiological studies, the variation in rates of prevalence of schizophrenia across the globe cannot be explained simply by the differences in the level of tolerance and social support within societies, but must also be explained by the contradictory injunctions that weigh upon social relations.[107] On a more everyday level, the clinical study of work gives innumerable examples of serious subjective harm brought about by contradictory injunctions (demands for autonomy in a context in which room for manœuvre is lacking, to increase in quality and productivity in a context of downsizing, etc.).[108]

Finally, the concepts of change of class (adjustment of habitus), of invisibilization, of stigmatization, of social rejection, of social contempt identify the way in which social contexts can impact psychosocial suffering. The symbolic components through which relationships of domination reproduce themselves and legitimize themselves are themselves the causes of different kinds of 'moral injuries' linked to the denial of recognition.[109]

These distinctions allow us, furthermore, to emphasize that the social context can play two different roles. It can intervene in the aetiology of structural factors in suffering, but also in that of its episodic factors. The topic of a 'complementary series' in the aetiology of neuroses relates to this fact. The social context can play a role in the aetiology of structural factors in neurosis by directly affecting anxiety, trauma, loss or psychological conflict. But the social context can also intervene as triggering factors in the form of socially conditioned individual behaviours or of collective phenomena.

Because one of the problems posed by the critical use of the concept of social suffering is that of shifting back from lived suffering to a general questioning of the social order, we should conclude by highlighting that macrosocial categories such as those of disaffiliation and domination designate factors which can be called transversal because they play a role in the three kinds of contents of suffering. The notion of disaffiliation refers to a macrosocial fragilization of social supports. Now, social support is generally considered a resource required for coping with violence and its traumatic effects, while the loss of social support increases social vulnerability and the probability of being a victim of violence.[110] Social supports are also a resource for protecting against the specific vulnerability of psychic structures and this resource defines a type of recognition fundamental to maintaining a positive relation to oneself.

In the same way, the concept of domination, when it is understood in the sense of the general form of social relationships of class, gender and 'race', designates, on the one hand, a principle of social hierarchy which limits the freedom of action of subordinated individuals and exposes them to be more likely victims of violence (whether they seek to transgress the limits of the freedom allowed them or interiorize their inability to resist the dominant members), and on the other hand, a principle of justification of social hierarchies which operates by legitimating the use of constraint and the modes of interiorization of obedience. Insofar as it increases the likelihood that dominated individuals will experience need and violence, domination is a factor in physical suffering. It is also a factor in psychic suffering because it can play a role in the aetiology of certain forms of traumatic violence and, more generally, because it impacts psychological conflicts by confronting individuals with their own ambivalent attitude to domination: we sometimes refuse with all our might even when we know that we have no other choice but to submit. Finally, insofar as it is bound up with symbolic hierarchies, it is also a factor of psychosocial suffering, in the form of 'invisible wounds' of class, race and gender.[111]

Dynamics of Suffering

What generally characterizes the sociological point of view on suffering is that it only makes the social factors and social effects of suffering explicit. Moreover, when the rebounding effect of suffering on its own social context is considered, as in the analysis of 'trajectories of suffering', the transformation of suffering is interpreted as a purely quantitative evolution and not as a process in the course of which suffering can undergo real mutations. It is argued, for example, that the triggering event induces a suffering which will have the effect of reducing social supports and the horizon of expectation, so that as the conditions attenuating suffering are undermined, suffering increases, dragging the individual into a catastrophic spiral. Here suffering develops only in a quantitative sense. With regard to the analysis of suffering itself, the sociological point of view is thus compatible with the static approach to suffering which has just been proposed in the form of a typology of 'contents' of suffering. But suffering is also caught up in a specific psychic dynamic.

To take into account its psychodynamic dimension, a new typology needs to be developed. In what follows, we will distinguish suffering that is *normal* (in the sense that it is a component of mental health), suffering that is *patho- genic* (in the sense that it defines a point of instability on the borderline between compensated suffering and severe suffering, on the border of health and pathology) and a *severe or pathological* suffering. These distinctions are based on the idea that neurosis, which figures here as the origin of pathogenic suffering, defines a space external both to mental health and to mental illness (or pathology). Here again, the distinctions must be taken not in the sense of exclusive definitions supported by strict demarcation criteria, but as delimita- tions of types. It is clear, for example, that the tendencies that characterize neurosis (and thus pathogenic suffering) are also found in health, but it still remains the case that they can acquire a type of predominance which results in the production of a specific form of suffering (Freud does not hesitate to speak in this context of 'neurotic suffering'[112]) and of specific difficulties which have to be faced.

This observation permits us to clarify the distinction between normal and abnormal suffering that we introduced in the first chapter, while emphasizing its importance for the critical use of the problematic of social suffering. There exists normal suffering in the sense that suffering is a component of all existence and that mental health, considered as a precarious balance attained by psychic work, is always in part linked to a struggle against suffering. We can say in this sense that 'normal suffering' is a relatively successful mode of appropriation of suffering, an integration of suffering with the psychic self and the social self. It can be based upon two processes.

A first type of appropriation of suffering has to do with the displacement mechanisms which make it possible to transform suffering into pleasure. What is displaced are the tendencies whose nonsatisfaction causes suffering. As for the objects towards which this displacement occurs, these are socially valorized objects which offer at once a compensation and a type of satisfac- tion of a superior order. Freud used the term 'sublimation' to designate this process without providing a worked out theory of it. A second type of appro- priation has to do with the strong evaluations and with the positive identifica- tions thanks to which the self can value the suffering arising from certain activities, compensating for it by a related intersubjective satisfaction or interpreting it as an aspect of its quest for autonomy and for self-realization. The Freudian theory of the ego ideal describes certain aspects of this second process, as does the theory of recognition. The two processes can intervene jointly and, according to the psychodynamics of work, the transformation of suffering at work into pleasure offers an illustration of this: the processes which make it possible to confront the harshness of the activity of work depend preeminently on the eroticization of the body and the capacity for sublimation. But this psychodynamics also draws on the themes of the recognition of the reality of the activity and of the social utility of work and of the value of an occupation, which are grounded in the theory that a positive relationship to the self is constructed in social interactions. [113]

In the second process, we can say that suffering is conscious in the sense that it is the object of a challenge. We all face the question of whether our efforts are justified, whether our projects are worth the trouble; furthermore, the experience of work sometimes takes the form of a display of our own suffering as an indicator of our merit and of the value of what we have produced. In the case of the first process, it is difficult to know if suffering can be totally transformed into pleasure or totally annulled by a shift in the tendencies that cause it (in which case it would disappear).

Here we encounter the ambiguities of the concept of normal suffering. Either it is understood in the sense of low-intensity harm against which the self does not need to struggle, and thus it may seem unjustified to speak of suffering, or suffering mobilizes different defences and other processes of integration into the self, in which case it can be experienced in a way that is even less painful or it can even disappear completely from the field of consciousness. To retain its meaning, the concept of normal suffering must designate the first stage of a dynamic of transformation of suffering and not of a primary suffering or an originary mode of relating to the world. [114] We can only ever identify the first stage of transformation of a suffering which never exists in a pure state. To summarize, let us say that normal suffering is always partially conscious, long-term and intrinsically hard to bear, but damped down either by sublimation or by valorization.

The idea of abnormal suffering must also be reworked as part of a theory of the struggle of the self against suffering. It can be understood either as a failure in this struggle or as a development of means of struggle whose effects are contradictory and partially unsatisfactory. The two explanations can be combined if we consider, along with Freud, that what triggers the intervention of a new form of struggle is the frustration of an effort to appropriate suffering, which, by seeking to destroy suffering itself, amputates the self from a part of its capacities. The difference between normal and abnormal suffering thus depends on the distinction between a form of struggle that we can call normal, in the sense that it is an undeniable component of health, and an abnormal form of struggle, not in the sense that it concerns illness, but in the sense that it leads to the uncertain and unstable space located between health and illness.

This second form of struggle is characterized by the mobilization of what Freud called 'defences' (excluding sublimation from 'defences' and thus understanding by defences only the psychoneurotic defences). It is clear that, in a way, psychoneurotic defences and the neurotic tendencies associated with them are part of normality. The idea of neurosis designates only a certain type of development and of predominance of these tendencies: these defences have the capacity to impose specific types of psychic organization which can no longer be considered, strictly speaking, as falling under the category of health. From a Freudian point of view, it must also be emphasized that when these defences structure an individual's psyche, there results both a loss of freedom of the individual in his or her relationships to the outside world and a type of adaptation both inert and fragilized.

When used against suffering in the form of denial, isolation, repression, introjection or suppression,[115] these defences lead to a transformation of suffering, to a transformed suffering that will be called pathogenic. It is certainly not pathogenic as such, but in the sense that it is inseparable from a structure which can be termed pathogenic because it results from an unstable compensation, and that is destabilization can give rise to severe (noncompensated) or pathological (psychotic) forms of suffering. The term 'pathogen' indicates a possible fate of this suffering, but 'neurotic suffering' also makes itself felt in the subject through an intolerable aspect which Freud regards as the principal motivation for undertaking psychoanalytic treatment; its rejection is the 'rational aim'[116] of the treatment.

If we concede that all defences are invariably defences against suffering, as Freud sometimes puts it, we can see that the question of transforming suffering is absolutely decisive in any psychodynamic approach: decisive in a dual way. On the one hand, it indicates that suffering is always expressed through defences in such a way that defences are always what analysts are dealing with.[117] On the other hand, it implies that suffering is not necessarily conscious or, more precisely, that one aspect of suffering is excluded from the field of consciousness by defences. Either suffering has become nonconscious (because it has been neutralized by isolation, denial or introjection) or it is conscious but in a form that is displaced by defences (defence by projection or return of the representations linked to the effects which are repressed because they are associated with suffering).

The passage from the second to the third stage of suffering is much the same as the passage from the first to the second: there are neither linear relationships nor necessary succession between them. It is only from a meta-psychological point of view that we can say of the failure of neurotic defences that it brings about a new transformation of suffering. This transformation can take different forms. It can be traced back first of all to the suffering caused by an episode of failed compensation, the uncompensated suffering being explained very directly by the destabilization of the neurotic defences whose function was to compensate for it. But we must also take into account the forms of suffering connected with the mobilization of new defences, such as those which characterize psychosis, which Freud sometimes considers the most desperate and radical attempt to struggle against suffering, a last resort when the other forms of struggle cannot or can no longer be mobilized. Psychosis, understood as a desperate struggle against suffering, mobilizes new defences and brings about a new transformation of suffering.

There are also other types of defence which appear neither neurotic nor psychotic in the strict sense, but which are just as desperate as psychosis and which are a response to suffering just as severe as that of decompensation; they are described by the clinical term 'extreme situations' (severe precarity and concentration camps for example[118]). In this case the defence operates via the sacrifice of certain psychological functions, a sacrifice which may be understood either as an attempt at neutralizing suffering by splitting or as a passage from the logic of defence against suffering (again in accordance with the pleasure principle) to a logic of destruction of the painful excitation (death drive). In certain cases, it is necessary to '"kill" oneself to survive'.[119] As in psychosis, the conscious aspect of suffering only allows one to identify a very superficial aspect of the transformation of suffering.

The contribution of the psychodynamic approach consists in making it possible to distinguish different stages of suffering. In itself, it tells us nothing about the social dimension of suffering, but it makes it possible to clarify the idea that societies can produce contrasting responses to suffering. On the one hand, the social context can positively produce suffering by playing a role either in the aetiology of pathogenic psychological structures or in that of episodic pathogenic factors. The social context thus comes into play in the aetiology of suffering that the ego seeks to appropriate to itself or against which it attempts to defend itself. The factors of this type of aetiological

approach that must be taken into account have been enumerated in the pre-
ceding subsection. They concern the social conditions of physical, psychic
and psychosocial suffering. But the social context can also impact the modes
of appropriation of suffering and of defence against it, and this in two different ways: either by providing means of appropriation and defence or by
undermining the social conditions of modes of appropriation and defence.

The social context can provide the self with means of struggling against
suffering at different stages of its development: by placing at its disposition
instruments of *appropriation* (normal suffering), *defences* (pathogenic suffering) and modes of *social integration* of madness (pathological suffering).
To identify the social conditions of this struggle against suffering, we need to
enlarge on the Freudian psychodynamic approach and take into account
psychosocial logics. To begin with, the role of the social context in the
appropriation of suffering concerns above all the collective dimension of the
ego ideal and the cultural conditions of sublimation. But social components
of identity and relationships of recognition also play a role in the valorization
of suffering. Next, the social context has a direct influence on the struggle
against suffering by providing collective defences (the theme of the cultural
unconscious and of forms of collective denial illustrates this point). Finally,
societies can supply means of socialization of pathogenic suffering by offering modes of normalized social expression for attacks of insanity (as in the
case of Amok crises[120]), special functions for mental disturbances (by means
of the institution of shamanism, for example) and rites of social reintegration
for psychotics (ceremonies of freeing from witchcraft).[121]

Inversely, the social context can intervene *by default* in the development
of suffering. Given that the presence of social support seems to play a decisive role in the appropriation of suffering and that the lack of it is doubtless
an aggravating factor in neurosis, even psychosis, we can advance the theory
that the lack of social support concerns all the three stages in the dynamic of
suffering. Furthermore, we can take the view that certain social situations no
longer provide individuals with the conditions of sublimation or transformation of suffering into pleasure by valorization (this is the case, for example,
when the destruction of work collectives and procedures for individualized
evaluation and for evaluation of overall quality no longer allow recognition
of the reality and value of work). The lack of social context can explain
suffering in a more indirect way: by causing modes of appropriation and
defence or available forms of social integration to fail. Certain social transformations and certain events can indeed cause the various forms of struggle

Chapter 3

against suffering to lose their meaning (for example, Freud interpreted war as a radical placing in doubt of the ego ideal, and perhaps even of sublimation)[122] or render them impracticable (for example, when the organization of work is such that the psychological cost of certain collective defences becomes too high for certain individuals).

Figure 3.2 attempts to clarify the idea of social suffering more precisely on the basis of the distinction between the social dimension of suffering (social modes of expression, social effects, types of interaction characterized by suffering) and social factors of suffering, while taking into account the existence of two types of social conditioning of suffering: one, direct, can be traced back to suffering produced directly or indirectly by the social environment; the other, which operates negatively, can be traced back to the absence of the social conditions for the struggle against suffering, whether the latter has been produced by the social context or not.

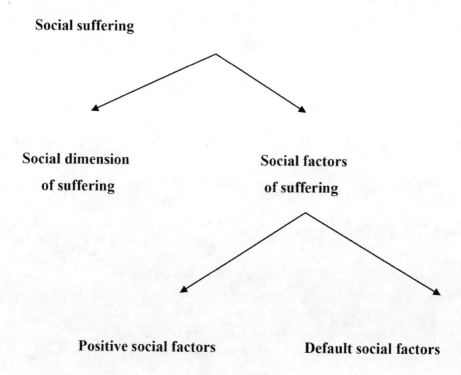

Social suffering

**Social dimension
of suffering**

**Social factors
of suffering**

Positive social factors

Default social factors

Figure 3.2. Social suffering.   Source: Author's own.

A Conception of Social Suffering

All social suffering lies at the intersection of a triple causality: positive social factors, negative social factors, a distinct psychic dynamic. The positive factors in suffering, as well as the negative factors, are distributed across the different strata of the social world: the civilizational and cultural, as well as general social relationships and social bonds which, in addition to conditioning institutions and frameworks of interaction, are the source of different types of privation and violence. Furthermore, as we have noted, the same positive social factors can affect two branches of the 'complementary series' (as structural conditions and situational conditions); this argument can also be applied to the shift from normal suffering to pathogenic suffering, as well as to that which leads to pathogenic suffering. In the same way, negative social factors can doubtless come into play in the two transitions. These different social conditions only apply to the psychological dynamic of individuals by connecting with specific social trajectories.

In this sense, the concept of social suffering does designate a complex interweaving of the psychic and the social, of life history and context, of structural and situational factors. It is only in light of this interweaving that the idea of social factors in suffering takes on meaning. Due to its internal complexity, two ways of using of the concept of social suffering are thus possible. The first attempts to give a global vision of suffering by seeking out the specific features of a determinate social diagnosis (of a social pathology) in the effects of one of the general components of suffering: for example, the weakness of social support, the violence of relations of domination or the disappearance of the symbolic order. The second use is oriented rather towards the analysis of particular configurations which, in a determinate social context, lead to a particular interweaving of the three causalities.

The first option thus makes global use of the concept of social suffering. In view of the different factors in suffering that the concept of disaffiliation allows us to group together, and due to the diagnostic aim of this concept, it is not surprising that it has led to such broad uses, for example when psychological suffering is explained as an 'indicator of precarity'.[123] The argument could be reconstructed in the following way: when society is pervaded by a general process of disaffiliation, it is characterized both by a greater social vulnerability to domination and violence and by a weakening of the social conditions of the struggle against suffering so that the development of positive factors in suffering reinforces that of the negative factors.[124] Understood in this sense, the concept of social suffering points towards a general social critique in terms of disaffiliation, the concept of disaffiliation allowing us both to interconnect a group of positive and negative social factors in suffering and to take into account the trajectories of suffering thereby engendered, while connecting a diagnosis in terms of suffering to a theory of social evolution.

A second option consists rather in attempting to determine the way in which the different dimensions of the concept of social suffering are interconnected in a specific social context. It is this approach that we will now pursue, considering the literature related to suffering at work and suffering in situations of severe precarity. The following analyses have a dual function: on the one hand, to subject our conception of social suffering to a test of relevance by confronting it with two modes of theorization of social suffering and by seeking to identify what is at stake in the controversies these raise, and on the other hand, laying down the foundations of a social critique in terms of social suffering, an alternative critique to that which is based on the assumption of disaffiliation. We believe that social critique must be applied not only to a general dynamic of the weakening of social supports, but also to the different interconnections of domination and disaffiliation which characterize two typical social phenomena: new forms of work and social exclusion. The clinical study of work and of severe precarity makes it possible to describe forms of suffering which characterize the one and the other.

At first glance, it may seem that only the first approach allows us to advance from suffering to a general interrogation of society, and thus to a criticism of social pathologies. But the second approach is also compatible with this type of social criticism, if the specific interweaving of social factors in suffering in determinate social spaces is related to the way in which structural social logics (like those which characterize the social relations of neoliberalism) give rise to different specific forms to domination and disaffiliation. We will develop this hypothesis in the next chapter.

Favouring the second of these two options over the first is not without consequences for the position one takes in the conflict regarding the social suffering which is played out along the borderline between disciplines. The first of the two options consists of only retaining from the conception of social suffering whatever can be integrated into a description of general social processes. It reunites with the classic sociological manœuvre of putting to one side the factors linked to life history and to specific contexts—as when Durkheim rejects the explanation of suicide by 'motivations' and 'circumstances'—in order to retain only what can be directly described in terms of general social facts.

The second approach is traceable, by contrast, to a clinical approach as proposed by clinical psychology or by a 'social clinical psychology'. When Daniel Lagache defined 'clinical psychology', he made it 'the study of the whole person in a situation', while setting it the following tasks: 'envisaging behaviour in its true perspective, tracing as faithfully as possible a concrete and human being's entire way of being and of reacting to the hold a situation has on him, seeking to establish the meaning, the structure and the genesis of this behaviour, untangling the conflicts that motivate it and the concrete steps which tend towards resolution of these conflicts'.[125] Insofar as clinical psychology attaches itself to 'the whole person in a situation', to the way in which this person experiences and reacts to the trials he or she faces, it is characterized by the attention paid to the social context of subjective disorders. In this sense, any clinical psychology is, or should be, a clinical social psychology.

The idea of clinical social psychology designates a specific approach centred chiefly on the ways in which the social is inscribed in the individual psyche and on the dynamic relations which exist between psychic structures and social systems. Its traditional concerns are the group, as an object of specific psychological investment, and the institution, as a system of rules and constraints liable to produce supports or conflicts, to give rise to collective identifications and to reinforce individual defences.[126] It is sometimes characterized by an insufficiently stratified conception of the social context and by an assumption of continuity between the psychic and the social that we have rejected by distinguishing between the psychic self and the psychosocial self. Even if the definition of the group and of the institution and, more generally, the broader problematic of clinical psychology seem too narrow to take into account the different elements of the concept of social suffering, it remains true that it is indeed within clinical psychology, completed by a sociological illumination of the general forms of domination (of class, gender and 'race') and of disaffiliation, which are played out in time in specific social contexts, that this concept can be most appropriately accommodated within a discipline. In a way, this is the project of a concrete psychology as Politzer envisaged it.

In the case of severe precarity (the situation of a 'tramp'), what seems determining at first glance seems to be the 'trajectory of suffering' itself, namely the catastrophic social career which leads an individual whose socialization has apparently been successful to his or her downfall. The concept of a 'trajectory of suffering' allows us to explain that this career depends as much on life history factors as on a social context. The condition of any social trajectory of this type is a life history marked by forms of humiliation and degradation which generally spring from physical or symbolic violence of which individuals have been victims or which they have witnessed during childhood. This biographical condition must be complemented by a contextual condition, that is, the existence of a disadvantageous or unstable social environment, in which the individual is placed in a position of structural vulnerability. It is on this triple condition (life history, contextual, structural) that an event can tip individuals over into a trajectory characterized by the progressive undermining of their different horizons of expectation, of their models for interpretating themselves and others, by the disappearance of all forms of trust in social relationships and, conseqently, by the destruction of their last relational supports and by a social incapacity which reinforces their suffering. [127]

But it would be a mistake to believe that analysis in terms of a 'trajectory of suffering' sums up all the social processes typical of severe precarity and the psychological disorders associated with it. On the one hand, the vulnerability of individuals to catastrophic social fates must be explained not only in terms of past humiliation or degradation and of weakness of support, but also by psychic structurations (implying this or that form of reaction to these weakenings of social support and to the triggering events) as well as by more general social forms (the class relationships which provide individuals with differentiated social resources in the face of hardship, the dynamics of disaffiliation which affects social support and protection). On the other hand, tramps are not only the victims of a desocialization process whose subjective logic the concept of a 'trajectory of suffering' hermeneutically captures; they are also familiar with forms of resocialization in contexts marked by situations of extreme violence and humiliation in which different structural dominations are played out. This resocialization not only shapes their logics of action, it also becomes deeply ingrained in the structures of the psyche by giving rise to quite specific disorders which, in their turn, call for a dual contextual and biographical explanation: not all individuals react in the same way to the violence and humiliation of the street and of the squats where the condemned of the city take refuge.

Conversely, what the concept of suffering at work designates is no longer a process of desocialization followed by resocialization, but the subjective effect of a stabilized type of socialization. To speak of suffering at work is, as we have said, to speak of a suffering produced by social relationships proper to a specific institutional context (the work context), but it is also to take into account the fact that the subjective effects of work relationships are mediated through 'psychic reality' in such a way that the analysis of the social context necessarily calls for the analysis of the individual life history.The analysis of the specific social context and of the life history must, moreover, be completed by taking into account other social constraints weighing on the individual and other difficulties encountered in the course of the social trajectory. In the work context, as well as outside it, the general forms of domination (of class, gender and race) and processes of disaffiliation may also on occasion intervene.

It is only in light of these biographical, contextual and structural factors that it will be possible to explain how certain individuals can manage to transform suffering produced by work into the object of a protective sublimation or neutralization, while others mobilize destructive defences against this suffering. On the basis of this analysis of the effect of work relations on the individual, we can now develop a dynamic analysis of the negative social trajectories which lead individuals either to a more or less incapacitating compensation or to a decompensation that ends in the loss of their job, even in suicide in the workplace.

The conception of social suffering that we have proposed offers a theoretical framework which can make apparent the suffering linked to exclusion and suffering at work, as well as permitting the achievement of a comparable step forward in the knowledge of the one and the other. Let us now see whether this conception also allows us to give an account of the theoretical conflicts running through the study of these topics.

CLINICAL STUDY OF WORK

The clinical study of work in France is divided between two main theoretical orientations: the psychodynamics of work and the clinical study of work activity. Based on a rich range of empirical material, they produce a similar diagnosis of current work conditions, of which we here give a summarized version,[128] before turning to their theoretical divergences.

The new working conditions make suffering at work a major issue. The current situation is indeed marked by an unprecedented mobilization of subjectivity in a context in which social support for employees is rendered fragile. Whereas Taylorism had sought to increase productivity gains by mobilizing the body in an efficacious way, post-Taylorism seeks to intensify work by mobilizing the responsibility and autonomy of employees, while struggling against dead time. In the context of a reorientation of activity towards services, the mobilization of subjectivity also extends to how to be' (*'savoir être'*) and the control of emotions. Overall quality procedures, individual evaluation of results, precarization and downsizing result furthermore in the atomization of workers' collectives and in the cooperative dimension essential to the activity of work becoming more difficult.

In this context, suffering can be explained by the conjunction of accumulated subjective pressure (designated notably by the popular category of 'stress') and new physical constraints (the number of employees assigned to repetitive tasks is increasing, like the prevalence rate of musculoskeletal disorders [MSD] and other pathologies of overstrain). Suffering also results from the contradictory injunctions of the different orders employees are subjected to: taking on the responsibility linked to autonomy in a context in which margins for manœuvre are lacking, contributing to the improvement of the business's productivity in a context of continuous downsizing, continuing to engage in work as a cooperative activity in a context of atomization of work collectives and increased pitting of employees against one another in competition. In the case of service work, suffering can be traced back, moreover, to the way in which the requirements of work 'with' the customer contradict those of work 'on' the customer, on the one hand, and the violence which results from the subjective taking on board of this contradiction and, on the other hand, to the difficulty of having to mobilize in a sustained and and public way emotions which are contradictory to the movement of one's own feelings.

At the same time, these different types of suffering are more difficult for the self to appropriate. On the one hand, it is, in actual fact, more difficult to find a recognition of the reality and of the value of work on the part of one's colleagues (due to the atomization of collectives) and within the management chain (due to the proceduralization of evaluation, to rigidity and to the unrealistic, even disorganizing aspect of the procedures). On the other hand, the development of internal and external flexibility tends to destroy the conditions for a lasting identification with one's work and, at the same time, undermine the conditions for finding validation through one's occupational identity. Under the effect of the new organization of work and the neoliberal transformations of the right to work, we observe, furthermore, a trend towards the disappearance (real as well as symbolic) of the limits of the working day, which has the effect of contaminating life outside of work more than ever with the difficulties of work and weakening the resources offered by nonwork which enables individuals to compensate—or struggle against—suffering at work.

According to Dejours, the suffering caused by these positive and negative social factors is caught up, furthermore, within the context of work itself, in a dual dynamic of deterioration. The first dynamic is the result of social obstacles to the expression of suffering, work being considered a privilege in a society affected by mass unemployment: suffering is all the more difficult to work through psychologically because it is rendered invisible and the discursive instruments for describing and articulating it are lacking. The second dynamic is linked to different managerial techniques for instrumentalizing defences (such as the valorization of the 'dirty work'), which tend to solidify these defences and to shrink individuals' margin of freedom in relation to their suffering.

If the psychodynamics of work and the clinical study of work activity differ, it is not so much in their description of contemporary pathologies of work as in their disciplinary roots and the definition they give of suffering. The psychodynamics of work constitutes an original synthesis of theoretical elements borrowed from psychoanalysis, psychosomatics, ergonomics and moral sociology.[129] The clinical study of work activity, for its part, is an element in a more traditional disciplinary framework, that of social psychology.[130] This traditionally awakens in psychoanalysts suspicions of superficiality, while psychoanalysts themselves are suspected by social psychology of placing too much emphasis on the typical forms of psychological disturbances without taking into account enough of the diversity of possible reactions to psychological hardships and the productivity of the transformative practices which can spring from them. However, the psychodynamics of work and the clinical study of work activity have numerous shared sources of inspiration (Politzer, Le Guillant) and the second, which acknowledges many theoretical advances made by the psychodynamics of work, makes use of psychoanalytic schemas. In the eyes of an external observer, what distinguishes the point of view of the psychodynamics of work and that of the clinical study of work activity are often differences of emphasis and terminology rather than fundamental divergences, even if divergences do exist.[131]

The most serious of these concern the definition of suffering. Clot rejects the claim that the work/defence pairing plays the fundamental role that Dejours gives it. Emphasizing that responses to suffering can be a defence just as much as riposte, he is led to interpret suffering in terms of 'hindered activity'.[132] It seems important to emphasize that the specific dynamic of suffering engages the individual in efforts at transforming the self and the world and that it can also involve a narrowing of the sphere of action. Nonetheless, it is difficult to agree that 'hindered activity' can offer a definition, a criterion or an explanation of suffering.

Far from contenting itself with analysing the suffering/defence relationship, the psychodynamics of work offers a theory of action which seems better able to give an account of how obstacles to action are linked to suffering. On the one hand, it relates action to the dynamism of drives and to individuals' efforts to think about their current situation and their perspectives of self-realization. On the other hand, it conceives of work activity as a 'deontic activity', that is, as an elaboration of the norms of living together within a work collective, the work activité being confronted with the hardship of the reality of work and its irreducibility to the instructions of the management chain. Ultimately, the clinical study of work is characterized by an analysis of suffering and of its psychological and social processes that is less developed and probably less convincing than that proposed by the psychodynamics of work. This is why we will take the latter as a guiding thread.

The principles of the psychodynamics of work can be summarized in a set of propositions: 1) all work activity causes suffering that the individual can only bear by using techniques that aim at transforming suffering into pleasure; 2) in this suffering there come into play the reality principle (the reality of work, constituted by the aim of the activity and the reality of the social context, represented by instructions and the management chain, on the one hand, and by types of interaction with colleagues, on the other hand) as much as the modalities of psychological investment in one's own body (the body being the first instrument of work); 3) the individual mobilizes different psychological procedures to struggle against suffering, among which are the use of a thought oriented towards appropriation of one's experience and the satisfaction of drives, individual defences (among them sublimation) and collective defences (among them 'defensive occupational ideologies'); 4) the successful transformation of suffering into pleasure depends upon specific psychic conditions (a psychic structure that is compatible with the accomplishment of drives and the mobilization of adequate defences) and on a social context that is not deficient (failures of the social context express themselves notably in the weakening of relations of intersubjective recognition of the reality and value of work and the absence of conditions for sublimation); 5) among the chief obstacles to this transformation of suffering into pleasure are relations of domination linked to employees' subordination: whether these have to do with the material embodiment of constraints (stopwatches, the rhythm of the assembly line, computer-based checking of activities, etc.) or with the orders issued by the management, they have the capacity to limit the conditions for thought and for sublimation and to create strong conflicts of ambivalence.

This theorization takes up in many respects the main theses of our conception of social suffering (which is not surprising, because it is one of the main sources of inspiration for our conception). It is, however, possible to identify three points of divergence, which will be considered in order. The first concerns the idea of positive social factors in suffering, the second the distinction between normal and abnormal suffering, the third the role of work in the interconnection of the psychic and the social.

In the work of Dejours, the definition of suffering has been subject to various modifications. In *Travail, usure mentale* (1980), suffering is defined in terms of unbearable dissatisfaction. It designates more specifically the experience of the unbearable and inevitable nature of constraints, an experience which opens the way to pathological decompensations: 'It is not so much the importance of the mental or psychic constraints involved in work that trigger suffering (even though this factor is evidently significant) as the impossibility of any development towards its alleviation. The certainty that the level of dissatisfaction that has been reached cannot diminish marks the entry of suffering onto the scene'.[133] The notion of suffering is, then, inseparable from that of collective defence, which can itself be traced back to situations in which the strenuousness of work is such that it brings about collective defence strategies, such as self-acceleration on the assembly line or ideologies of manly courage in risky jobs (as with roofers or police officers).

Beginning with the texts of the seminar *Plaisir et souffrance dans le travail* (1988), the concept of suffering is reformulated: from this point on, it is understood as an absolutely general given of the activity of work and a component of normality. Dejours writes nowadays 'that it is originary and consubstantial with all work situations since work is first of all a confrontation with systemic and technical constraints'.[134] This 'originary' suffering can be integrated into two different psychological dynamics: no longer simply the mobilization of defences, but also its transformation into pleasure (following the sublimation model).

The reformulation of the hypotheses defended in *Travail, usure mentale* has to do chiefly with a critique of the idea that work situations make it possible to identify positive factors in mental illness. Dejours emphasizes that this idea, which forms a shared assumption in traditional approaches in work pathology, is bound up with a group of mistaken theses: work organization is taken for granted as a group of inert constraints, it imposes itself upon work activity in an unequivocal way, the normal and the pathological can be interpreted as 'the mechanical result of a summation of actions and reactions'.[135] Noting, first of all, that work organization results instead from compromises between the social actors and, secondly, that prescribed activity is always different from real activity, that freedom is thus engaged in work activity and, finally, that 'normality appears right from the start as an unstable, fundamentally precarious equilibrium between suffering and defence against suffering', Dejours stops regarding pathology as his object of study and defines the psychodynamics of work as the study of the psychic and intersubjective dynamics which allows the individual to cope with suffering at work.

It is striking that this shift leads to withdrawing the notion of positive social factors in suffering and that it is correlated with a certain ontologization of suffering. Starting from the idea that suffering is fundamentally bodily (in the sense that it is always experienced in the body) and interpreting it, in light of Michel Henry's ideas, as the very form of original affectivity, Dejours and Molinier are led to posit suffering as a fundamental ontological structure: 'ontologically primary, existential and prior to work'.[136] This claim seems disputable. That suffering is essential to affectivity is more than contestable if, for example, there exists something like a primary eroticism or if play defines a fundamental affective function.

The idea of the originary status of suffering goes hand in hand with the idea according to which the social context only intervenes in the struggle against suffering, in such a way that the social factors of suffering are reduced to negative factors. The ontologization of suffering thus gives rise to an explanatory deficit, if not to a relativization of the role played by the positive social factors in suffering. By this the limits of ontologization of suffering are also revealed. The enquiries of researchers working with psychodynamic frameworks unceasingly emphasize, in fact, the importance of the specific constraints bearing on work in general, as a repetitive activity subject to cooperative and technical constraints, and on salaried work in particular, with the dominations which accompany it. Furthermore, it is hard to agree that a factor contributing to the transformation of suffering into pleasure, such as recognition, can only explain social suffering by default. Relationships of negative recognition such as invisibilization (of staff located on the lowest rung of the work hierarchy ladder) and devalorization (of unqualified staff) are a source of subjective suffering. It is to this type of causality, and to its influence on depressive experiences, that *Travail, usure mentale* refers in raising the three recurrent themes of workers' discourse: indignity (the shame of being made robotic, depersonalized, dirty), uselessness (lack of representation of the usefulness of the work within and outside the firm) and disqualification.[137] Furthermore, domination seems to intervene at once as a negative factor in suffering (as an obstacle to thought and sublimation) and as a positive factor (a factor of ambivalence in relation to our own obedience, even in relation to our own aggressiveness). Even if these ideas are still present in its clinical studies and its theory, the psychodynamics of work no longer allots them a main role as positive factors of suffering.

A second topic of debate has to do with the distinction between normal and abnormal suffering. In the thought of Dejours, the idea of health designates an ideal that is never attained, and normality is the space which separates health from illness. It is thus unfair to reproach him for confusing health with conformity to norms and to argue against him that it is characterized rather by the capacity to create norms:[138] his concept of 'normal' is not defined by 'norms' but by the precarious balance which indicates that at least partial success has been achieved in a struggle against suffering.

It remains to specify the way in which the distinction between 'suffering normality' and pathology can be founded and in what precisely it consists. On this point, the psychodynamics of work does not seem to defend an unequivocal position. In *Plaisir et souffrance au travail*, Dejours used the term 'suffering' to designate nonpathological disturbances, that is to say precisely one of the characteristics of the space (of 'normality') which separates health from illness. In 'De la psychopathologie à la dynamique du travail' (1993), the concept of suffering comes to define a general characteristic of work (ordinary suffering), which leads to an implicit distinction between a normal suffering (transformed by a successful struggle against suffering) and an abnormal suffering: 'If the dynamic of recognition is paralysed, suffering can no longer be transformed into pleasure, it can no longer find meaning. In such a case, it can only accumulate and draw the subject into a pathogenic dynamic leading finally to psychiatric or somatic decompensation. Between suffering and illness can be inserted defensive strategies which have been discovered since the beginnings of the psychopathology of work'.[139] Molinier makes use of another conceptual pair to express these same distinctions: 'The notions of "creative suffering" and of "pathogenic suffering" do not designate the existence of *two* different sufferings, but designate the different fates of *the one and only* type of suffering'.[140]

Two theses could be debated here: Is it really illegitimate to distinguish different types of suffering and are there only two fates of suffering? Insofar as originary suffering never exists in a pure state but is always caught in transformations which result from a struggle against it, we could just as well say that 'suffering' only exists as an abstraction because what actually exists is only 'creative sufferings' and 'pathogenic sufferings'—here again, it seems, we would come across our 'normal suffering' and our 'pathogenic suffering'. Moreover, it seems difficult to distinguish only between 'creative suffering' and 'pathogenic suffering' without taking into account the possible pathological fate of pathogenic suffering—thus we again encounter our distinction among normal, pathogenic and pathological suffering.

One could certainly dispute the idea that the distinction between 'creative suffering' and 'pathogenic suffering' corresponds, in effect, to our distinction between 'normal suffering' and 'pathogenic suffering'. The psychodynamics of work has accumulated a vast amount of clinical material making it possible to back up the idea that the struggle against suffering does not only take the form of defensive strategies and that as well as the (psychological) mechanism of sublimation, the psychic logics of recognition and construction of identity through work activity play a determining role in the transformation of suffering into pleasure (it also takes the view that 'ethical suffering', which corresponds to our 'moral suffering', is part of this last process). Whereas we seemed to be of the opinion that the intervention of psychoneurotic defences characterizes the shift from normal suffering to pathological suffering, Molinier emphasizes that these defensive strategies come into play in normal suffering: 'The fate of creative suffering is to transform itself into pleasure and into a structuring experience. The fate of pathogenic suffering is the illness which comes into play when defences no longer fulfil their protective function'.[141]

However, if we trace psychoneurotic defences back to pathogenic suffering, this is not to deny that they are always at work in health (just as neurotic tendencies are present in it), but to emphasize that these defensive strategies can lead to psychological structures that are dominated by a defensive rigidification, marked by fixation in a type of adaptation synonymous with the loss of the normativity which defines health and with a new form of fragility. In other words, defences are not pathogenic in themselves, but a certain type of hegemonic immobilization of defences can tip the individual over into a pathogenic dynamic. The psychodynamics of work seems moreover to make use of this type of distinction when it explains that collective defences can supplement individual defences, to help individuals remain in normality, while at the same time distinguishing among these collective defences 'defensive occupational ideologies' of a pathogenic nature, where conformity to the defensive strategy becomes a criterion for distinguishing friends from enemies, and a false promise of happiness (for example in the ideology of manly courage in certain risky occupations). [142]

A third debate is connected with the role of work in the interrelation of the psychic and the social. Dejours defends a radical thesis which ends up making the psychodynamics of work the only possible theory of social suffering: 'A Key conclusion of the psychodynamics of work ends is that there is no direct link between the subject of the unconscious and the social field. This relationship is always mediated by the reference to an action on the real which mobilises work activity. In this, the psychodynamics of work confirms its distinctiveness with respect to psychosociology, which most often seeks to grasp a direct relationshp between subject and society, as a result of its analysis of small groups'. [143]

This thesis calls for several explanatory remarks. It is first of all based on the argument for the centrality of work: love and work are the only two activities which cause subjectivation effects deep enough to alter psychic structures, and they produce the same effects on mental health: they are capable of sustaining individuals who are not 'doing well', but also of profoundly weakening those who are 'doing well'. But work is the only one of these two activities which is social in a strong sense, and no other social activity can bring about this type of effect. Moreover, this thesis is based on the idea that the processes which govern the individual psyche are of another character than those which govern society (the social bond cannot be conceived of as the unity of a crowd ensured by narcissistic projections onto a 'leader') [144] and that nowhere else but in work are individuals confronted with the reality of the social world (that of the material and symbolic objects which mediate their work activity, but also the constraints of interaction in the work collective and the hierarchical constraints proper to salaried work institutions).

Each of these arguments has in our eyes an undeniable relevance, but it is not obvious that they imply a justification of the hegemony of the psychodynamics of work with respect to social suffering. In reality, the importance of the psychic stakes of work does not stop mental health from depending on other factors than work activity strictly speaking: the analysis of the psychological effects of the denial of recognition (the specific effects of racism and colonialism studied by Du Bois and Fanon, for example[145]) and the study of the different stages which characterize trajectories of suffering (the specific effect of the deteriorations of the environment outside work) prove the contrary. It is in the clinical study of severe precarity that the specific effects of the components of the trajectories of suffering which cannot be traced back to work are best brought to light.

This type of clinical study describes a form of suffering which no doubt negatively proves the importance of work for mental health, as Dejours and Clot emphasize,[146] but whose characteristic traits cannot be explained by the lack of work alone. In Dejours's view, suffering linked to exclusion is chiefly explained by lack of the protections which should surround work for it to fulfil its structuring function; not only does unemployment constitute a deprivation of work, but the phenomenon of exclusion also includes the condemnation of entire populations to forms of work characterized by extreme precarity (temporary work) or by a relationship with violence (under the two symmetrical forms of drug-related crime and security work, which, together with social work, are often the only legal occupational avenues for 'inner-city youth'). According to Clot, it is within the framework of a theory of psychological function of work that we must analyse the subjective impact of social exclusion, which he analyzes using the model of unemployment, itself conceived of as a deprivation of work. The psychological function of work has to do with its capacity to produce specific subjectivation effects. The demanding experience of reality and of cooperation brings about, in work, a process of distancing from our other concerns which constitutes one of the main conditions for the subjective appropriation of the hardships of existence.[147] When work is lacking, individuals have difficulty detaching themselves from their problems, as is illustrated by the profiles of the long-term unemployed, crushed by a feeling of uselessness.[148] If the explanatory power of the psychodynamics of work and the clinical study of work activity is undeniable with regard to exclusion, these theoretical undertakings, developed to address another topic, can nevertheless only deal with one part of the data relevant in the study of exclusion.

CLINICAL STUDY OF SEVERE PRECARITY

The notion of the clinical study of severe precarity refers here to the totality of observations and theoretical and therapeutic proposals connected with the particular aspect of exclusion exemplified by the extreme social situations of individuals living on the street. It thus constitutes only a part of the clinical study of exclusion, but we shall see that its theoretical proposals often lead it to speak of exclusion and precarity in a more general way.

Like the clinical study of work, the clinical study of severe precarity uses tools from psychoanalysis and clinical psychology, it focuses on psychological disorders whose social dimension is fundamental, it refuses to describe its subjects in the classical terms of psychiatric nosography and it sets up therapeutic procedures using forms of intervention in the specific social context in which the individuals concerned live. Both the clinical study of work and the clinical study of severe precarity refer to suffering in a situation, but they relate to social situations in different ways.

In the case of the clinical study of work, situations produce a psychological dynamic which is difficult to bear and either leads individuals to an exit from the situation (in the form of resignation from job, decompensation, even suicide) or provokes a questioning of the social characteristics of the situation (a crisis of the organization of work which motivates a recourse to clinicians of work or other forms of collective action); the first outcome can give rise to the second. The aim of intervention in the workplace by a clinician is to contribute to the collective development of the understanding of suffering at work, with a view to bringing to light the reality of work, of identifying the social component of the difficulties (thus abandoning self-incrimination or moral denunication of the 'harassment' type) and giving the individuals concerned the possibility of acting collectively on the context of their work activity.

The clinical study of severe precarity, for its part, takes on its subjects in the aftermath of catastrophic social trajectories. The type of defence brought into play during these trajectories leads these subjects to a situation in which they find themselves stuck fast in a condition marked by a dual disconnection: in relation to reality and in relation to others. Treatment practices do not aim so much at contributing to a personal or collective elaboration of the psychological or social factors of their current condition so much as at restoring the minimum level of a relation to oneself and to reality which permits the forming of social bonds, the reestablishment of self-confidence and the possibility of facing reality, of projecting oneself into the future. [149]

As we mentioned at the end of the third section of this chapter, we are here dealing with two totally different forms of the interweaving of biographical and social factors in social suffering, with two types of dynamic relation between social condition and social trajectory. We can also anticipate that the social dimension of suffering will be thought of within almost contrary schemas: while the theatre of suffering at work is a universe saturated with social and intersubjective constraints, the psychological suffering specific to severe precarity is characterized by a spiral of reciprocal intensification of desocialization and its psychological effects: the 'clinical picture of desocialisation' [150] is characterized by a sort of sacrifice by the individual of his or her own social life (described by notions such as 'loss of social objects', [151] 'fragility of bonds' [152] or 'melancholization of the social bond' [153]). Nevertheless, this suffering can also be explained in terms of the dual causality of the positive and negative social factors in suffering.

The presentation of the debates related to suffering is not so easy here. While the psychodynamics of work and the clinical study of work activity are both successors to the psychopathology of work, the clinical study of severe precarity confronts subjects who call into question the paradigms of psychiatry, psychoanalysis and social psychology. Even if a clinical psychology inspired by psychoanalysis seems called for, nothing allows us to decide a priori the way in which relevant hypotheses should be formed. Furthermore, certain elements of the clinical picture seem to call for approaches of the psychosocial type with Meadian inspiration, even more directly than for psychoanalytical approaches. A reference to Winnicott makes it sometimes possible to join these two types of inspiration. [154] In the clinical study of severe precarity, theoretical concepts, paradigms and hypotheses vary and today they still only define a field of research and controversy. In what follows, we will deal with the two following questions: Is the clinical study of severe precarity really a clinical study of suffering and, if yes, in what sense can we speak of suffering? What are the factors making it possible to give an account of the symptoms proper to the situation of severe precarity?

The idea that the clinical study of severe precarity is a clinical study of social suffering is the subject of two symmetrical objections: for some, the subjective harm observed does not really have a social origin; for others, it does not merit being described in terms of suffering. The first position is formulated in the work of Patrice Declerck, who, opposing the view of a tramp as a victim of the economic crisis, maintains that the desocialization evident in his behaviour is, on the contrary, the effect of a psychic structure whose origins go back to life in the womb. The syndrome of desocialization does have suffering as its distinctive indicator, but it is an originary suffering based on an 'anal foreclosure': 'The psychoanalyst can imagine that the subject's suffering can only be perceived by him on condition of emerging from a background (of sensations, affects, memories etc.) from which it is distinguished. A suffering deeply immersed in the psyche of the subject, a suffering dating from forever, which occupies the entire psychic stage, would no longer be perceptible to him. This is to form the hypothesis of a background suffering which not only pervades and permanently accompanies the subject, but has become the subject him- or herself, and constitutes a psychic signature'.[155]

This hypothesis is as debatable as the book was successful, a book which is anyway more interesting for its ethnographic dimension than for the theory accompanying it. The simple fact that there are suitable treatment mechanisms proves that the suffering of homeless people is not the sign of such a primordial illness. As well as encouraging the development of the theory of new treatment practices, our objection leads us to suspect that Declerck is developing the theory of the failure of his own mode of treatment rather than that of the individuals he dealt with using a wrong type of treatment. In the context of the hospital downsizing, it is undeniable that different forms of psychosis lead to individuals ending up on the street.[156] But as Olivier Douville emphasizes, the clinician must take note of three things: 1) the social conditions of the street have specific subjective impacts which can be extremely severe; 2) the street can function as a specific form of socialization, even of stabilization, of certain psychotic profiles; 3) but it can also be an environment that further aggravates these profiles.[157]

Unpacking the first observation leads to a conception of social suffering which jointly mobilizes consideration of the social and psychodynamic factors. As Sylvie Quesemand Zucca comments, 'For some, ending up on the street is evidence of long-"forgotten" psychic traumas onto which are grafted all kinds of violence, which over time merge together. The survival mode of the street multiplies repetitions of trauma, continously reminding the man or woman of old wounds that have not scarred over. The memory of what once was seems, then, to cause splitting, but also denials'.[158] Even if the specific social context of the street affects the aetiology of a suffering which can in this sense be called social, this action is always mediated by the specific structures of an individual psyche. The situation in the street cannot itself be correctly understood without reference to the traumatic experience of crossing thresholds which have led from normal life to a situation of severe exclusion.

Today, nearly all practitioners of the clinical study of severe precarity consider that there are certain kinds of subjective harm linked to the forms of desocialization characteristic of the street, and that a double social context explains this subjective damage: that which, at an earlier date, played a role in the catastrophic social trajectory and that of the violence, the humiliations and the fears typical of the street.[159] An approach in terms of social suffering is thus required in a double sense.

A second objection concerns the relevance of the use of the notion of suffering to describe the subjective harm of severe exclusion. A first argument involves the worry, expressed by Sylvie Quesemand Zucca, 'that this notion licenses an amalgamation with everything that features as a symptom in severe precarity'.[160] There are two ways of responding to this point: demonstrating that the specific symptoms of severe precarity are explained by a specific type of defence against suffering and demonstrating that suffering takes a specific form due to a specific syndrome of precarity. To illustrate this second response, we could base our argument on the fact that severe precarity is prominently characterized by a loss of the corporeal and social analysis of psychic life, a loss which pushes the individual into a state of distress marked by a 'polymorphy of symptoms', by a lack of distinction between psychological, physical and external (specifically social) reality, and that this results in a 'diffuse' psychological suffering.[161]

It is also worth emphasizing that the clinical study of severe precarity is a clinical study of survival and that, as such, it can only be conceived of as involving the mobilization of defences against particularly acute forms of suffering. This makes it possible to explain the recourse to different types of narcotic anaesthetising agents, and particularly to alcohol, so decisive in the clinical picture of severe precarity.[162] It also makes it possible to give an account of the processes of 'progressive psychic anaesthesia',[163] which include renunciation of the body (revealed by desensitization, but also by the abandonment of one's body to defilement and illness),[164] even renunciation of thought and of certain essential dynamics of psychic life,[165] and the 'total disintegration of subjectivity'[166] through denial and splitting. It also makes it possible to explain a type of conjoined omnipresence and disappearance of suffering, which revives the hypothesis of a 'background suffering'. Finally, it enables us to understand that self-inflicted suffering can also constitute an attempt to recover contact with oneself, as in the case of self-harm.

Ferenczi noted long ago that 'as soon as the quantity and nature of suffering surpass a person's capacity for integration, one gives up, one can no longer stand it, it is no longer worth grasping these painful things together as a whole, one breaks into pieces. I no longer suffer, I even cease to exist, at least as a total self'.[167] In this way he emphasized that suffering includes thresholds and degrees and that taking these into account makes it possible to bring to light specific psychodynamic processes. These seem to be absolutely decisive in accounting for the clinical picture of precarity because in many of its features it represents a clinical picture of survival in a situation of unbearable suffering.

But the argument from the clinical picture of survival raises an objection in its turn. One can indeed argue that it is no longer relevant to speak of suffering to describe the subjective impact of extreme social situations such as concentration camps or life on the street. According to André Roussillon, the severity of the traumatic impact of these situations can be measured by its incommunicable aspect. At this point, the term 'suffering' can cause its user to run the risk of euphemization when it is applied to severe precarity: 'The concept of psychic suffering is the concept most often used, but suffering designates an affect which has a meaning, it belongs to the human condition; extreme situations confront an affect that it would be better to define as "acute pain", sometimes physical pain, but above all psychic pain, pain without "acceptable meaning", dehumanising pain'.[168]

The term 'psychic pain' is, however, difficult to apply here as it indicates an impact which does not have the same duration as suffering and causes us to lose sight of the combined suffering/defence mechanism which remains central in the work of Roussilon. Ultimately it seems that his arguments lead to a distinction between different types of suffering rather than to an opposition between suffering and psychic pain. To clarify the way in which the clinical study of severe precarity backs up this type of distinction, let us turn to Jean Furtos, who has attempted to defend the relevance of the use of the concept of 'psychic suffering' as part of a typological approach to suffering.

As we explained in the first chapter, the term 'psychic suffering' is often used in a general sense with respect to severe precarity (it corresponds to our 'social suffering'), whereas we have given a more restricted meaning to this notion (making it a form of psychological suffering, itself distinguished from physical suffering). Apart from this terminological divergence, Furtos's typology corresponds to ours (which is not surprising in this case either, as his clinical study was one of our sources of inspiration).

Starting from a definition of mental health as a capacity to cope with suffering, he distinguishes 'a suffering which helps us to live; a suffering which begins to prevent us from living; a suffering which prevents us from suffering, thus from living'.[169] The first suffering corresponds to our 'normal suffering', in which suffering constitutes an object and a component of the work of the appropriation of the self and the world which defines health: 'We must underline the important role of the suffering which maintains the link with oneself and with others: it is agonic in the etymological sense of the struggle (*agon*) thanks to which the subject does not give up . . . ; we are in a zone of sound mental health where suffering does not prevent us from acting'.[170] The social conditions required for suffering to retain this form are work, on the one hand, and a stable and valorizing social situation, on the other. By contrast, the loss of these 'social objects', of these fundamental bases of security, which allow individuals to believe in the promise of narcissistic contracts, contribute to the emergence of other forms of suffering.[171] The second kind of suffering corresponds to our 'pathogenic suffering'. It takes two different forms. One relates to types of psychic precarity in which the fear of the loss of social objects is accompanied by stress, self-devaluation and loss of confidence: 'We are in a zone of pre-pathology, even of acknowledged pathologies of the somatic, depressive or pseudo-depressive type'.[172] This suffering is associated with the precarization of work, which leads to stress and fear of breakdown by causing a first level of vulnerability of the narcissistic contract.[173] The other corresponds to psychic precarity which is explained by the effective loss of social objects, that is to say to the subjective difficulties which are met in the field of social work, which have sometimes been grouped together under the concept of 'syndrome of exclusion':[174] 'Let us cite . . . shame and discouragement, which, along with inhibition, constitute in the view of the psychiatrist Jean Maisondieu the triad of exclusion'.[175] The social context of this suffering is an effective loss of social objects, which leads to increased vulnerability.[176]

The concept of 'suffering which begins to prevent us from living' takes on meaning not in the framework of a general theory of suffering but in that of a theory of the psychosocial processes which can lead to severe precarity. It aims to theoretically formulate the observation that exclusion is the stepping stone to severe precarity not only from a social, but also from a psychological point of view. The invalidating dimension of this suffering is really a factor in play in the catastrophic trajectories which can lead to severe precarity. But the distinction between suffering which 'begins to prevent us from living' and that which 'prevents us from living' also has the function of identifying what separates the clinical picture of exclusion from that of severe precarity, for which Furtos reserves the concept of 'self-exclusion syndrome'.[177] In the context of the loss of social objects and the fracturing (or the reversal) of narcissism, suffering takes the form of terror, of despair, and it leads to a mobilization of paradoxical defences to avoid psychic agony and breakdown.[178]

Drawing inspiration from Roussillon's clinical study of survival, he thus emphasizes that the reality of subjective disturbances cannot be explained simply by the effect of a failing or traumatizing environment; we must also take into account the strategies employed to cope with a suffering that has become unbearable due to a situation of radical lack and of violences of various kinds: 'Choosing the term self-exclusion makes it possible to highlight the activity of the human subject in certain situations where, to survive, she is obliged to exclude herself from her own subjectivity. So as not to suffer the intolerable, she cuts herself off from her suffering, anaesthetises itself. To live, she prevents herself from living, an extremely serious paradox'.[179] This provides an explanation for the inhibition of thought and emotion, the partial anaesthesia of the body, the abolition of shame, and self-neglect, but also for sudden upsurges of violence, as soon as the guard is lowered under the effect of alcohol or of a restoring of confidence (return of anaesthesia).[180] To describe the specific nature of this third stage of suffering, we could also say that it is marked by different forms of identification with the unbearable, as witnessed by forms of identification with the scrap.[181] We could also say of this third stage that it consists in a passage from a struggle against suffering that is still governed by the pleasure principle to a struggle governed by the death drive,[182] as indicated most notably by what has been termed a process of 'asphaltization'.[183]

Distinguishing among these three forms of suffering allows us, then, to establish a continuum between pathogenic suffering and pathological suffering which shows at once the irreducible specificity of severe precarity and its general link with the difficulties experienced in a situation of exclusion. It is also the indicator that the analysis of the social factors of severe precarity cannot be limited to the study of the situation of severe precarity itself, in abstraction from the general social processes which cause exclusion.

What, then, are the social factors which make it possible to speak of social suffering in the case of severe precarity? The answers are necesarily complex because they must adopt a point of view that is at once dynamic and static. From the dynamic point of view, that of the trajectories of suffering, two types of process can be mentioned. The first can be traced back to negative social factors. It is the general process of social disaffilation which is in question here, either in the form of precarization and the fear of losing social objects that it implies or in the form of exclusion (unemployment, loss of housing, breakdown of significant relationships) and of the effective loss of stable and valorizing intersubjective relationships with which it is bound up. The traces of this lack of social world remain present in the reality of the suffering of severe precarity, and perhaps it is against this which the syndrome of self-exclusion takes shape: 'Disaffiliation, disqualification are notions which help us to identify something of the social history of the patient, of the meaning or the lack of meaning of which it conveys at the symbolic level'.[184]

But the social context can also intervene as a positive factor. It is chiefly under the concept of trauma that it is identified in this case. The traumatic impact of collective redundancies and their triggering role in catastrophic social trajectories are then emphasized. Stress is also put on the fact that traumatic experiences are accompanied by effects of identity and relationship breakdown and of a desymbolization and an identification with suffering that can also be observed in situations of severe precarity.[185] Past traumas are certainly part of the suffering of individuals in situations of severe precarity, as witnessed specifically by the delusional narratives with which they often seek to make public, in the street, their own story.[186] To be sure, not all traumatic effects are connected with social logics, but potentially traumatic violence is nonetheless shared out in an unequal way and, from the macrosocial point of view, the analysis of the distribution of potentially traumatic events, as well as of the probability of experiencing them in a manner that is actually traumatizing, certainly leads to an intersection of an analysis in terms of disaffiliation with an account of the structures of domination.

The analysis of trajectories of suffering must combine the two explanations: an explanation by positive social factors (potentially traumatising collective events, forms of domination) and an explanation by negative social factors (disaffiliations). A potentially traumatizing event can only become so as a function of the specific psychic balance of an individual, and his or her social support also has direct implications for the individual's capacity to appropriate suffering. But specifically, the context of social disaffiliation,[187] like that of the sudden destructuring of social groups,[188] produce specific effects of the weakening of collective supports. Within groups in a situation of collective weakening, the most socially vulnerable and those who are situated at the intersection of different types of domination will in addition risk experiencing traumatic harm in the form of violence exercised by the group.[189]

Suffering is social, then, mainly from the point of view of the catastrophic trajectories which lead to the street. The breaking of bonds is so determinant in the symptoms specific to the psychic suffering of severe precarity and is so active in what is played out over and over again in interactions among homeless people and with social workers (interactions which are often structured by a repetition of 'failed encounters', in which the subject ends up cutting off his or her relation to the other by divorcing him- or herself from the language[190]) that, at the end point of catastrophic trajectories also, in the specific social context of the street, the squat and the homeless shelter, suffering no longer seems explicable by negative social factors. But the idea of an explanation in negative terms is paradoxical here anyway. In actual fact, if severe precarity is indeed characterized by an absence of stable and valorizing intersubjective relationships, this lack of a social context is an effect just as much as a cause because, very often, it is the individuals themselves who cut themselves off from social relationships. Already, in the trajectories of suffering, the weakness of social support bolstered a suffering which in return caused further weakening. But here, the breaking of bonds is a protection against suffering. It thus appears as an expression of suffering in interactions, but equally as a cause or a recoil effect of suffering.

The expression of suffering in interaction takes numerous forms: that of avoidance of the conditions for any encounter, that of the intrusion of markers that are normally supressed during interaction (resurgence from the interior of the body, the general effects of lack of shame) and that of indecent exposure. The malaise experienced during contact with homeless people by passersby as well as by those who take care of them does confirm one of the ideas put forward in the first chapter, to explain the difficulty of expressing suffering: the grammar of ordinary interactions is oriented towards an intersubjective validation which always presupposes forms of dissimulation of suffering. As Olivier Douville comments, 'these patients, caught in the reality of exclusion, can free some of our repressions. They render our relation to our own bodies awkward, embarrassing, difficult to bear, they seriously disrupt our narcissism'.[191] As noted by Jean-Pierre Martin, 'the extreme destitution, the expressed suffering, the violence of the street to which they witness deeply affect the interlocutor as existential wounds, an unspoken threat. After these encounters, the word which comes to mind each time is "exhaustion"'.[192]

But suffering itself can end up disappearing. As Sylvie Quesemand Zucca emphasizes, when bodily wounds become chronic, something observable in certain severely excluded people, this must be interpreted as an attempt to exist in the eyes of others and of oneself, in other words, as an effort at reestablishing self-awareness, 'as though [the] wound, sometimes monstruous, represented itself the ultimate proof of an existence in the world'.[193] The dramatic expression of suffering is sometimes, no doubt, a means of existing in the eyes of others, despite everything. Conversely, in the context of the invisibilization and social death specific to severe precarity, the loss of the regard of others and of the possibility of announcing one's suffering to them will play a role in corporeal and psychological anaesthesia.

To give an account of these intersubjective aspects of suffering, we must analyse it not only as corporeal and psychic suffering, but also as psychosocial suffering. The clinical picture of severe precarity can be traced back in different ways to relations of recognition. If the destruction of the narcissistic mirror, which characterizes this clinical picture, must be explained psychodynamically in terms of defences and psychological survival strategies, it must doubtless also be explained according to the psychosocial logic which makes one's self-image depend on the gaze of others. It is doubtless also because they no longer exist in the eyes of others that certain severely excluded people cease to invest their own image libidinally (this is expressed notably in an avoidance of mirrors) and even lose the image of themselves.[194]

But relations of recognition do not only have an effect as a negative social factor in this suffering. If severe precarity no longer bears the traces of stable and valorizing recognition, it is nevertheless organized by a multiplicity of social relationships which the inhabitants of the street or of squats have both among themselves and with others. From this standpoint, suffering is explained anew by positive social factors. For these social relationships are indeed marked by instability, unpredictable violence and constant humiliation. In this clinical picture, the question of shame is central, a shame often related by former sufferers from severe exclusion to the contempt conveyed by the gaze of others, a humiliation whose subjective effects are so deep that they appear almost indelible.[195] This shame amounts to a narcissistic suffering so intense that it too can contribute to the destruction of the narcissistic mirror and hence to the shamelessness which so often characterizes the clinical picture.

NOTES

1. Ch. Laval, *Les réaménagements de la relation d'aide à l'épreuve de la souffrance psychique* (doctoral thesis, Lyon II, 2003), 11.

2. Fassin, *Des maux indicibles*.

3. For the first principle, see the critique of Marxist and Nietzchean functionalism in the introduction to Weber, 'The Social Psychology of World Religions'; Weber, *The Protestant Ethic and the Spirit of Capitalism* (New York: Oxford University Press, 2011), first part, second section.

4. For an illustration of this principle, see Renault, 'Le discours du respect'.

5. This analysis is developed in the French version of this work.

6. Perrot, *Enquêtes sur la condition ouvrière en France au 19e siècle*, 30: 'Over and above the acuity of their vision, doctors brought to social research a broad set of scientific requirements and practices; a concern for measurement, for the observation of a series of facts, for correlations, for causal connections'.

7. On the relationship between 'social science' and 'political economy' in the first half of the nineteenth century, see G. Procacci, *Gouverner la misère. La question sociale en France, 1789–1848* (Paris: Seuil, 1993), 161 et seq. Analysing the politics of health in the eighteenth century, Foucault had already suggested: 'A "medico-administrative" knowledge begins to develop concerning society, its health and sickness, its conditions of life, housing and habits; this serves as the basic core for the "social economy" and sociology of the nineteenth century' ('The Politics of Health in the Eighteenth Century', in *Power. Essential Works of Michel Foucault* [New York: The New Press, 2000], 3:100).

8. This analysis is developed in chapter 4 of the French version of this work.

9. In attempting to develop a coherent conception of social suffering, we do not claim to deliver a series of definitive decisions on the nature of suffering and its social dimension; we do not believe, either, that we are forging a concept from the point of view of a new psychosocial science which, by philosophical decree, could take the place of psychology, sociology, medical anthropology or ethnopsychiatry. The aim is rather to proceed with an attempt at critical synthesis based on theoretical elements developed by the human sciences, whether in the classics or by the main protagonists in the contemporary debate on social suffering.

10. On the role of religion as a traditional form of justification in the face of suffering associated with inequalities, see Weber, 'The Social Psychology of World Religions', 270–72.

11. Farge et al., *Sans visages*, 28: 'The great catastrophe of 1784, during which the generality of Rouen alone would count 34,950 beggars and workers would sell their furniture, forming long processions of the wretched heading towards the capital, would send panic through France'; 'Between the 1st of July of 1722 and the 11th of November of 1731, the registers of the Bicêtre hospital in Paris would record the entry into the hospital of more than 30,000 beggars'.

12. Ibid., 28–29.

13. On this subject, see A. Clément, 'La représentation du pauvre dans la pensée économique classique (1780–1880)', *Storia del Pensiero Economico* Vol. 1, no 1 (2004), 53–84, which we follow here.

14. Th. R. Malthus, *An Essay on the Principle of Population*, sixth edition, in *The Works of Thomas Robert Malthus* (London: Wrigley and Pickering, 1986), 3:536.

15. On this subject, see A. Rabinbach, *The Human Motor: Energy, Fatigue and the Rise of Modernity* (New York: Basic Books, 1990), and F. Vatin, *Le travail. Économie et physique. 1780–1830* (Paris: PUF, 1993).

16. Th. R. Malthus, *An Essay on the Principle of Population*, first edition (London: Penguin Books, 1970), 98.

17. Ibid., 355.

18. E. Buret, *De la misère des classes laborieuses en Angleterre et en France: de la nature de la misère, de son existence, de ses effets, de ses causes, et de l'insuffisance des remèdes qu'on lui a opposés jusqu'ici, avec les moyens propres à en affranchir les sociétés* (Paris: Paulin, 1840), 1:46.

19. Ibid., 13: 'Is not the study of poverty an integral and necessary part of political or social economy, or of the physiology of society, as some would call it?'

20. Ibid.

21. Ibid., 34.

22. Ibid., 43.

23. Ibid., 41.

24. Ibid., 80: 'However much one may preach providence, recommend to the poor that precious capacity which embraces the future in its conceptions, encourage economy and sobriety, one will not prevent the poor from being improvident, from being prodigal and intemperate, if they remain subject to an economic regimen which . . . forcibly pushes them to improvidence, prodigality and intemperance'.

25. Ibid., 77.

26. For an overall introduction to 'social economy' in the first half of the nineteenth century, see Procacci, *Gouverner la misère*, 161–225.

27. L. R. Villermé, *Tableau de l'état physique et moral des ouvriers employés dans les manufactures de coton, de laine et de soie* (work undertaken by order of the Académie des sciences morales et politiques; Paris: J. Renouard, 1840), 2:253–55: 'As for the spinners and weavers, whose life at all stages has the highest mortality rate (depending on age, three times, double and even several times that of cotton printers, millers, manufacturers) it has doubtless not been forgotten how poor they are, how thin, how haggard with hunger and fatigue. . . . The excessive mortality which cuts down the families of the weavers and cotton spinners of Mulhouse more particularly affects the earliest stages of life. In reality, while half the children born in the class of manufacturers, businessmen and factory directors will reach their twenty-ninth year, half of the children of weavers and of humble spinners will have ceased to exist, and this we scarcely dare to believe, before having reached the age of two years. . . . But how can we admit that our state of society actually implies conditions in which death devours half of the infants before they have reached the age of two? What privations, what sufferings does that not lead us to imagine?'

28. Ibid., 349.

29. Ibid., 258.

30. See L. R. Villermé, *Sur les cités ouvrières* (Paris: J.-B. Baillière, 1850).

31. L. R. Villermé, *Des organisations ouvrières* (Paris: Imprimeries de Firmin-Didot frères, 1850), 99: 'I hope that the heads of industry will apply themselves to further development to

the very useful system of bonuses, and that they will concern themselves more with the good conduct, the moral instruction and the improvement of their workers'.

32. Ibid., 99–100.

33. Villermé, *Sur les cités ouvrières*, 19.

34. A. E. Cherbuliez, *Étude sur les causes de la misère tant morale que physique et sur les moyens d'y porter remède* (Paris: Guillaumin, 1853), 121.

35. It is sometimes maintained that this approach is bound up with a projection of a distinction of the normal and the pathological onto the social body and that this is entirely characteristic of the social medicine of the time (of which Villermé is moreover a representative) (Procacci, *Gouverner la misère*, 1993). It is true that medicine can back up the liberal denial of social suffering in different ways, but we shall see that the social medicine of the first half of the nineteenth century also developed other conceptions of social suffering and proposed another model of social pathology. Ultimately, what seems decisive for social economy is more the economic measurement of what is necessary and what is incidental than the medical distinction between the normal and the pathological.

36. M. Loriol, *Le temps de la fatigue. La gestion sociale du mal-être au travail* (Paris: Anthropos, 2000), 35.

37. Ibid., 42.

38. Ibid., 45.

39. Ibid., 68 et seq.; see also F. Vatin, *Le travail, sciences et société* (Brussels: Éditions de l'université de Bruxelles, 1999).

40. Loriol, *Le temps de la fatigue*, 93.

41. Ibid.

42. O. Lewis, *La vida: A Puerto Rican Family in the Culture of Poverty* (New York, San Juan: 1967; Paris: Gallimard, 1969). For a critique of this type of approach, see Bourgois, *In Search of Respect*, 16–18.

43. Here again, cultural relativism could well be an easy defence for an observer faced with the suffering he or she observes in another. Its effect is to enclose social groups in situations that the observer refuses to judge, but that those concerned may judge severely. On these questions, see Devereux, *De l'angoisse à la méthode*, 131 et seq.

44. See the synthesis presented by R. H. Shryock, *The Development of Modern Medicine: An Interpretation of the Social and Scientific Factors Involved* (New York: Alfred A. Knopf, 1936). For a discussion of the catastrophist interpretation of the trajectory of the standard of living and of living conditions during this period, see Thompson, *The Making of the English Working Class*, part two.

45. See the synthesis by Perrot, *Les enquêtes ouvrières*.

46. Jules Guérin was head editor of the *Gazette médicale de Paris*. From February to June 1848, he campaigned for doctors to participate in the social revolution and made 'social medicine' one of the *Gazette*'s main headings.

47. On this point, see G. Rosen, *A History of Public Health* (New York: MD Publications, 1958), 192 et seq.; and 'What Is Social Medicine', in *From Medical Police to Social Medicine* (New York: Science History Publications, 1976), 60–119.

48. The terms of the editorial in the first number of *Die medicinische Reform* are unambiguous: '"Medical reform" is seeing the light at a time when our old political institutions have not yet been superseded, and yet from all sides plans are being constructed and steps are being taken towards the construction of a new political structure. . . . In such a situation, medicine cannot remain alone unscathed; it cannot postpone for long a radical reform in its domain' (*Die Medecinische Reform. Eine Wochenschrift, erschienen vom 10. Juli 1848 bis zum 29 Juni 1849* [Berlin: Druck und Verlag von G. Reimer], no. 1, 1).

49. For a criticism of the Foucauldian interpretation of the emergence of social medicine, see E. Renault, 'Biopower and Social Pathologies', *Critical Horizons* 7 (2006): 159–77.

50. J. R. Guérin, 'Au corps médical français', *Gazette médicale de Paris*, no. 11, March 11, 1848, 184: 'We have already had occasion to stress the numerous relationships between medicine and the public interest; but at a time when the social framework was too narrow and too antiquated to contain them, these relationships could only be pointed out as particular applications of a medicine that was in some way merely ideal; but today, now that all the barriers of the past are falling before the march of progress, this ideal medicine can and must enter into reality'. See also 'La République et la médecine', *Gazette médicale de Paris*, no. 9–10, February 26 and March 4, 1848, 153: 'Even yesterday, we were straining to fit into a worn and narrow framework new views on the reorganisation of medicine; and at each moment we were held up by obstacles that we believed insurmoutable, and we cast into the wind ideas for which no ground seemed to us to be ready'.

51. J. R. Guérin, 'La République et la médecine', *Gazette médicale de Paris*, no. 9–10, February 26 and March 4, 1848, 153.

52. *Die Medizinische Reform*, quoted by Grotjahn, *Soziale Pathologie*, 3.

53. On the relationship between medical reform and socialism, see Rosen, *A History of Public Health*, 250–52; Coleman, *Death Is a Social Disease*, 283; and La Berge, *Mission and Method*, 23–24, 162–63.

54. R. Virschow, 'Die öffentliche Gesundheitspfege', *Die Medecinische Reform* 5 (1848) (H.-U. Deppe and M. Regus, *Seminar: Medizin, Gesellschaft, Geschichte. Beiträge zur Entwicklungsgeschichte der Medizinsoziologie* [Frankfurt/Main: Suhrkamp, 1975], 171): 'The term "public medicine" conveys, to him who understands all its meaning, a full and radical modification in the relationships that we establish between the State and medicine. We have only had one sanitary police force—and in fact, as Mr Schmidt has put it very well, we have only had one one treatment for the *illnesses* of the poor—in certain large cities, and in truth more as management of the sick poor than as treatment of the sick poor'.

55. Guérin, 'Au corps médical de France', 184: 'In place of the indecisive and separated applications that had been gathered under the name of the medical police, of public hygiene, of legal medicine, the moment has come to bring together all the scattered deeds, to regularise them in a group and to raise them to their highest meaning under the appellation best suited to their goal, that of *social medicine*. . . . It is not a revelation that we can claim to be making to our brethren, but it is a formula that the weight of circumstances commands us to propose to them as illuminating clearly and accurately the nature of the totality of services that they are called to render for the public good' (continuation of the previous quotation from the same article).

56. J. R. Guérin, 'La médecine sociale et la médecine politique', in *Gazette médicale de Paris*, no. 13 et seq., March 25, 1848. Replying to the Medical Union, which had seized on his conception of social medicine and interpreted it as a project in 'political medicine', Guérin explains that the relationship between social medicine and political medicine is the same as that between a social revolution and a political revolution, the first encompassing the second: 'A social Revolution is the one which enters into the bowels of society, which shifts its innermost elements, which places them in new relations. . . . Social medicine comprises all the points of view, all the relations which can exist between medicine and society, while political medicine is restricted to the relation of medicine with governmental interests, political interests'.

57. Guérin, 'La médecine sociale et la médecine socialiste', 203.

58. See, for example, the distinction between natural and artificial epidemics in R. Virschow, 'Die Seuche', in *Die Einheitsbestrebungen in der wissenschaftlichen Medizin* (Berlin: 1949) (Deppe and Regus, *Seminar*, 202–4).

59. J. R. Guérin, 'De l'organisation médicale du point de vue de la situation actuelle', *Gazette médicale de Paris*, no. 12 et seq., March 18, 1848, 212. This article aims to justify the model of professional organization and apply it to the medical profession while responding to the liberal criticism of professional associations.

60. R. Virschow, 'Der Armenartz', in *Die Medicinische Reform*, March 11, 1848 (Deppe and Regus, *Seminar*, 175–78).

61. R. Virschow, 'Die öffentliche Gesundheitspfege', in *Die Medicinische Reform*, March 11, 1848; Guérin, 'Au corps médical français'.

62. On this subject, see J. Guilhaumou, 'Sieyès et le non-dit de la sociologie: du mot à la chose', *Revue d'histoire des sciences humaines*, no. 15 (November 2006).

63. Guérin, 'Au corps médical de France', 184.

64. The term was coming into existence at the same time in Britain, and if we are to believe an author like Durkheim, this is its true origin: 'It was coined in England in 1835. In that year a group which took the rather emphatic name of "Association of All Classes of All Nations" was founded under the auspices of Robert Owen and the words "socialist" and "socialism" were used for the first time in the course of the discussions that took place on that occasion. In 1839, Reybaud used it in his book on Modern Reformers, in which the theories of Saint-Simon, Fourier and Owen are studied. Reybaud even claims authorship of the word' (*Socialism*, 29).

65. J. Leroux, 'De l'individualisme et du socialisme', in *De l'Egalité* (Paris: Slatkine, 1996), 47: 'the human sciences are very close to finding the solution [to the social question]'.

66. Ibid., 67: 'Our perplexity will continue until the social sciences manage to bring these two principles into harmony, when our two tendencies will be satisfied'.

67. Ibid., 63: 'We are socialists if socialism is understood as meaning the Doctrine which does not sacrifice any of the terms of the formula *Freedom, Brotherhood, Equality, Unity*, but reconciles them all'.

68. Rosen, *From Medical Police to Social Medicine*, 97–98.

69. S. Neumann, *Die öffentliche Gesundheitspflege im Staate des Eigentumsrechts, ihre rechtliche Begründung und zweckmässige Organisation* (1847) (Deppe and Regus, *Seminar*, 164).

70. Guérin, 'Médecine sociale et médecine socialiste', 203.

71. Guérin, 'Au corps médical français'.

72. Guérin, 'Médecine sociale et médecine socialiste', 203.

73. Ibid.

74. Virschow, 'Der Armenartz' (Deppe and Regus, *Seminar*, 175–76).

75. Guérin, 'La médecine sociale et la médecine socialiste'.

76. Grotjahn, *Soziale Pathologie*, 3–4.

77. The concept of a 'need of the self' is moreover scarcely compatible with Freudian orthodoxy. In reality, the domain of needs can be traced back more to physiology than to psychology, and the way in which the 'self' takes on the tendencies anchored in needs would be better described in terms of the 'interests of the self'. Moreover, Freud distinguishes between the libido and the 'drives of the ego' in such a way that within the interests of the self, a new distinction seems necessary (if we admit that drives can be presented as needs). The 'ego', understood in the Freudian sense, pursues its interests and not needs: in other words, it sets up as means of providing what it interprets as a possible satisfaction of needs or of drives which are themselves clearly distinguished from needs.

78. On this point, see T. W. Adorno et al. (New York: Harper and Bros., 1950).

79. The concept of the 'needs of the self' comes from Winnicott, and we draw inspiration from Winnicott when we speak here of a 'metapsychological' self. René Roussillon ('Les situations extrêmes de la clinique de la survivance', in *La santé mentale en acte*, ed. J. Furtos

and Ch. Laval, 230) writes on this subject: 'Winnicott did not really define the "needs of the self", but logically it can be suggested that they are "everything a subject needs to carry out the work of integration and symbolisation of his or her lived story"'.

80. Marx, *Early Writings*, 389–90.

81. These terminological conventions are arbitrary in nature and do not correspond exactly to what is understood by these notions within the framework of the contemporary debate. We will take our distance therefore from a terminology which we have generally made our own up until this point and will postpone until the following section the confrontation of our conventions with the uses accepted in the clinical study of work and exclusion.

82. On these different points, see Ch. Dejours, *Le corps d'abord. Corps biologique, corps érotique et sens moral* (Paris: Payot, 2001).

83. In a certain sense, the distinction between a 'psychic self' and a 'social self' is constitutive of social psychology. There are other social psychologies than that of Mead, and some among them tend to conceive of the social self as a self distinct from the psychic self. Thus Gérard Mendel maintains that, in the same way that psychoanalytic treatment is based on a mechanism making it possible to isolate the characteristic processes of the 'psycho-familial' self and aims at producing a 'neo-child' independent of an unchanged social self, the objective of 'sociopsychoanalysis' should be the construction of mechanisms making it possible to bring out the specific processes of the 'social self' and to act upon this self (see *La société n'est pas une famille*, introduction: 'De l'aporie générale de la psychanalyse à la psychologie sociale comme aporie'). While the first self is defined by the processes that constitute the psychological unconscious, the second would be characterized by a heterogenous process: 'We give this process the name of "movement of appropriation of the act". In each individual there exists a force of an anthropological nature which expresses itself in an non-conscious manner within the psychological dimension, and which impels the subject to "appropriate" to himself the voluntary and conscious act which he accomplishes, the activity, the action that he elaborates. This movment has two aims: taking control of the process of the act, and the appropriation of the effects of the act' (*La société n'est pas une famille*, 15).

84. Freud, 'Introduction to Psychoanalysis and the War Neurosis'; 'Beyond the Pleasure Principle', section II.

85. Freud, *Introductory Lectures on Psychoanalysis*, *Standard Edition*, vol. 16, p. 362.

86. Ibid., 364.

87. G. H. Mead, *Mind, Self and Society* (Chicago: University of Chicago Press, 1967).

88. For a presentation of a synthesis, see J. Cl. Croizet and J. Ph. Levens, ed., *Mauvaises réputations. Réalités et enjeux de la stigmatisation sociale* (Paris: Armand Colin, 2004).

89. V. de Gauléjac, *Les sources de la honte* (Paris: Desclée de Brouwer, 1996).

90. Honneth, *The Struggle for Recognition*. Honneth's theory identifies a group of specific needs of the self which can be said to belong to the psychosocial self in that they are specifically oriented towards others (the tendencies stemming from them take the form of demands for recognition) and whose content is determined by interaction frameworks. Each institutional sphere gives its particular content to expectations of recognition (what is at stake in recognition varies in the institutions of intimacy, of work and of the public political sphere) and tends to produce specific recognition effects, so that it is possible to describe different forms of socially produced denial and recognition of so many specific factors in 'moral injuries' or in suffering (Renault, *L'expérience de l'injustice*, chap. 3).

91. See, for example, Thierry's comment, reported by S. Quesemand Zucca, *Je vous salis ma rue. Clinique de la desocialisation* (Paris: Stock, 2007), 112: 'I've suffered a lot from people's contempt when I was begging in front of a post office or in a market. When you stop doing that, you're really paranoid because you think people are still seeing you do it. . . . I'd

like to have been homeless yesterday and not still be hearing about it today. But that's not at all the way it goes. . . . That is to say, in the street, you're hurt by people looking at you, and then you're hurt by looking at yourself'.

92. Ibid., 83–84.

93. For an example of the interweaving of these different processes, see S. Beaud, 'Postface', in *Pays de malheur. Un jeune de cité écrit à un sociologue*, ed. Y. Amrani and S. Beaud (Paris: La Découverte, 2004) 207–31.

94. W. E. B. Du Bois, *The Souls of Black Folk* (New Haven: Yale University Press, 2015); F. Fanon, *Black Skin, White Masks* (London: Pluto, 1986).

95. Dejours, *Souffrance en France*, 89 sq.

96. Freud, 'The Claims of Psychoanalysis to Scientific Interest', *Standard Edition*, 13:188.

97. S. Freud, 'Group Psychology and the Analysis of the Ego', *Standard Edition*, 18:129: 'Each individual is a component part of numerous groups, he is bound by ties of identification in many directions, and he has built up his ego ideal upon the most various models. Each individual therefore has a share in numerous group minds—those of his race, of his class, of his creed, of his nationality, etc.—and he can also raise himself above them to the extent of having a scrap of independence and originality'.

98. Honneth, *The Struggle for Recognition*.

99. On this point, see A. Honneth, *Reification* (Oxford: Oxford University Press, 2008). Notably because the question of which individuals are capable of providing a satisfactory recognition is part also of the sociological analysis of class and social conflict (being recognized by 'them' does not have the same significance as being recognized by 'us').

100. Even if the members of stigmatized social groups tend to minimize the reality of stigmatization so as not to lose all social hope, they are well enough aware of their social disadvantage to consider themselves more meritorious in obtaining results analogous to those of individuals coming from advantaged social groups, while at the same time, they also tend to limit their hopes to less valued social activities in which they can succeed more easily due to low levels of social competition. On these questions, see J.-Cl. Croizet, 'Stigmatisation et estime de soi', in *Mauvaises réputations. Réalités et enjeux de la stigmatisation sociale*, ed. Croizet and Levens.

101. On these questions, see Renault, *L'expérience de l'injustice*, chap. 5, and J.-Ph Deranty and E. Renault, 'Politicizing Honneth's Ethics of Recognition', *Thesis Eleven*, no. 88 (2007) 92–111.

102. P. Bourdieu, *Pascalian Meditations* (Cambridge: Polity Press, 2000), 140–41.

103. Ibid., 160.

104. Ibid., 191.

105. The originality of the Bourdieusian theory of social suffering is its attempt to propose a strictly sociological explanation short circuiting the psychosocial moment (identity) as well as the psychic moment (drives and the fate of drives). In so doing, it also reveals the limits of his theory of action. In developing his study within the framework of a dispositional analysis of action, theory can take account neither of the suffering which is produced by the very dynamism of action (inasmuch as it is sustained by tendencies founded in needs and drives, and not only in flexible and inventive modes of reaction to social situations) nor of the suffering induced by the lack of objects to satisfy needs and drives (objects which cannot be reduced to instruments of action that must be available to reach socially legitimate goals) nor of the suffering which is induced by failures of the cooperative dimension of action (regardless of whether intersubjectivity intervenes as a condition of normal progress of the action or of validation of its success). Just as social action cannot be adequately explained within the framework of theories of action which do without an analysis of the dynamism of agency as it is founded in the constraints of drives (psychic self) and in needs for recognition from signifi-

cant others (social self), suffering cannot be adequately explained within the narrow framework of such theories. For a general critique of this type of theory of action, see G. Mendel, *L'Acte est une aventure. Du sujet métaphysique au sujet d'actepouvoir* (Paris: La Découverte, 1998); F. Fischbach, *L'Être et l'acte. Enquête sur les fondements de l'ontologie moderne de l'agir* (Paris: Vrin, 2002); and Haber and Renault, 'Une analyse marxiste des corps?'

106. On the link between violence and psychological suffering, see the synthesis proposed in the report edited by A. Lowell, *Violence et santé mentale* (Ministère de la santé, 2004), III–B, www.sante.gouv.fr/htm/dossiers/violence_sante/sante_mentale.pdf.

107. For a discussion of these questions, see E. Corlin, R. Thera, and R. Padmaranta, 'A la recherche d'une texture dans les recherches interculturelles sur la schizophrénie', *L'Evolution psychiatrique* 69, no. 1 (2004): 91–112. On this topic, see D. Cooper, 'Families and Schizophrenia', in *Psychiatry and Anti-Psychiatry* (London: Routledge, 2001).

108. Y. Clot, *La fonction psychique du travail* (Paris: PUF, 1995), 7: 'It is . . . a complete mobilisation of one's person which is required to take upon oneself the task of reconciling the irreconcilable: regularity, speed, quality, security. The psychological interiorisation of the conflicts of criteria associated with objectives that are too often unrealisable leads to new dissociations'. See also the interpretation of Le Guillant's psychopathology proposed by Clot: 'His conception is not narrowly determinist. In reality, it is not the social condition which is inherently pathogenic, even if it can become so in its own terms. It is rather its discordances, the conflicts which this condition harbours and which it imposes upon the subject' ('Après Le Guillant: quelle clinique du travail?', in *Le drame humain du travail. Essais de psychopathologie du travail*, ed. L. Le Guillant [Toulouse: Erès, 2006], 24).

109. On this point, see in particular E. Renault, 'Le discours du respect', in *La quête de reconnaissance*, ed. A. Caillé (Paris: La Découverte, 2007), 161–81.

110. On the subjective impact of the cycle of disaffiliation and violence, see in particular E. Renault, 'A propos de la violence en situation de sous-emploi: récit et tentative d'analyse', in *Conjurer la violence*, ed. Dejours.

111. R. Senett and J. Cobb, *Hidden Injuries of Class* (Cambridge: Cambridge University Press, 1977); G. Cowlishaw, *Blackfellas Whitefellas and Hidden Injuries of Race* (London: Blackwell, 2003).

112. See, for example, Freud, *An Outline of Psychoanalysis*, 53.

113. On the psychodynamic function of recognition in work, see Ch. Dejours, 'Psychanalyse et psychodynamique du travail: les ambiguïtés de la reconnaissance', in *La quête de reconnaissance*, ed. A. Caillé. For a comparison of the concepts of recognition developed by Dejours and Honneth, see E. Renault, 'Reconnaissance et travail', *Travailler*, no. 18 (2007): 115–35.

114. The necessity of the dynamic point of view makes apparent the insufficiency of all purely 'phenomenological' approaches to suffering (such as Ricoeur and Lévinas have proposed); see P. Ricoeur, 'La souffrance n'est pas la douleur', *Psychiatrie Française*, special issue, 1992; E. Lévinas, 'La souffrance inutile', *Les Cahiers de la Nuit Surveillée*, no. 3: *Emmanuel Levinas* (Paris: Verdier, 1984).

115. On the concept of psychic defense, see Anna Freud, *The Ego and the Mechanisms of Defense*, London: Karnac books, 1992.

116. Freud mentions the patient's rational aim of becoming healthy and free from his ailments: 'An Outline of Psycho-Analysis', *Standard Edition*, 23: 175, and counts among the factors acting in favour of successful treatment 'the need for recovery which has its motive in [the patient's] sufferings (ibid., 181).

117. Ibid., chap. 6.

118. Observing the similarity between two clinical objects does not entail that the phenomena are comparable in other ways.

119. Roussillon, 'Les situations extrêmes de la clinique de la survivance', 226.

120. In certain South Pacific cultures, running Amok, or mad dog races, are an institutionalized means of expressing of psychological disturbance, which have been notably been described in the eponymous short stories of S. Zweig.

121. On these points, see Devereux, *Essais d'ethnopsychiatrie générale*.

122. S. Freud, 'Thoughts for the Times on War and Death', *Standard Edition*, 14: 275–300.

123. Report of the Haut Comité de Santé Publique: 'La progression de la précarité en France et ses effets sur la santé', February 1998.

124. This type of argument is found in the work of M. Joubert, 'Précarisation et santé mentale. Déterminants sociaux de la fatigue et des troubles dépressifs ordinaires', in *Précarisation, risque et santé*, ed. M. Joubert et al. (Paris: Inserm, 1999).

125. D. Lagache, *L'unité de la psychologie* (Paris: PUF, 1979), 32.

126. See the synthesis offered in Lhuilier, *Cliniques du travail*, 26–42.

127. Schütze, 'Verlaufskurven des Erleidens als Forschungsgegenstand der interpretativen Soziologie'.

128. Dejours, *Souffrance en France*; *L'évaluation du travail à l'épreuve du réel. Critique des fondements de l'évaluation* (Paris: INRA Éditions, 2003); 'La flexibilité, ou l'autre nom de la servitude'; DeJours, *Conjurer la Violence*; Y. Clot, *Le travail sans l'homme. Psychologie des milieux de vie et de travail* (Paris: La Découverte, 1995); *La fonction psychologique du travail* (Paris: PUF, 1999); 'Après Le Guillant: quelle clinique du travail'.

129. For an overall introduction, see Molinier, *Les enjeux psychiques du travail*.

130. For an overall introduction, see Lhuilier, *Cliniques du travail*.

131. As D. Lhuilier writes: 'The points of convergence between the psychodynamics of work and clinical social psychology seem not only numerous (dynamic conjunction of the psychological and the social, reference to a theory of the subject which recognises the hypothesis of the unconscious, constructivist-subjectivist paradigm and comprehensive approach, conjunction of research and action . . .) but fundamental' (ibid., 51).

132. Y. Clot, 'Psychodynamique du travail et clinique de l'activité', *Education permanente* 146 (2001): 35–51.

133. Dejours, *Travail, usure mentale*, 78–79.

134. Ibid., 224.

135. Ibid., 206–7, 212–16.

136. Ch. Dejours and P. Molinier, 'De la peine au travail', *Autrement* 142 (1993): 138–51. For the comparison with Michel Henry, see Molinier, *Les enjeux psychiques du travail*, 60–64.

137. Dejours, *Travail, usure mentale*, 74.

138. As done by Lhuillier, *Cliniques du travail*.

139. Dejours, *Travail, usure mentale*, 226.

140. Molinier, *Les enjeux psychiques du travail*, 60.

141. Ibid.

142. On this distinction, see Dejours, *Travail, usure mentale*, 60–61, note.

143. Ibid., 224–25.

144. as in Freud's 'Group Psychology and the Analysis of the Ego'.

145. Du Bois, *The Souls of Black Folk*; Fanon, *Black Skin, White Masks*.

146. Dejours, *Travail, usure mentale*, 49–60; Clot, 'Après Le Guillant: quelle clinique du travail'.

147. Clot, *La fonction psychologique du travail*.

148. Y. Clot, 'Métier en souffrance et clinique du travail', in *Répondre à la souffrance sociale*, ed. Joubert and Louzoun.

149. For an introduction to the particulars of these practices, see notably Orspere, *Points de vue et rôles des acteurs de la clinique psychosociale* (Ministère de l'Emploi et de la Solidarité, FNARS, 1999); J.-P. Martin, *Psychiatrie dans la ville. Pratiques et cliniques de terrain* (Toulouse: Erès, 2000).

150. Zucca, *Je vous salis ma rue*.

151. J. Furtos, 'Epistémologie de la clinique psychosociale (la scène sociale et la place des psy)', *Pratiques en santé mentale*, no. 1 (2000): 23–32.

152. G. Charreton, V. Colin, and B. Duez, 'A la rencontre de sujets SDF, demandes de traces ou traces de demandes?', *Psychologie clinique*, no. 16 (2004): 73–86.

153. O. Douville, '"Mélancolie d'exclusion". Quand la parole divorce du corps et retour', in *Psychanalyse et malaise social. Désir du lien?*, ed. F. de Rivoyre (Toulouse: Erès, 2001).

154. This is the case in the work of Furtos.

155. Decklerck, *Les naufragés*, 308.

156. Zucca, *Je vous salis ma rue*, chap. 6.

157. O. Douville, 'Notes d'un clinicien sur les incidences subjectives de la grande précarité', in *Psychologie clinique*, no. 7 (1999): 58–59.

158. Zucca, *Je vous salis ma rue*, 113.

159. On this point, see the discussion by P. Declerck in P. Pichon, 'Intervention d'urgence et désocialisation: éléments généalogiques', in *Travail social et souffrance psychique*, ed. Ion et al.

160. S. Quesemand Zucca, 'A propos de la banalisation du terme "souffrance psychique"', *Psychologie clinique*, no. 16 (2004): 101–4: Rupture des liens, clinique des altérités.

161. D. Mellier, 'Précarité du lien, détresse sociale et mechanisms de contenance', *Psychologie clinique*, no. 16 (2004): 87–100: Rupture des liens, clinique des altérités.

162. On this point, see Zucca, *Je vous salis ma rue*, 93–99, and J. Maisondieu, 'Alcool, alcoolisme, exclusion et précarité', in *Précarisation, risque et santé*, ed. Joubert et al.

163. Zucca, *Je vous salis ma rue*, 116.

164. Douville, '"Mélancolies d'exclusion"'.

165. R. Roussillon, 'Les situations extrêmes de la clinique de la survivance', in *La santé mentale en actes*, ed. Furtos and Laval, 229: 'Survival strategies are always based on the sacrifice of one or the other of the major processes of psychic life: sacrifice of the drive, sacrifice of temporality, sacrifice of emotional life and of the experiencing of it'. Douville, '"Mélancolies d'exclusion"', 48: 'For certain patients and at certain points, there can occur such disappointments in encounters, and indeed such real, concrete risks in encounters, that it is entirely possible for the subject to assume that it is no longer worth having a psychic life at all'.

166. Zucca, *Je vous salis ma rue*, 83.

167. S. Ferenczi, *Infantil-Angriffe! Über sexuelle Gewalt, Trauma und Dissoziation* (Berlin: Verlag Autonomie und Chaos, 2014) (only available as a free download from http://www.autonomie-und-chaos.de), 112.

168. Roussillon, 'Les situations extrêmes de la clinique de la survivance', 224.

169. J. Furtos, 'Souffrir sans disparaître (pour définir la santé mentale au-delà de la psychiatrie)', in *La santé mentale en acte*, ed. Furtos and Laval.

170. Ibid., 18.

171. Furtos, 'Epistémologie de la clinique psychosociale', 23–25.

172. Furtos, 'Souffrir sans disparaître', 19.

173. Furtos, 'Epistémologie de la clinique psychosociale', 26.

174. J. Maisondieu, *La fabrique des exclus* (Paris: Bayard, 1997).

175. Furtos, 'Souffrir sans disparaître (pour définir la santé mentale au-delà de la psychiatrie)', 20.

176. Furtos, 'Epistémologie de la clinique psychosociale', 26.

177. Furtos, 'Souffrir sans disparaître', 21.

178. Furtos, 'Epistémologie de la clinique psychosociale', 26, 29–31.

179. Furtos, 'Souffrir sans disparaître', 21.

180. Ibid., 21–22. Which Douville describes as an inversion of shame into hatred; Douville, '"Mélancolies d'exclusion"'.

181. Douville, 'Notes d'un clinicien sur les incidences subjectives de la grande précarité', 64: 'An identification which has given up the ideal points which maintain the narcissistic mirror will move towards a desperate collusion with rejection'.

182. Roussillon, 'Les situations extrêmes de la clinique de la survivance', 229: 'As is immediately noticeable, the clinical study of extreme situations concerns less the register of desire—which is maximally relevant when the psychic economy is clearly organised under the primacy of the pleasure principle—than that of need, which has primacy when, above and beyond the pleasure principle, the clinician is confronted with the question of the damaging effects of the death drive, of the disappearance of the difference between the thing and the representation of the thing'.

183. Zucca, *Je vous salis ma rue*, 93: 'The more the person is desocialised, the more he or she strikes roots, directly into the ground. . . . In extreme cases, the man or the woman "asphaltise" him- or herself, as though welded to the earth, their feet stuck in asphalt, to the point where it is impossible to tell if they are able to stand upright. Sitting down, leaning against something, propping up their backs, lying down, surrounded by a mass of bags, bottles, food items, they become a vague shape'.

184. Martin, *Psychiatrie dans la ville*, 133. In the work of Furtos, the typology of forms of suffering is constructed on the basis of the analysis of disaffiliation proposed by Castel.

185. B. Doray, 'Du "traumatisme social" au traumatisme psychique', in *Répondre à la souffrance sociale*, ed. Joubert and Louzoun.

186. A. Lovell, 'Les fictions de soi-même ou les délires identificatoires dans la rue', in *La Maladie mentale en mutation. Psychiatrie et société*, ed. A. Erhenberg and A. Lovell (Paris: Odile Jacob, 2003).

187. Joubert, 'Précarisation et santé mentale'; Colin and Furtos, 'La clinique psychosociale au regard de la souffrance psychique contemporaine'.

188. Doray, 'Du "traumatisme social" au traumatisme psychique'.

189. On this point, see Grenier-Pezé, 'Un cas de violence au travail', in *Conjurer la violence*, ed. Dejours.

190. Douville, '"Mélancolies d'exclusion"'.

191. Ibid., 44; see also Charreton, Colin, and Duez, 'A la rencontre de sujets SDF, demandes de traces ou traces de demandes?', 77: 'While what is touched on in the exchange could create a bond of familiarity between him and me, on the contrary it is an sensation of intrusion that I feel'.

192. Martin, *Psychiatrie dans la ville*, 120.

193. Zucca, *Je vous salis ma rue*, 84.

194. Ibid., 106–9.

195. Ibid., 111–13.

Chapter Four

Social Suffering and Social Criticism

Prior to forging new policies or lubricating creaky policy discourses, these essays argue, we need first to examine the most basic relationships between language and pain, image and suffering. The authors discuss why a language of dismay, disappointment, bereavement and alarm that sounds not at all like the usual terminology of policy and programs may offer a more valid means for describing what is at stake in human experiences of political catastrophe and social structural violence, for professionals as much as for victims/perpetrators, and also may make better sense of how the clash among globalising discourses and localised social realities so often ends up prolonging personal and collective tragedy.

—A. Kleinman, V. Das, M. Lock, *Social Suffering*, x–xi

With only the old-fashioned category of the 'social' at their disposal to think about these unexpressed and often inexpressible malaises, political organisations cannot perceive them and, still less, take them on. They could do so only by expanding the narrow vision of 'politics' they have inherited from the past and by encompassing not only all the claims brought into the public arena by ecological, antiracist or feminist movements (among others), but also all the diffuse expectations and hopes which, because they often touch on the ideas that people have about their own identity and self-respect, seem to be a private affair and therefore legitimately excluded from political debates.

—P. Bourdieu, *The Weight of the World*, 1450

All political concepts are 'essentially contested' in the sense that the political conflicts in which they are involved enter into them, thus conferring on them contradictory meanings. The political concept of suffering is also essentially contested, and doubly so: the questioning has to do with its political value

167

(does this vague category not risk screening out all the classic social problems which are still decisive and which can be designated in another way?) as well as with its political dimension (can it legitimately be used in a genuinely political, not simply moral or medical, way?).

If we were to stop at the analysis of the linguistic uses of the term 'suffering', we would have to content ourselves with simply noting these aporia, in other words give up on political theory, which consists specifically in taking sides in this type of debate. We would also have to take refuge in scepticism and reserve judgement when actually existing forms of social critique use the term. But by taking sides in favour of the critical use of the term 'suffering', we have rather attempted to connect a political defence of a specific use of the term 'suffering' (a critical use) with a resolution of the epistemological aporias of the conception of social suffering. To this end, we have paid attention not only to common or institutionalized political discourse, but also to scholarly uses, where the logical difficulties of the concept of social suffering cut across theoretical conflicts. We have thereby moved towards a critical examination of theories of social suffering, of which we have been led to develop a synthetic conception.

But the project of a theoretical defence of critical reference to suffering includes other tasks. It also requires, on the one hand, a justification of the claim that a reference to social suffering can genuinely call into question the contemporary world, with its specific characteristics, and, on the other hand, a demonstration of the benefit of this model of social critique as opposed to others which, by contrast, are more current and less problematic.

We will begin by distinguishing between two styles of social critique in which the theme of social suffering can be drawn upon (1), before explaining the norms of a critique of social suffering (2) and the way in which a description of the different contemporary forms of social suffering can lead us back to a generalized questioning of the current social order in terms of social pathology (3).

TWO STYLES OF THEORETICAL CRITIQUE

Like any political discourse, the discourse of social critique can be evaluated from the point of view of its social objects and of the political subjects that it presupposes. On the one hand, we can actually measure the relevance of a model of social criticism by asking ourselves about its capacity to apply to the ills on which the effort of social transformation must focus. On the other hand, its relevance depends on the existence of political subjects capable of carrying out these transformations, as well as the subjectivation effects that it has on potential political actors. Any consistent critical theory must doubtless adopt the goals of producing a relevant description of social ills and of finding or producing political subjects who can intervene in a relevant way in a process of social transformation. But these two aims can be pursued in different ways.

According to a first style of critical theory, these aims are taken on board directly. Theoretical criticism sees itself in this instance as the expression and justification of a practical social criticism (social movements, social struggles, ongoing political processes), which itself proceeds to identify the specific ills of society and which itself institutes the relevant political actors. In its legitimating function, theoretical critique then turns to demonstrating that the highlighted ills actually count among the principal ones and that there is nothing inevitable about them, as well as to defending the well-foundedness of the intended social transformations and the legitimacy of the political actors who are determined to undertake the task of carrying them out.

It is by taking this type of theoretical criticism as a model that different objections to the critical reference to social suffering can be dealt with: we would be running the risk of concentrating our attention on ills which are not the principal ones (the superficial effects of social transformations on individuals) or which are inevitable (the unpleasant aspects of existence), thus blocking a perception of the true social problems (injustices). We would moreover induce modes of subjectivation which would be vehicles of depoliticization by transforming potential political actors into powerless victims waiting for moral (compassion) or medical (care) responses. But we have seen that struggles against social injustice can take suffering as one of their main themes (*Écho de la Fabrique*) and that in the course of them political subjects can characterize themselves in terms of suffering (the '*Armée souffrante*' or 'suffering army').

The second style of theoretical criticism is distinguished from the first in that it presupposes neither a prior identification of social ills by existing social and political movements, nor an already constituted political subjectivity. Even if the first style of theoretical criticism constitutes the classical model since the emergence of the social question, there are cases in which political struggles and social movements clearly do not manage to identify more than a fraction of the social ills which must be taken into consideration. Political and social struggles can also be so weak that political subjectivity

appears as a problem to be resolved rather than as a foundational fact. Theoretical critique is in these cases stripped of its cognitive and practical guarantees.

Twentieth-century critical thought offers different examples of discourses
which have adopted the style of theoretical critique which results from this
type of situation. In the context of the emergence of fascism as a mass
phenomenon, Adorno thus explained that critical theory should be interested
not only in the forces making it possible to combat fascism, but also in those
which explain support for injustice and domination.[1] He offers the example
of a movement for redefinition of critique which, from Gramsci to Althusser,
aims at explaining the failures of the working proletariat as a revolutionary
subject and which finally leads our contemporaries explicitly to pose the
question of political subjectivity as a problem (Balibar, Badiou, Rancière,
Butler, Zizek)[2] or as a messianic horizon (Derrida).[3]

It is doubtless in the work of Adorno that reflection on the status of a
social critique with neither cognitive nor practical guarantees has been
pushed the furthest. A lack of confidence in the pretheoretical identification
of social ills led him to see forms of domination and reification in nearly all
contemporary institutions and cultural products. Insofar as praxis is always
caught in dilemmas of the totalizing and mutilating rationalization of the
modern world, theoretical critique is in the last analysis the only form of
legitimate critique. It is striking that in Adorno's work suffering serves precisely to supply a *substitute* pretheoretical guarantee for critique; in the absence of a practical guarantee of struggles for emancipation worthy of the
name, philosophy finds its source of legitimacy in the anthropological war-
rant of lived suffering. The scandal of the suffering produced by the modern
world suffices not only to justify a philosophical critique of this world, but
also to refute any attempt at contesting the well-foundedness of criticism:
'The undiminished persistence of suffering, fear and menace necessitates that
the thought which cannot be realised [in practice—E.R.] should not be dis-
carded. After having missed its opportunity, philosophy must come to know,
without any mitigation, why the world—which could be paradise here and
now—can become hell itself tomorrow. Such knowledge would indeed truly
be philosophy. It would be anachronistic to abolish it for the sake of a praxis
that at this historical moment would inevitably eternalise precisely the
present state of the world, the very critique of which is the concern of philosophy'.[4]

But the reference to suffering can also fulfil another function in this second type of criticism. It can offer another response to the absence of practical and cognitive guarantees by being mobilized to identify a certain number of social ills insufficiently taken into account by institutionalized political processes and by social movements. And specifically, we have seen that many social ills characteristic of the current period do not seem capable of being better described than in terms of social suffering (the new forms of suffering at work and suffering linked to exclusion) because ordinary theoretical and political vocabulary seems to be unable to capture the seriousness of these ills. As witnessed by the texts quoted as the epigraphs to this chapter, this is the conviction underlying the references to suffering in the work of Bourdieu and of authors such as Kleinmann and Das.

The concept of suffering can also allow us to reflectively focus on the absence of practical guarantees of criticism by designating a constellation of factors which are an obstacle to social and political struggles either because the suffering of individuals blocks their engagement in social movements, even their narration of this suffering, or that the invisibilization of suffering leads to a delegitimation of any engagement in the public political sphere. In the work of authors such as Bourdieu and Das, the writing and theorization of social suffering have the specific function of contributing to the visibilization of social suffering and bringing about a new relationship of individuals to their suffering which can return to them their capacity for political action and engagement. This is also one of the mainsprings of Dejours's criticism of suffering at work.

In Bourdieu's view, a group of social problems that are invisibilized and forgotten by classic social movements are brought to light in terms of suffering (the poverty of position in opposition to the classic faces of inequality).[5] Sociology thus makes use of the lexicon of suffering not only to proceed with a purely theoretical critique (as Adorno does), but also to give a voice back to those whose voices have been taken from them and to supply models which can be endorsed by social agents and contribute to the relaunch of a practical social criticism.[6] Dealing with the consequences of the mass rape which took place when India was partitioned and the invisibilization they have undergone, Das considers, for her part, that anthropology has an obligation to struggle against collective denial and the dynamics of self-destruction in those who are victims of it, that it must make an effort to break the cycle which leads the victims of violence and social injustice to wall themselves away in silence and that it must make an effort to develop suitable forms of visibilization and collective expression.[7] In the work of these authors, theoretical criticism attempts to supply the subalterns with cultural tools to describe their own experience and raise demands in a dynamic of empowerment which is a response to the lack of a practical guarantee of critique. Whereas in Adorno's view philosophy constitutes itself as a bearing of witness, sociology and anthropology here constitute themselves as 'spokespersons' for suffering.[8]

The notion of a spokesperson certainly merits more precise description. In the first type of social critique, theoretical criticism can also make itself a spokesperson for suffering. This was the case for example when the *Écho de la Fabrique* introduced itself as the spokesperson of the *canuts* in the process of constructing a workers' voice: theoretical critique espoused the point of view of social practices, proceeding to a co-construction of their aims and making an effort to intensify the struggles. To this end, the discourse of suffering became part of a strategy of legitimation, of identification of adversaries and of motivational support. It is here that the question of the political function of the spokesperson arises in new senses: on the one hand, in the sense of a critical operation aimed at neutralizing the obstacles preventing certain subjects from accessing a place where they can express their suffering and make demands in the public political sphere, and on the other hand, in the sense of a critique of all the discourses which fraudulently present themselves as spokespersons for their suffering.

In Bourdieu's as well as Das's view, the spokesperson is a critic who struggles against institutional spokespersons who instrumentalize suffering or who contribute to its euphemization. Bourdieu criticizes the politicians and sociologists who use their symbolic capital via the mass media to impose their interpretation of social suffering.[9] In her analysis of the Bhopal disaster, Das, for her part, criticized the way in which the state, relying on medical and legal expertise, referred to suffering to legitimize its right to be the sole negotiator with the multinational Union Carbide, all the while denying the reality of this suffering (reduced to a mere 'verbal object'[10]) as well as the right of the victims to make demands themselves in the name of suffering: 'Suffering was cut off from the victim in order to be refashioned as a trope which legitimised the producers of judicial discourse. The more suffering was talked about, the more it was used to extinguish the sufferer'.[11] Even more than Bourdieu, Das highlights the aporia which any spokesperson for suffering must confront. When suffering subjects are muzzled by the convergence of symbolic and social logics of subalternity (as was the case of the inhabitants of Bhopal), the closeness of these aporias to those of witnessing is real.[12] Nonetheless, there is no other critical function than that of the spokesperson if we are to reject the invisibilization of the social suffering of the subalterns as well as the way in which institutional spokespersons claim to explain this suffering.

To conceptualize the originality of the type of social criticism proposed by Das and Bourdieu, when they explicitly put forward ethnographers or sociologists as 'spokespersons' for social suffering, it may be useful to refer to the concepts of 'social pathology' and of 'criticism as disclosure' developed by Axel Honneth. 'Pathologies of the social' are here presented as the other of justice.[13] While the question of justice is oriented towards the problem of equal respect for universal rights, the idea of social pathology designates the effects of institutions upon the forms of individual existence. These are no longer evaluated on the basis of the principles to which they must conform but on the basis of the effects which they produce. And these effects are themselves evaluated from the point of view not only of respect for individual rights, but also of the types of existence produced by institutions. Manifestly, the criticism of social suffering is part of a critique of social pathologies understood in this sense. It is, on the one hand, a criticism of institutions and of social arrangements based on the effects which they produce (and not on the basis of normative principles to which their rules of operation and their justificatory principles ought to conform). On the other hand, it is also a criticism adopting the point of view of the kind of painful experiences which, in the eyes of the individuals concerned, can make demands for the respect of rights, and the normative principles of institutions lose their meaning and their value.

Honneth maintains that political deliberations tend to favour the point of view of justice (we must clarify: of an overly narrow definition of justice) and to invisibilize the set of problems connected with social pathologies. In this sense, criticism of social pathologies takes the form of 'disclosing criticism' (*erschliessende Kritik*).[14] Disclosure means here both a rendering visible of social problems which are denied or euphemized by ordinary political discourse and a legitimation of the right to make them fully a part of political deliberations.

Moving towards 'disclosure' in this sense is one of the aims of the reference to suffering in Bourdieu's *The Weight of the World*:[15] contributing to a transformation of invisibilized social problems into an object of public concern and political confrontation. It is also the function of Das's reference to suffering: struggling against the collective denial of the rapes committed at the time of partition, denouncing the euphemization of lived suffering in the discourse of medical or legal experts and the deprivation of the power to make demands which results from such euphemization.

But in Honneth's view, the concept of 'disclosing critique' also has a pragmatic function. By making the corrupt and intolerable aspects of the real world which social discourse tends to hide appear in all their crudity, 'disclosing critique' contributes to a neutralization of social legitimations. On the one hand, it describes a reality which is often at odds with what can be justified with the logical and normative resources of the discourse of legitimation; confronted to disclosing critique, these discourses may appear false or mystifying. On the other hand, disclosing critique tends to undo our spontaneous identifications with the world, spontaneous identifications which constitute another powerful vehicle of social justification. At a time when social justifications seem to rely less and less on discourses of legitimation (on 'grand narratives' or 'ideologies' in the broad meanings of the terms) and more and more on descriptions of reality as desirable, on performative images and identificatory narratives to which correspond different forms of invisibilization of the disagreeable, intolerable and unbearable aspects of social experience and the social environment,[16] it would be damaging to give up this type of social criticism.

In the work of authors such as Bourdieu and Dejours, Das and Kleinman, the critique of social suffering also attempts to produce such pragmatic effects. In Dejours's approach for example, the aim is explicitly to transform the pathic relation which individuals have to their own suffering so that they may perceive that of others afresh. In Bourdieu's view, the aim is to neutralize the justifications for the new social order by emphasizing the harshness of the experiences of domination and misery which are their real counterpart. In Das's and Kleinman's view, the aim is to make apparent 'the clash between globalising discourses and localised social realities'[17] by bringing to light the mystificatory effects of the absorption of political discourse by global questions in the age of globalization. If we wish to resist the depoliticization effects inherent in the globalization of institutionalized politics, and if we wish to resist the abstraction effects which a struggle against neoliberal globalisation that would restrict itself to the internationalist space of the anti-globalisation movement risks producing, we must return to the local spaces in which social issues arise in the first place.[18] Social suffering is, to be sure, not the only social problem in which concrete citizenship can be anchored, but to give up criticism of social suffering would mean depriving ourselves of an indispensable vehicle for making forms of politicization more concrete.

For all of these authors, it is a matter of drawing on the resources—both cognitive and affective—of critique by offering ways of understanding the social world which contribute to bringing about new relations to one's own suffering and that of others and thus to bringing about a new practical relationship with the world which produces suffering and new possibilities for making political demands. [19]

Disclosing critique is especially suitable for the second type of social criticism, characterized by an absence of practical and cognitive guarantees. It is doubtless because we are accustomed, first, to thinking of social criticism in terms of the first model, second, to reducing the critique of suffering to a use of the second model, and finally, to thinking of the second model as a kind of bearing witness that we feel some reticence about acknowledging its political fruitfulness. Nonetheless, this fruitfulness is real, in the specific context of an absence of practical and theoretical guarantees of criticism, and it is quite general, in the current context of a public political sphere characterized by depoliticization, as a consequence, on the one hand, of the loss of meaning of the conflicts between the discourses of legitimation, and on the other hand, of the abstraction of political discourse, that is, of its poor fit with the problems encountered in social experience. To the extent that constituted social movements also sometimes have to struggle against the invisibilization of social problems, the first type of social criticism is also sometimes led to make use of the operator of disclosing social suffering. And in the context of contemporary depoliticization, it is probable that these movements will always gain by doing so.

Criticism of social suffering attempts to produce effects both cognitive (legitimation or change of the perception of the social world and the validty of its justifications) and practical (refusal of the unacceptable and of the unbearable). It states that societies must conform to the requirements of a struggle against the suffering which they produce. But what kind of standard can we appeal to when we demand that social suffering be one of the topics of public discussion and political confrontation? And, more generally, how can we establish that the refusal of suffering can be set standard in matters of social criticism?

JUSTICE, SELF-REALIZATION AND ALIENATION

That suffering is a constitutive part of existence and that it cannot, therefore, be the basis of any criticism is an argument that we have met in various forms. To respond to it, it is sufficient to defend the well-foundedness of the distinction between normal and abnormal suffering. As we have seen, another recurring argument is that this distinction runs the risk of opening the way to a pathologization of the social world. We have already replied to this type of objection that not all abnormal suffering is pathological. This distinction is presupposed when the individuals concerned testify to the pain and trauma, the discouragement, the stress, even the depression which are caused by certain social contexts, while at the same time distinguishing them from what belongs to the domain of medical and psychiatric nosography. For their part, the sociology of exclusion and the clinical study of work and of severe precarity make it possible to confirm this distinction, while showing furthermore that pathology can indeed be one of the fates of abnormal, though nonpathological, suffering. The proportion of individuals affected by pathological suffering of social origin will generally remain too small for social critique to find a point of solid support in pathology. The forms of pathogenic social suffering linked to a specific social context are more widespread.

When criticism turns to pathogenic suffering, to a suffering which no longer belongs to the domain of health without being strictly speaking pathological, from what standard does it derive the authority to bring an accusation against the social context? The most obvious answer points towards justice. If the idea of social justice in fact refers to the way in which institutions shape the satisfaction of universal aspirations by distributing the means of their satisfaction, if, more specifically, it requires that this distribution be subject to a principle of equality when fundamental expectations are in play,[20] this idea seems applicable to health. Indeed, it seems that health is the object of a universal (moreover proverbial) expectation and that institutions engage in a distribution of the conditions of health, which can thus be considered as a good that is unequally distributed.

Among the current social uses of the theme of social suffering, some clearly belong to this problematic. It is clearly an interpretation of health in terms of injustice which motivates public health studies on inequalities of health on the national or global scale. The objective in this case is to identify injustices and determine the best responses, taking into account the cost and efficacity of different possible measures. Sometimes public health reports interpret psychological suffering as an indicator of precarity, thus emphasizing that social inequalities extend into in inequalities in terms of suffering. Even if criticism of social suffering in terms of injustice presupposes a widening of the traditional definitions of justice,[21] it seems entirely legitimate. But it also seems that it will not suffice to exhaust the demands implied by the critique of social suffering. In these, health designates something more than the satisfaction of a fundamental expectation or the use of a primary good.

Indeed, critique of pathogenic suffering also seems refer back to a demand for self-realization, understood in the two forms of the 'good life' and of freedom realized in desired actions ('positive freedom'). We wish for health because it defines a fundamental condition of quality of life and, inversely, because the absence of health can remove all value from our existence. A whole philosophical literature has emphasized that a good life depends on self-realization, in the sense of the capacity to lead a life which fits with our identifications and our strong evaluations.[22] We have seen that these components of identity play a part in the social genesis of suffering in such a way that we could say that the absence of self-realization may be at once cause and consequence of the absence of health; in this casual circle, which can take the form of a spiral of constant deterioration, the absence of health appears as a fundamental obstacle to any good life. When the study of social suffering is taken on by the public health authorities under the heading of 'quality of life indicators',[23] it is in this sense that it paves the way for social interventions.

The idea of self-realization can also be understood in the sense of our capacity to translate our freedom of choice (negative freedom) into satisfactory actions (positive freedom). And here also, health appears to play a decisive role, in the sense that ill health can be conceived of as a handicap, a source of increased social difficulties, even an impediment to action. Again, a whole philosophical literature has sought to identify the capacities which allow individuals to make use of the freedom which is important to them. In the list of 'capabilities' proposed by M. Nussbaum, numerous ones concern physical and mental health: lifespan, physical integrity, good nutrition and housing conditions, emotional maturity and capacity to play and to think.[24]

Here again, social suffering seems caught in a spiral because suffering is an obstacle to action when it is accompanied by a constriction of social relations and a collapse of horizons of expectation, while difficulty in acting is itself a factor in suffering when it brings about a feeling of social uselessness, even shame and guilt. Often the criticism of social suffering is accompanied today by a demand to restore the capacity for action of individuals trapped in their difficulties. This is the case when suffering is characterized in terms of 'invalidating suffering' or 'suffering as a handicap', when social workers intervene in the framework of empowerment dispositives and when the clinical study of work or of severe precarity adopts the goal of reestablishing the individual or collective capacity for action.[25] The link betwen criticism and the norm of positive freedom is even clearer in the clinical study of work activity in which suffering is defined in terms of 'hindered activity'.

But the idea of self-realization does not allow us to adequately formulate all the normative content of the critique of social suffering either. Not wanting to experience abnormal suffering is sometimes the refusal of something which cannot be reduced, except by way of a euphemism, to poor quality of life. Certain social contexts render the search for quality of life redundant, for instance when the issue is far more getting by from day to day, as in the numerous pockets of severe poverty in third-world countries, or even survival, in many other extreme social situations.

The approach in terms of 'capabilities' seems able to answer this type of objection by giving an account of suffering as a handicap or invalidating factor, but it overlooks the fact that if health is not a simple expectation neither can it be treated as a simple condition of our expectations of freedom. The capabilities approach is based on a critique of definitions of poverty in terms of a failure to satisfy needs, but it seems clear that the value which is spontaneously accorded to health is accorded to a set of needs.[26] It is important to take the question of needs seriously, as lack of satisfaction of fundamental needs imposes upon individuals the need to ward off lack and deficiency, to adapt to them, even to identify oneself with them. No more than approaches in terms of justice or the good life does the approach in terms of 'capabilities' make it possible to satisfy the normative demands arising from suffering that are linked to its dynamic core. These demands are clearly part of a critique of alienation, and it is not surprising that certain theories of social suffering, in particular the psychodynamics of work,[27] allot a decisive function to this concept.

What should we understand in general by alienation? As this is quite a tangled question, we should pause for some time over it. Here again, it may be useful to take a detour through Marx. One of the remarkable characteristics of the critical model which he develops in the *1844 Manuscripts* is connected with his attempt to link: a) the idea of a separation from the world (an alienated world) and b) that of a separation from oneself (self-alienation)[28] c) by making a social activity (in this case alienated work) the site where these two components of alienation become entwined. The assertion that the separations from the world *and* from oneself are interdependent, the search for a social origin for this double separation, and the claim that they can be connected with a domination of activity by its own product is what defines the problematic of alienation in the work of Marx—and what, moreover, will turn out to be the template for most later theories of alienation.[29] Not all of them allow us to capture the normative content of the rejection of suffering with the same accuracy.

A first option consists of thinking of alienation in the framework of a philosophy of life. It consists in effect of interpreting alienation as a separation from oneself and one's world which results from blocking and frustrating the activity of a living being in its environment.[30] In this same blocking and frustration, the world appears as an obstacle to action (alienated world) and the effective existence of the subject is separated from the values which it sought to realize (self-alienation). We have already noted that, in certain problematics, suffering is sometimes related to the theme of blocked activity and a failure of self-realization, problematics which we have found to have many deficiencies: the framework of a theory of blocked activity seems too narrow to give an account of the psychic dynamism of suffering. It could be added that the normative content of such a critique of alienation, that is the critique of the reduction of life possibilities by an objective environment, does not allow us to take account of the content of the normative issues in the critique of social suffering, which are irreducible to the demand for self-realization.[31]

According to this model, individuals are defined by a group of intrinsic potentialities (positive anthropology) rather than by the socially and culturally compensated indeterminacy which characterizes the human self (negative anthropology). It is not obvious that the model of life takes the fact that individual subjectivity is inherently intersubjective and institutionalized seriously enough,[32] and that for this reason it is marked by the heterogeneity of physiological and social conditioning. This heterogeneity is expressed in the existence of qualitatively different needs (the difference between the corporeal, the psychic and the social self) and in the fact that the psychic self, for its part, is structured by the conflict between the drive-dominated and nonsocialized part of the psyche (the id) and its socialized part (the superego).[33]

Philosophies of life risk underestimating the heterogeneity of physiological dynamism and psychic functioning, and if they go so far as to transpose the scheme of the 'organism' onto the psyche, they risk underplaying the structural nature of psychological conflicts. But in fact we have seen that many aspects of social suffering can be traced back to this heterogeneity and to these conflicts.

Criticism of social suffering thus needs a more differentiated conception of alienation than one based on the idea of blocked life activity. It must integrate the theme of blocked action into the more dynamic and more differentiated framework of a theory of the different types of needs of the self. Just as these do not seek their satisfaction so much in the deployment of a vital dynamism as in the effort of conflict resolution and the reciprocal transformation of the self and the environment, so the failures and frustrations of this effort lead us to think of alienation along the lines of defective appropriation. But this model can itself be thought of in two different ways: as the frustration of the appropriation of the objects of needs or as the frustration of the activity dynamized by needs. Let us now consider the way in which the first of these two versions allows us to think of social suffering.

The relation which individuals maintain with themselves is always also the relation which they maintain with needs and desires oriented towards the external world, in such a way that the relation to oneself is insepararable from the relation to the world. If, now, the world presents itself in social activity as an environment incapable of satisfying our needs and our fundamental aspirations, then, in the same movement, it becomes foreign to us and the relationship which we maintain with ourselves as bearers of needs and desires becomes problematic. This model can be inflected in different ways, depending on whether needs are conceived, for example, as extensions of organic and psychic activity (of the corporeal self and psychological self) or as intersubjective needs (of the social self).

We find in Freud's work an example of the first orientation. Freud is indeed led to a conception of alienation when he emphasizes in *Civilisation and Its Discontents* the difficulties of finding one's place in a world which represses the libido and is based on the denial of the death drive, while analysing the effects of the splitting which results from the fact that the self is thus constrained to repress essential aspects of its existence. It is because the cultural and civilizational context forbids the satisfaction of the needs of the physical and psychological self that the outside environment appears as a relatively alien world and that individuals attempt to separate themselves from a fundamental part of their organic and psychological existence.

In a different perspective, one can also seek the origin of alienation in the intersubjective needs of the individual. If we follow Honneth, the positive relation which individuals can maintain with themselves is intersubjectively constituted in relation to recognition. If the social world structures intersubjective relations in such a way that it inflicts a denial of recognition on individuals, it emerges as an alien or hostile world which weakens or destroys the positive relation to oneself by engendering a feeling of injustice and 'moral injury'.[34]

Neither Freud nor Honneth refer to alienation when they elaborate these themes, but they can be considered thinkers seeking in the lack of satisfaction of fundamental needs the origin of a type of relation to the world and to oneself which can be traced back to the problematic of alienation because it conjoins separation from oneself and from the world within the framework of a theory of social action. This is a psychogenetic theory of the effects of socialization in the case of Freud and a theory of the normative presuppositions of social interaction and of identity in the case of Honneth.[35] Both make it possible to advance the idea that, in the critique of suffering which results from alienation, a normative content can be defined which can be reduced neither to the demand for a good life nor to a reduction of life possibilities, but which rather also concerns the rejection of distorted forms of existence in which individuals adapt themselves to unresolved conflicts (Freud) or to a negative relation to themselves (Honneth).

Among the needs of the self is also the maintenance of a certain form of unity of the self: the unity of the different components of the psychic self (id, ego, superego), as well as of the social self (identity). Starting from the principle that personal identity specifically designates a certain type of integration of the plans of action and the roles by means of which we negotiate social worlds, adding that it is always in the confrontation with social reality that the individual psyche struggles against its potential breakdown, we reach the idea that the appropriation of one's self and that of the world constitute two tasks which are both inseparable and fundamental.[36] Their failure defines a new form of alienation. On this model, one can explain alienation by the fact that social experience can be structured so that individuals cannot manage to appropriate some of the reality of their activity, so that the institutions in which the activity occurs, as well as the subjective components (social roles) through which institutions are sustained remain partly foreign to the individual. Because we are constituted by the roles that we play, the alienated world is also accompanied here by an alienation from the self.[37]

The general logic of this last argument brings into play a problematic idea: that of an experience which is inappropriable because of its intrinsic characteristics and no longer only by reason of fundamental desires or needs relating to the external world. To establish the possibility of such a structure of social experience, two situations can be mentioned. The first, which plays a decisive role in the thought of Bourdieu, corresponds to cases in which social experience is traversed by contradictory normative logics, whether this is a matter of the existence of an individual involved in institutions whose normative logics are conflictual (the 'torn habitus' of which immigration and 'dual absence' provide examples) or that the habituses bear the trace of normative logics incompatible with the institutional contexts to which individuals must adapt ('symbolic violence').

The second situation corresponds to circumstances which impose a mutilating and imprisoning mode of appropriation. Alienation is in this case attributed to a failure of appropriation which is not conceptualized as the encountering of an insurmountable social obstacle and a blocking of the process of appropriation, but as a defective mode of appropriation. Dejours suggests a theory of the defences against suffering at work which develops this line of argumentation by analysing the psychodynamic mechanisms by which individuals subjected to painful or dangerous conditions of work attempt to merge into the work activity itself. When all of the conditions for appropriating suffering through thought and sublimation are no longer present, it sometimes only remains to numb oneself through identifying oneself with the rhythm of the assembly line, for example, even through attempting to accelerate it.[38] We have also observed this psychological dynamic in the clinical study of precarity, in the theme of 'desperate collusion with the garbage',[39] that ultimate means of defence by identification with what symbolizes suffering.

It will perhaps be objected that there is nothing objectively unbearable in this, certainly, because everything depends on the social context in which we confront that which may become unbearable and because, moreover, it is possible to adapt even to what has become totally unbearable; but this is precisely the problem. When something places the psychic economy in grave danger and is nevertheless inevitable, when the only means of satisfying fundamental needs involves accepting the imposition of a profound lack of satisfaction on the self, the only recourse is the mobilization of psychic defences such as identification with the inappropriable. To identify with something amounts to bearing it, but at what psychological, social and political price? This question also counts among the normative issues of the critique of social suffering.

THE CRITIQUE OF NEOLIBERALISM

We have already examined numerous general objections to the political relevance of the problematic of suffering, and some of them bear more specifically on the usage of this problematic in a model of social criticism in terms of social pathology. They can be placed under the rubric of 'expressivism', that is to say, of a move which contents itself with displaying the pathologies of the present-day world to make its criticism.[40] Because the critique of social suffering may be tempted by expressivism, it could get caught in two traps. The first can be traced back to a tendency to exaggeration which could lead to seeing severe suffering everywhere and comparing the most ordinary social situations to the most extreme ones. This argument does not count against a procedure like ours, which attributes a specific meaning to the idea of suffering, distinguishes different types of suffering and makes the problem of the social aetiology of suffering one of the principal challenges to be confronted.

The second trap consists in only considering the pathologies of the present-day world in terms of the effects produced on individuals, leaving in the shadow the social structures which produce these pathologies and thus condemning criticism to analytical and political sterility.[41] In a way, this argument points once again to the necessity and the difficulty of integrating the critique of suffering into a model of social pathology: a decisive issue is tracing local scenes of suffering back to the general structures of the social formation. More precisely, today it is a matter of determining the way in which the forms of domination and the general dynamics of disaffiliation combine in different ways under the constraints of the logic of neoliberalism.

Another source of objections has to do with the capacity of the critique of social suffering to compete with a critique based on the norms of justice (liberalism), democratic nondomination (republicanism) or self-realization (communitarianism and perfectionism). The substitution of the ambiguities and narrowness of the former for the clarity and the general nature of the others is sometimes deemed too perilous. But it could well be that the problem is poorly expressed in this form. Indeed, we have seen that we do not need to choose between the critique of suffering and the critique of injustice, of domination or of lack of self-realization. Quite the reverse: the standards of justice and of the good life and of positive freedom can be the foundation for the criticism of suffering. The fact that social suffering constitutes an obstacle to political mobilization implies, moreover, that the norms of democratic nondomination can also function indirectly as the basis of such criticism. But the foundations of a model of social critique and its political value are two different things, even when the social critique is based on such norms. We have said that a model of social critique must seek to account as far as possible for the characteristic ills of a social formation and for the potentialities and obstacles related to political subjectivation. Now the objectifying and comparative vocabulary of justice, as much as the objectifying and relational vocabulary of domination (as a form of nonfreedom), are insufficient for explaining the subjective impact of injustice and domination, which define both social ills and specific forms of subjectivation, and the perspective of the good life is not enough to complement them on this point. As we have noted several times in the foregoing, to formulate the critique of injustice and domination from the point of view of the experience of injustice and domination, it seems especially useful to take social suffering into account.

Moreover, we have noted that there are also a certain number of normative problems which cannot be adequately explained only in light of the standards of justice and self-realization. We have just seen that the concept of social suffering designates a certain number of specific social ills which social critique must not gloss over and which should rather encourage an approach in terms of alienation. Even if the criticism of social suffering can be advantageously integrated into a critique of injustice and the lack of self-realization, it is also complementary because it can claim a certain independence, making explicit the normative problems linked to the forms of alienation produced by disaffiliation and social relations of domination.

Hence, a first type of objection concerns the way in which a reference to suffering can contribute to a social diagnosis, while a second concerns the critical perspective associated with such a diagnosis. These objections converge in the following question: In what sense does a critique of social suffering add something to the criticism of neoliberalism in terms of injustice, of democratic deficit and of failure to respect the conditions of self-realization? To answer, it may be useful to begin from the specific function which these three classic forms of social criticism fulfilled in Fordism, where it seemed quite easy to do without a critique of suffering, and to try to determine what has changed with neoliberalism.

What is Fordism? As the regulation school of political economy has shown, it could be considered a specific framework of support for the dynamics of capitalist accumulation within a determined institutional system. This mode of regulation is characterized, first, by a particular type of employee relationship based upon a group of juridical (labour law) and social (notably different forms of indirect salary) protections, as well as on a sharing of the gains of productivity; second, a set of institutions intended to make Keynesian economic policies aiming at cushioning economic cycles and at full employment on a national scale possible; and finally, a specific type of democracy which understands itself as the result of an extension of the sphere of private rights to political and social rights and which was based, moreover, in certain nation-states, on a combination of political and trade union representation within the general framework of a redistributive social compromise.

Considered from the point of view of the history of capitalism and the different phases it has passed through, Fordism undoubtedly ensured a maximum of democracy and social justice. By doing so, it contributed to conferring a specific social validity on demands for democracy and justice, demands traditionally suspected by the workers' movement of paving the way for all kinds of ideological mystifications. Seeming to prove empirically that capitalism does not necessarily condemn the proclaimed requirements of justice and democracy to flip over into their opposites, that is to say into a legitimation of social injustice and of class domination, it contributed to convincing people that the problems of democracy and of justice ultimately encompass all the social and political questions worthy of consideration. By means of a specific institutional mechanism (interventionist state, co-management with trade unions, joining together of unions and political parties), it transformed the norms of justice and democracy into a process of social transformation, whereas they had previously seemed to designate either ideal requirements (on the utopian or programmatic level) or principles making it possible to measure the value of societies. At the end of the Fordist period, a renewal of the theories of justice and democracy, by authors such as Rawls and Habermas, sought to draw the conclusion that societies cannot reasonably be criticized from any another point of view.

It is not surprising that Fordist institutional mechanisms led to the rise of a third type of normative demand making, which set up the recognition of dominated cultures and the preservation of minority cultures as conditions of self-realization, that is to say of the good life and of the realization of freedom in desired actions (positive freedom). As the institutions which are supposed to administer democracy and justice are national ones, and nation-states retain the marks of their colonial past, in terms of different forms of cultural restriction of the exercise of the rights of citizenship as well as different types of ethnoracial classification, we can understand that the demand for self-realization has been the favoured way of making apparent the inability of the norms of democracy and justice to embrace all the significant issues. The debate setting liberalism in opposition to communautarianism, which dates from the 1970s, was the occasion for developing and formalizing the different aspects of the problem raised by the structure of a good life and by the strong evaluations which structure collective identities and which individuals aspire to make real in their social experience.

It thus seems that Fordism has contributed directly to conferring social validity on the standards of democracy and of justice and, indirectly, upon the question of self-realization, the first two standards justifying its institutional functioning, the third bringing to light the limits of its legitimation. This institutional framework also contributed to the double disappearance of the question of suffering from the political vocabulary. If there were no reasons to believe that suffering was disappearing from the Taylorian factory, it was nonetheless difficult to think of the political problem of work in terms of suffering. In accordance with an institutionalized political compromise, the management and organization of work were left to the heads of businesses, whereas the demands of the workers focused on remuneration. The question of suffering at work thus found itself subordinated to that of redistributive justice. Moreover, the reduction of inequalities made it possible to hope that suffering linked to poverty was decreasing. The problematic of the good life could have contributed to again raising the question of a suffering linked to the interiorization of the negative images generated by colonialism and the prejudices and the practices marked by ethnoracial logics, but the formulation of these problems on the terrain of justice or of the restrictions of democracy meant granting little importance to the lived experience of these forms of domination.

Today, political discourse is still shaped by the norms of democracy, of justice and of the good life. Even if their social validity relied on specific institutional mechanisms, there is no reason to think that the disintegration of these mechanisms automatically implies the loss of critical relevance of these standards. However, such a disintegration does necessarily bring about a modification of their social and political meaning. They certainly remain the implicit standards of a certain number of transformative social struggles, but the fact is that their current unmooring from the social and institutional dynamics of Fordism tends to relativize their transformative power and their capacity to give an account of main social ills characteristic of neoliberalism.[42] If they are to remain the fundamental norms of political judgement, we must also take into account the emergence of a set of public problems for which they are poorly suited and which are, nevertheless, not reducible to mystifying social constructions. It is precisely among these problems that we find the emergence of suffering linked to the mobilization of subjectivity in the new organization of work, suffering linked to the vulnerability to domination that is characteristic of disaffiliation, suffering caused by extreme poverty and the inhibition of the capacity to make demands which results from it.

Neoliberalism has been accompanied by the appearance of new forms of work and of the mass phenomenon of social exclusion, in the form of disaffiliation in the countries at the centre and the reduction to forms of extreme poverty in the countries on the periphery. In this regime of accumulation centred on finance, an elevated rate of short-term profit (above 10 percent) is a constraint in the face of which factors such as the direct or indirect wage, the duration of the work day and the right to social benefits appear as adjustable variables.[43] In the workplace, a double dynamic of the intensification and precarization of work results. As profit is monopolized by shareholders to the detriment of investment, productivity growth can no longer be based upon technical progress. Rather, it is based upon the reduction and flexibilization of the scale of organizations (slimmed down business model, internal and external flexibility, outsourcing), employees' ability to self-organize (teamwork and project-based employment), quantitative (elimination of idle time and acceleration of the rhythm of work) and qualitative (subjective investment and responsibility) intensification of work and increase in working time (raising of the legal limit, tendency to eliminate the symbolic limit of the working day and outsourcing to countries where labour laws are less restrictive). In other words, neoliberalism is returning to primitive forms of extraction of surplus value: it is not so much based on technical progress (relative surplus value) as on an increased quantity of work (absolute surplus value).[44]

Fordist workers could consider their activity at work as contained within a circumscribed sphere of their existence, in which they endured a suffering compensated for by purchasing power, social relationships and social security, allowing them to envisage self-realization in the sphere of their free time and their family life.[45] But, the division of life into the sphere of work and the sphere of nonwork is rendered ever more difficult when work no longer offers the security making it possible to project one's existence outside of life at work and when employees are no longer judged only upon their professional capabilities and *savoir-faire*, their know-how, but also upon their '*savoir-être*', their knowing how to be, when they are asked to involve themselves body and soul in their work and to take on the responsibilites which accompany the autonomy which is supposedly granted to them. Moreover, the idea of a 'limit' of the work day is losing its meaning and time spent at work is continously increasing. The conditions which reduced the experience of work to a secondary topic no longer apply. In this context, the question of suffering at work becomes a public problem whose political stakes are fundamental.

Social existence outside of work, for its part, is deeply marked by dynamics of disaffiliation and social polarization. On the one hand, the precarization of work and the progressive dismantling of various social protections are producing convergent effects which have been designated by the concept of disaffiliation. On the other hand, the reestablishment of rates of profit to the detriment of real-term wages and the link of Fordist standards of consumption (mass consumption) converge in a dynamic of social polarization. Combined with the general dynamic of disaffiliation and with the process of competitive marketization of all economic activity (notably that of the traditional peasantry), this explains the appearance of new forms of poverty (such as underpaid workers, the phenomenon of a long-term exclusion from the labour market, and the explosion of shanty towns on a world scale). The fact that the perspective of a tendental reduction of these forms of poverty is becoming ever less credible, and that belief in the capacity of societies to provide effective social remedies is fading away, the fact moreover that the dynamics of disaffiliation are leading an ever-increasing number of individuals to envisage such a social fate for themselves, all this helps to focus public attention on the question of the basic experience of poverty, that of the homeless, of the badly housed, of the undocumented, that of populations condemned to the desperate attempt to emigrate.

It would be absurd to maintain that the shift away from Fordism invalidates any criticism in terms of democracy, of justice or of the good life. The contrary is evidently the case. On the one hand, under the combined effect of the dynamics of liberalization, and interconnection of financial markets and of deregulation spurred on by neoliberal policies, nation-states have lost control of a certain number of their instruments of economic policy. The shift away from Fordism has thus been accompanied by a withdrawal from the democratic control of social change, so that the demand for democracy has become a watchword for resistance and remains a central demand, as much in struggles for an alternative globalization as in political experiments like that of local democracy.

On the other hand, neoliberalism has seen the inversion of redistributive dynamics and a considerable increase in inequalities on the national as well as on the global scale. Demands of social justice are thus all the more urgent because the context of globalization has led to the opening of a new debate on global justice. Finally, economic (interconnection of markets) and technological (diffusion of information technologies) globalization has been accompanied by a cultural globalization which operates via dynamic of cultural imposition. The question of the recognition of collective identities is thus raised anew at the very moment when the conjunction of the increase of global inequalities with economic globalization is accelerating immigration flows and relaunching the debate on the postcolonial nature of the nation-states of the centre.[46]

Moreover, the dismantling of the institutional framework of social democracy has been accompanied by different forms of depoliticization of politics, by abstraction and qualitative (number of questions deemed worthy of political attention) and quantitative (number of social actors participating) reductions in the public political sphere, but this new conjunction also makes the capacity of democracy and the compromises around justice to hide a certain number of social pathologies apparent. In such a context, disclosing critique appears as an important tool in the struggle against the tendencies which are constantly shrinking a public political sphere that is ever more abstract, and the question of suffering comes to designate a group of phenomena for which an approach in terms of justice or democracy does not permit clarification of all of the issues.

To be sure, the forms of social suffering linked to the growth of poverty (whether that of poor workers in the countries at the centre of the world economy or extreme poverty on the periphery) must certainly be denounced, at least in one aspect, as an injustice, just as the forms of social suffering brought about by the different forms of cultural and institutional (post)colonialist racism may also be, at least in part, in the name of the good life. Certainly, the different incapacitating effects of the suffering caused by exclusion and the new experiences of work may, at least in part, be criticized as an obstacle to or restriction upon self-realization. Similarly, the denunciation of the restrictions on the public democratic sphere which lead to the invisibilization of social suffering or to the blocking of its narration must join with demands for a broadening of democracy. But there are also particular features revealed by social suffering, which indicate rather a problematic of alienation.

One of the most noteworthy consequences of the transformation of work is connected with the mobilization of subjectivity at work: at a time when short-term profit has become an imperative constraint, while the level of investment in materials and in research and development is collapsing, research into productivity gains deals today as much with a management of subjectivity[47] as with the organization of activity. The combination of an intensification of work and of growing precarity, the contradictions felt between the demand for autonomy and responsibility, on the one hand, and the reality of situations in which most of the time there is no room for manœuvre, on the other hand, lead to new painful experiences which can be measured notably in the worsening of indicators of health at work (sick leave, work-related accidents, consumption of psychotropic drugs, decompensations linked to work situations),[48] while along with this there are new forms of denial of illness to maintain the appearance of a high-performing worker and avoid penalizing teams which are already under pressure developing.[49] Some commentators have interpreted the shift from Fordism to post-Fordism as an attempt to supersede the forms of alienation targeted by the leftism of the 1960s.[50] Neoliberalism deserves to be interpreted rather as a 'false supercession of alienation'[51] and as the site of 'new forms of alienation'.[52]

The neoliberal reorganization of work is accompanied by a reduction in collective control of production and by new injustices in the remuneration of work, so that demands for democracy and justice remain relevant for framing a critique. Moreover, the retreat of labour law causes further exposure to the domination inscribed in the employer-employee relationship, at the same time as the dismantling of work collectives reduces the possibilities of collective resistance to domination. But the description of the experience of these injustices and of these forms of domination raises specific normative problems which justify a critique in terms of alienation. To be sure, the subjective impact of working conditions and of the worsening of domination can be described in fairly traditional political language: that of the loss of collective identifications, of the worsening of quality of life and of obstacles to self-realization. But in thus describing them we are missing the problems linked to the fact that suffering is not only a consequence of domination, but can also explain a defensive adherence to domination. It would be difficult to give an account of the subjective aporia posed by 'forced commitment', by the necessity of having to take on the responsibilities to stay in the workplace after the dismissing of one's colleagues ('survivor's guilt'), by the duty of accepting the worsening of working conditions and of remuneration in order to keep one's job, without bringing in the language of 'voluntary servitude'.[53] It would be just as difficult to understand the way in which the new conditions of work contribute to spreading phenomena of denial of illness and of suicides in the workplace[54] without considering the processes by which subjective structures are erected to bear the unbearable. It is then in the language of alienation that the critique of suffering must be undertaken.

Similarly, the effects of the dynamics of exclusion in the countries in the centre of the world economy cannot be brought to light by a mere criticism of injustice or deprivation of the conditions of self-realization. Here again, the problematic of suffering is absolutely determinant in accounting for the experience of the injustices and forms of domination which characterize these situations, in which fundamental needs seem satisfied, but which are accompanied by considerable subjective difficulties due to the loss of social support and to social disqualification[55] (symbolic violence or imposition of a negative identity) which goes along with the precarization of work and mass unemployment. And here again, it is in terms of alienation that certain normative aspects of the phenomenon should be focused upon. Is exclusion not essentially characterized by an indissoluble link between forms of subjective collapse (separation from the self) and of the narrowing of social relationships (separation from the world)—a loss of the world accompanied by a loss of the self, causing a further reduction of the world?[56] As for situations of severe precarity, as we have seen it is sometimes within the framework of a problematic of identification with the unbearable that social suffering can again be traced back to alienation. Moreover, the theme of identification with the unbearable makes it possible to give an account of the specific subjective effects of the suffering linked to extreme poverty: it is especially applicable to the considerable section of humanity whose activity is reduced primarily to living from hand to mouth and the struggle for survival.

Criticism of social suffering makes it possible to denounce a part of the injustice and of the loss of the value of existence which is brought about by the deep social dynamics of liberalism, but it also makes it possible to bring to light the social pathologies of alienation which count among the most specific characteristics of present-day social development: those which play out in the theatre of the new social relations of work and those whose context is the different forms of exclusion (mass unemployment, severe precarity, shanty towns and severe poverty). To be sure, not all individuals are affected by these social pathologies, but those who experience them deserve to figure in our critical models.

Let us reiterate that the concept of social suffering cannot in any way develop a general critical model, comparable in its ambitions to that which the demands of justice or of freedom make possible. This concept is, to be sure, inextricably descriptive and normative, but it needs other concepts, such as those of justice, self-realization or alienation, to determine its normative content. Furthermore, the legitimate extension of these concepts should not be limited to the field of what can be described in terms of suffering. The criticism of suffering should thus be based on and integrated within a comprehensive model of social critique: it must be combined with a criticism of the different forms of injustice, of domination and of alienation, none of which can be reduced to critiques of suffering. Nothing, moreover, entails that once integrated into such a comprehensive model of social criticism, it must necessarily play the main role, on the principle that the forms of injustice, of lack of self-realization or of alienation accompanied by suffering are more serious than other forms of these phenomena. To avoid the politically ruinous consequences of setting up a hierarchy of injustices and of forms of domination and alienation, consequences which are inevitable in any model which gives one factor priority, it is best to reject this path.

Even when integrated into this broader whole, the critique of social suffering cannot hope to be based on criteria that make it possible to distinguish with certainty between legitimate and illegitimate suffering. But when dealing with social critique, the question of criteria allowing us to settle a debate remains secondary to that of the legitimate domains of political deliberation and confrontation. It will surely be acknowledged that we do not need to possess a watertight criterion of poverty to concede the legitimacy of a struggle against poverty! The same holds true for freedom, democracy and many other fundamental political goals. Ultimately, it is enough that the principle of a distinction between a normal and an abnormal suffering be established in order to legitimate the question of socially induced suffering as one of the focal points of political battles, and of collective deliberation concerning how we wish to refashion the world we inhabit. We are confronted, then, with the challenge of framing a social critique which can do justice to this insight.

NOTES

1. T. W. Adorno et al., *The Authoritarian Personality* (New York: Harper and Bros., 1950) (see the general introduction).

2. On this question, see in particular Zizek's critical synthesis in *The Ticklish Subject: The Absent Centre of Political Ontology* (London: Verso, 1999).

3. On this subject, see V. Houillon, 'Les avances de Marx', *Actuel Marx*, no. 39 (2006): 173–91.

4. T. W. Adorno, 'Why Still Philosophy?', in *Critical Models: Interventions and Catchwords* (New York: Columbia University Press, 1998), 14. On suffering in the work of Adorno, see notably J. M. Bernstein, 'Suffering Injustice: Misrecognition as Moral Injury in Critical Theory', *International Journal for Philosophical Studies* 13, no. 3 (2005): 303–24.

5. See the text quoted in the epigraph to this chapter.

6. In his *Interview* with R. Maggiori and J.-B. Marongiu, *Libération*, February 11, 1993, Bourdieu presents the motivations of *The Weight of the World* in the following way: 'It was, perhaps, an opportunity to resolve the problem that I have had since beginning in sociology: how to give back to people what we have learned? How to find an adequate form of expression?' On this point, see Cl. Gautier, *La force du social: enquête philosophique sur la sociologie des pratiques de Pierre Bourdieu* (Paris: Cerf, 2012). We could compare Bourdieu's approach to Dejours's on this point. In the latter's view, references to suffering aim at explaining consent to domination and the decline of assertive action. For Dejours, the point is to propose a modification of the self-understanding of agents and to bring about a new cognitive and practical relation to their social environment, but it is no longer possible to speak here of a spokesperson from the moment when the meaning of the situation is the object of a co-construction and the theorist intervenes only as the occasion and instrument of a collective development (within the framework of action research).

7. V. Das, *Critical Events. An Anthropological Perspective on Contemporary India* (Dehli: Oxford University Press, 1995), 196: 'The healing force of social anthropology can come if the experiences of suffering . . . do not become cause for consolidating the authority of the discipline, but rather an occasion for forming one body, providing voice, and touching victims, so that their pain may be experienced in other bodies as well'.

8. On sociology as a 'spokesperson', see Bourdieu, *Méditations pascaliennes*, 220–24. On the political function of the 'spokesperson', see Renault, *L'Expérience de l'injustice*, conclusion.

9. P. Bourdieu, 'Intellectuals Must Give a Voice to Those Who Have None!', *L'Événement du jeudi*, September 10–15, 1992: 'Among the functions which intellectuals can fulfil, and which they have often fulfilled poorly in the past, in presenting themselves as exclusive, possessive, spokespersons, there is one which sociologists can fulfil (after all they are paid to do so by the public), which consists of giving a voice to those who, for all sorts of reasons, have

been denied theirs. In so doing, they can complicate things for all those spokespersons, whether legally elected, such as politicians, or self-designated, such as media intellectuals, who rush into the newspapers or in front of cameras, armed only with their claim to the intellectual magisterium, to speak in terms of the social world. But, without abandoning their role to lapse into prophecy, they can do rather more: try to disclose the realistic vision of the social world which they seek collectively to produce. The sociological eye, which reports that these people are and make the social conditions of which they are the product, inclines us to an understanding of others which is neither that of an indulgence which forgives and tolerates everything, nor that of a resignation which accepts the world as it is'.

10. Das, *Critical Events*, 164; see also 142–43: 'This denial did not occur through repression and censorship alone, but rather by talking about suffering in such a way that it came to be constituted purely as something verbal. Language came to be deployed as an end in itself, creating a discourse of which the function was to dissolve the concrete and existential reality of suffering victims'.

11. Ibid., 174.

12. V. Das, 'The Act of Witnessing: Violence, Poisonous Knowledge, and Subjectivity', in *Violence and Subjectivity*, ed. Das et al.

13. Honneth, 'Pathologies of the Social'.

14. Honneth, 'The Possibility of a Disclosing Critique of Society'.

15. This is also one of the functions of Dejours's reference to suffering at work.

16. On this point, see E. Renault, 'L'idéologie comme légitimation et comme description', *Actuel Marx*, no. 43 (2008): 80–95.

17. Kleinman, Das, and Lock, *Social Suffering*, xi.

18. See on this subject the defence of 'critical regionalism' by G. C. Spivak (J. Butler and G. C. Spivak, 'A Dialogue on Global States', *Postmodern Culture* 17, no. 1 [September 2006]: doi: 10.1353/pmc.2007.0012), which involves not so much a criticism of the alternative globalization movement as an attempt to take into account politically those who have access neither to the national public political sphere nor to the alternative globalization public sphere.

19. Bourdieu, *The Weight of the World*, 629: 'As sceptical as one may be about the social efficacity of the sociological message, one has to acknowledge the effect it can have in allowing those who suffer to find out that their suffering can be imputed to social causes and thus to feel exonerated; and in making generally know the social origin, collectively hidden, of unhappiness in all its forms, including the most intimate, the most secret. Contrary to appearances, this observation is not a cause for despair: what the social world has done, it can, armed with this knowledge, undo'.

20. For an illustration of this type of theory of justice, see J. Rawls, *A Theory of Justice* (Oxford: Oxford University Press, 1973).

21. Renault, *L'Expérience de l'injustice*, chap. 6–7.

22. See, for example, Ch. Taylor, 'Le juste et le bien', *Revue de métaphysique et de morale* 93, no. (1988): 33–56; 'What's Wrong with Negative Liberty?', in *Philosophy and the Human Sciences: Philosophical Papers 2* (Cambridge: Cambridge University Press, 2012).

23. See the use of HRQoL (Health-Related Quality of Life Years) and of QUALY (Quality Adjusted Life Years).

24. M. Nussbaum, *Woman and Human Development: A Study in Human Capabilities* (Cambridge: Cambridge University Press, 2000).

25. Bernard Doray's formula could be applied to both: 'What is urgent is to transform the energy of life shut away in suffering to come back into harmony with oneself' ('From "Social Trauma" to Psychiatric Trauma', in *Répondre à la souffrance sociale*, ed. Joubert and Louzoun, 88).

26. For a defence of the approach in terms of needs against the theory of 'capabilities', see S. Reader, 'Does a Basic Needs Approach Need Capabilities?', *Journal of Political Philosophy* 14, no. 3 (2006): 337–50. This approach gains contemporary relevance as soon as we observe many current social and political problems (such as suffering linked to poverty) require a reflection on fundamental needs. See on this subject L. Hamilton, *The Political Philosophy of Needs* (Cambridge: Cambridge University Press, 2003), which defends the view that political theory should put more emphasis on the satisfaction of certain categories of need instead of paying exclusive attention to the problem of protecting rights.

27. On this point, see Ch. Dejours, 'Aliénation et clinique du travail', *Actuel Marx*, no. 39 (2006).

28. *Selbstentfremdung*.

29. We have developed these points in E. Renault, 'From Fordism to Post-Fordism: Beyond or Back to Alienation?', *Critical Horizons* 2 (2) (2007): 205–22.

30. On this point, see S. Haber's remarkable study *L'Aliénation. Vie sociale et expérience de la dépossession* (Paris: PUF, 2007).

31. For an interpretation of suffering in the framework of a problematic of 'psychological life', which leads notably to taking sides against the 'psychodynamics of work' in favour of the 'clinical study of work activity', see G. Le Blanc's proposals, *Les maladies de l'homme normal* (Bègles: Editions du Passant, 2004).

32. On this point, see Mead, *Mind, Self and* Society.

33. On this point, see A. Honneth, 'Appropriating Freedom: Freud's Conception of Individual Self-Relation', in *Pathologies of Reason: On the Legacy of Critical Theory* (New York: Columbia University Press, 2009), 126–45.

34. For this theory of the intersubjective construction of the relationship to oneself, see Honneth, *The Struggle for Recognition*, chap. 5–6.

35. Honneth has furthermore recently suggested a reformulation of these themes within the framework of a theory of 'reification' (Honneth, *Reification*).

36. On the link between the social self and the appropriation of activity, see Mendel, *La société n'est pas une famille*.

37. On this point, see R. Jaeggi, *Alienation* (New York: Columbia University Press, 2014).

38. Dejours, *Travail, usure mentale*.

39. Douville, 'Note d'un clinicien', 64.

40. Voir E. Pineault, 'Au-delà de l'expressionnisme et du marxisme: éléments pour une théorie critique des structures sociales du capitalisme avancé', https://depot.erudit.org/bitstream/002221dd/1/pineault-dec-2006-2.pdf.

41. This is E. Pineault's argument against different contemporary forms of social criticism. Even if this argument is not in his work explicitly turned on the criticism of social suffering, it could be.

42. For an introduction to the shift away from Fordism to neoliberalism, see G. Duménil and D. Lévy, *Crise et sortie de crise. Ordres et désordres libéraux* (Paris: PUF, 1999); D. Harvey, *A Brief History of Neoliberalism* (New York: Oxford University Press, 2005).

43. On financial hegemony and its social consequences in neoliberalism, we suggest a synthesis of the following works: S. de Brunhoff, F. Chesnais, G. Duménil, D. Lévy, and M. Husson, *La finance capitaliste* (Paris: PUF, 2006), and E. Pineault, 'What Accumulation Regime? The Social Structures of Financialised Accumulation, a Canadian perspective', https://depot.erudit.org/id/002221dd.

44. On the tendency to shift from the production of absolute surplus value to that of relative surplus value, see K. Marx, *Capital*, vol. 1, parts III–IV. Today we are witnessing the reversal of this tendency.

45. For the contrast between the Taylorist worker and the wage earner in contemporary conditions of precarity, see S. Paugam, *Le Salarié de la précarité. Les nouvelles formes de l'intégration professionnelle* (Paris: PUF, 2000).

46. For an introduction to the different aspects of the return of the problem of racism and colonialisms see *Actuel Marx* no. 37 (2005).

47. See, for example, Brunel, *Les Managers de l'âme*; de Gauléjac, *La Société malade de la gestion.*

48. See, for example, S. Volkoff and A. Thébaud-Mony, 'Santé au travail: l'inégalité des parcours', in *Les Inégalités sociales de santé*, ed. A. Leclerc et al. (Paris: La Découverte/Inserm, 2000), 349–61; Askenazy, *Les Désordres du travail*; A. Thébaud-Mony, *Travailler peut nuire gravement à votre santé: Sous-traitance des risques, Mise en danger d'autrui, Atteintes à la dignité, Violences physiques et morales, Cancers professionnels* (Paris: La Découverte, 2006).

49. On the question of the new forms of denial of illness, see H. Kocyba and S. Voswinkel, 'Krankheitsverleugnung. Das Janusgesicht sinkender Fehlzeiten', *WSI-Mitteilungen* 60 (March 2007): 131–37, and www.ifs.uni-frankfurt.de/forschung/krankheitsverleugnung/index.htm.

50. L. Boltanski and E. Chiapello, *The New Spirit of Capitalism* (London: Verso, 2005).

51. H. Kocyba, 'Die falsche Aufhebung der Entfremdung. Über die normative Subjektivierung der Arbeit im Postfordismus', in *Psychoanalyse und Arbeit: Kreativität, Leistung, Arbeitstörungen*, ed. M. Hirsch (Göttingen: Vandenhoeck and Ruprecht, 2000); H. Kocyba, 'Selbstverwirklichungszwänge und neue Unterverfungsformen. Paradoxen der Kapilalismus Kritik', in *Ökonomie der Subjektivität—Subjektivität der Ökonomie*, ed. Arbeitsgruppe SubArO (Berlin: Sigma, 2005).

52. See the contributions collected in *Actuel Marx*, no. 39 (2006): 'Nouvelles aliénations'.

53. J.-P. Durand, *La Chaîne invisible. Travailler aujourd'hui: flux tendus et servitude volontaire* (Paris: Seuil, 2004); Dejours, 'La flexibilité: l'autre nom de la servitude'.

54. Dejours, 'Nouvelles formes de servitude et de suicide'; A. Thébaud-Mony, 'Le travail, lieu de violence et de mort. Recrudescence des suicides et des cancers professionnels', *Le Monde diplomatique*, July 2007.

55. S. Paugam, *La disqualification sociale* (Paris: PUF, 1991).

56. See, for example, D. Linhardt, *Perte d'emploi, perte de soi* (Toulouse: Ères, 2002).

Index

About the Author

Emmanuel Renault is Professor of Social and Political Philosophy at the University of Paris Nanterre. He is the author of several books on Marx, Hegel, social philosophy and contemporary critical theory. He is the former editor of the journal *Actuel Marx* and co-editor of *Critical Horizons.*